THE INVISIBLE BANKERS

Everything the Insurance Industry Never Wanted You to Know

Andrew Tobias

THE
LINDEN
PRESS/Simon & Schuster
NEW YORK
1982

Designed by Irving Perkins Associates
Manufactured in the United States of America

10 9 8 7 6 5 4 3

Library of Congress Cataloging in Publication Data
Tobias, Andrew P.
      The invisible bankers.

      Bibliography: p.
      Includes index.
      1.Insurance—United States.   2.Insurance
companies—United States.   I. Title.
HG8531.T6   338.4'7368973   81-18564
ISBN 0-671-22849-8   AACR2

The author gratefully acknowledges permission to quote from the following:

Best's Aggregates & Averages, 1981. Copyright © A. M. Best Company.
Blye, Private Eye by Nicholas Pileggi. Playboy Press. Copyright © 1976 by Irwin Blye
Investigations, Inc., and Nicholas Pileggi.
Marketing Life Insurance, by permission of The McCahan Foundation, Bryn Mawr,
Pennsylvania. Copyright © 1969 by The McCahan Foundation. All rights reserved.
Medical Selection of Life Risks by R. D. C. Brackenridge, M.D. The Undershaft Press.
Copyright © 1977 by R. D. C. Brackenridge.
Lloyd's of London by Antony Brown. Stein & Day. Copyright © 1973 by Antony Brown.
Restraints on Underwriting by Robert B. Holtom. The National Underwriter Company.
Copyright © 1979 by The National Underwriter Company.
"The Day the Sky Fell In" by Rachel Lavoie. *Money,* July 1977.
"Integrity Test" by Jane Berentson. *The American Lawyer,* May 1980.
Analysis of Workers' Compensation Laws. Copyright © 1980 by The Chamber of Commerce
of the United States.
*Summary of Selected State Laws and Regulations Relating to Automobile Insurance, 1981
edition.* Copyright © 1981 by American Insurance Association.
Fun with Dick and Jane. Copyright © Columbia Pictures Industries, Inc.
The Fortune Cookie. Copyright © United Artists Corporation.

For Dad

acknowledgments

In the preparation of this book I have been enormously aided by conversations with industry insiders who might prefer not to be singled out here, and by a wealth of published material described in the bibliography. The bibliography is, in effect, an extension of this page. I also had the help of two wonderful research associates, Lee Aitken and Don Trivette.

Endless manuscript revisions were typed without complaint by my Qyx Intelligent Typewriter, then fed by telephone into a computer-driven phototypesetting machine. In other words, it didn't have to be typed all over again. This is a book about cutting costs.

I am greatly indebted to my friends, relations and publisher for putting up with a project that has wound up spanning five years instead of two.

Needless to say, however, the responsibility for all that follows is my own.

contents

THe INVISIBLe BankeRS

Isolation is comfortable. How satisfying to
be sure that no one understands us but ourselves.
—NEW YORK'S INSURANCE SUPERINTENDENT,
SPEAKING TO INDUSTRY EXECUTIVES, 1969

Author's Note

I believe in capitalism. I own stocks. Even a few insurance company stocks. I believe in free enterprise and incentives, and, by and large, in less government spending, less government regulation. I have "vested interests." What's more, I have never personally suffered at the hands of an insurance company. I have never had a policy canceled for making a claim, never been harassed by an unscrupulous agent, never been fired (or employed) by an insurance company, never witnessed at close range anyone who *was* so victimized. Nor, indeed, am I desperate to stir up a little trouble and profit thereby. (Eager, perhaps, but not desperate.) I raise all this because to the not inconsiderable extent this book is critical of the insurance industry and its regulators I hope it will not be taken, or dismissed, as the howlings of "yet another anti-establishment liberal who doesn't understand what made this country great." I happen to believe that our howling anti-establishment liberals have *themselves* helped to make this country great; but on economic matters, at least, I am not one of them.

1

THE BIGGEST GAME IN THE WORLD

They Just Want Us to *Think* It's Boring

*I've never understood one goddamn
thing about insurance, except that
I don't want to have any.*
—Paul Cabot, Financier

If you took all the men and women employed in the U.S. insurance industry and laid them head to toe, starting on New York's William or John Street—the little-talked-about insurance industry equivalents of neighboring Wall Street—they would stretch up the West Side Highway, head to toe, over the George Washington Bridge into New Jersey, down the New Jersey Turnpike to the Pennsylvania Turnpike, across Pennsylvania into Ohio, through Ohio along Interstate 80 past Chicago, past Des Moines, past Lincoln, Nebraska— still head to toe, one after another—past Cheyenne, Wyoming, to someplace just shy of Salt Lake City. No one of them *produces* anything as such—insurance is a risk-spreading, paper-shuffling business—but each one, on average, gets paid in the vicinity of $20,000 a year. One million eight hundred ninety-five thousand employees, or very nearly as many people as constitute the Armed Forces, twenty times as many as are required to collect all of the nation's federal income and excise taxes, and three times as many people as it takes to run the Postal Service.

Consider: the Postal Service pays a personal visit, albeit a brief

11

one, to almost every home and office in the country five or six times a week, processes more than 100 *billion* separate pieces of mail each year (no small portion generated by the insurance industry) and, incidentally, runs 30,000 retail "stores" where you can walk in and buy stamps, register letters, apply for passports, send money orders or collect your mail. And it does all that with *one-third* as many people as sell and process the nation's insurance.

Which suggests two things. First, that the insurance industry is enormous, which it is. Second, that it could perhaps be a bit more efficient.

That the insurance industry is enormous no one would dispute. The roughly $200 billion in annual premiums the industry collected in 1981 comes to $900 for every living American, $3,600 for a family of four. Tot up the sales of every clothing store in America, every liquor store, every drugstore, every restaurant, every bar and fast-food place—every one of them—and you will just about match the sales of the insurance industry. And none of this includes what we pay for Blue Cross or for government-administered programs like unemployment insurance and—the giant—Social Security.

There are life insurance and health insurance and auto insurance and homeowners insurance, of course—the so-called "personal lines" that you and I buy. But also "commercial lines." There are crop and hail insurance, cargo and hull insurance, flood insurance, flight insurance, insurance against roof collapse ("The roof fell in on Allendale Mutual Insurance Co. last year," reported *Forbes* in 1979—"98 of them to be exact") and insurance against bridge collapse. Of the estimated 560,000 bridges in the United States, three-fourths were built prior to 1935 and 105,000 are considered in some way unsafe.

Also: title insurance (lest someone show up with the true deed to the home you thought you'd purchased title to), workers' compensation insurance (lest you be injured on the job), insurance against political upheaval, riot insurance, ransom insurance . . . malpractice insurance (for doctors and dentists, yes, but also for lawyers, travel agents, architects, accountants, insurance adjusters, animal trainers and clergymen), directors-and-officers liability insurance (which is simply malpractice insurance for corporate executives), product liability insurance, insurance on satellite launches, insurance against earthquakes, insurance against boiler explosions (a line all to itself) . . . "excess and surplus" insurance for really big risks, reinsurance to spread those risks, self-insurance (when you decide to bear the risk yourself), "retroactive" insurance against disasters that have already occurred (like the MGM Grand fire in Las Vegas, after which MGM chose to pay one gigantic insurance premium rather than have a mega-loss of indeterminate size hang over its head for years as the lawsuits plodded through the courts), "modified coinsurance" (an arcane arrangement between life insurers designed solely to foil equally arcane federal tax statutes) . . . race horse insurance (in case of the animal's death or, for an extra premium, impotence), bad-debt insurance, business interruption insurance, burglary insurance, bank-heist insurance, cancer insurance ("Exploiting Fear for Profit," as the House Select Committee on Aging titled its March 1980 report on the subject) . . .

And! Electronic-data-processing insurance, war-risk insurance, spectator insurance (as in the case of the radio-controlled model airplane, part of a half-time show, that crashed into a hapless sports fan's forehead); insurance on roller coasters, state fairs and rock concerts; insurance to protect corporations from the costs of fighting hostile takeover attempts (thereby to help management keep their jobs, at the expense of the shareholders); nuclear power insurance, insurance on mortgages, credit cards and municipal bonds; disability insurance, libel insurance, liquor liability insurance (for the bar whose well-lubricated patron swerves into oncoming traffic on the way home), theatrical insurance (Betty Grable's $250,000 legs, Jimmy Durante's $140,000 nose)—and more. There is even insurance publishers will occasionally take out on their authors' lives, lest the author die before finishing his work but after spending his advance.*

Basically, the industry is two industries: life insurance companies, which sell life and health policies; and property/casualty companies, which sell everything else. I have endeavored to cover not just life insurance—the usual topic of such books—but the property/casualty side of the business as well. On one hand, this is a nigh ludicrous undertaking. (The corporate history of The Equitable Life Assurance Society of the United States *alone* consumes 1,475 pages of text—and leaves off with the year 1966.) On the other

---

*In at least one case, the author did die while the insurance was in force—so the publisher collected; but the manuscript *had* been completed—so the publisher published it and "collected" again.

hand (assuming you have not yet *shot off* your other hand, to collect dismemberment benefits), if one cannot say at least a good deal of what needs to be said about insurance in 300 pages, one is perhaps missing the forest for the trees.

It is a big business. More than 4,800 insurance companies are domiciled in the United States. They include National Fidelity, National Guardian, National Home, National Benefit, National Investors, National Life & Accident, National Life, National Public Service, National Reserve, National Travelers, National Western, Western National, Washington National, American National, National American, National Auto & Casualty, National Casualty, National Fire & Indemnity, National Fire, National Fire & Marine, National Grange, National Guaranty, Guaranty National, National Indemnity, National Mutual, National Standard, National Trust Fire, National Union Fire, National Unity (a member, unlike any of the others on this list, of the National Group), National General, Nationwide General, and about 4,750 more.

Most are relatively small, but some are all-embracing. One life insurance company not long ago had no fewer than five agents surnamed Patel—Chandrakant, Jayanti, Jaydev, Vishnu and Viren—and no fewer than three Sidney Millers—Sidney A., Sidney J. and Sidney M.

The capital underlying the operation of the State Farm Mutual Automobile Insurance Company at year-end 1980, $4.6 billion, was greater than that of either Citicorp or Bank of America, double that of the Chase Manhattan Bank.

While there is an element of apples-and-oranges in comparing such things, the assets of the U.S. insurance industry—in excess of $700 billion in 1981—were greater than the combined worldwide assets of the nation's fifty largest industrial corporations. Only the banks sit steward over a greater share of American wealth. For, of course, most of that $700 billion doesn't belong to the insurance companies; it belongs to us. It is our collective savings against catastrophe, mishap, malfunction and misfortune.

We deposit our money with insurance companies to assure nest eggs for our families if we die, money for a new house if ours burns down, cash to fix the car if ours is in a wreck. The insurance companies manage that money until we need it, lending it out to others in the meantime. Insurance companies are thus very much like savings banks—with one crucial difference: the amount of money any one of us may withdraw is based not on what he has deposited by way of premiums, but rather (within strictly defined limits) on what he *needs*. The aforementioned $700 billion that we have, as a group, saved up through private insurance companies comes to more than $8,500 for each of the nation's 82 million households. Hence, "the invisible bankers."

The analogy to banking is an important one. In both cases, the product is really only money. Banks—and insurance companies— are "financial intermediaries." They collect deposits from people and businesses with extra cash and lend it to people and businesses (and governments) that need to borrow some. The difference, as I say, is that with a bank you are entitled to withdraw 100 percent of what you deposit, often with interest. With an insurance company, you and your fellow insureds as a *group* will wind up withdrawing much of what you put in, but just how much any *individual* can draw out depends on his luck. The worse his luck, the more he is allowed to withdraw. This is the deal we make, implicitly, with our fellow depositors, just as, millennia ago, Phoenician shippers agreed to share the hazards of the sea.

But there is a second difference as well. Where a bank is able to safeguard your money, process all your checks, insure your account with F.D.I.C., pay for all those radio jingles, pay the rent on its building, and so on, at little or no charge to you—living off the investment income your deposit earns—insurance companies are unable to do this. For every dollar we collectively "deposit" with an auto insurer, for example, only 65 cents or so is available for our collective withdrawal. (Some will withdraw much more, many will withdraw nothing, but *on average,* for every dollar Americans pay in auto insurance premiums, 65 or 70 cents gets paid back out.) Some bank! Deposit a dollar, withdraw 65 cents. The rest of our dollar, *plus* the interest the insurance company earns on it, goes to expenses, overhead and profit.

What kind of bank gives back just 65 percent—often less—of what you deposit? Indeed, when you compare the services of a bank and an insurance company, common sense suggests something is out of whack. Think how often you deal with your bank, how many checks it clears for you in the course of a year, how many statements it mails you, loans it discusses with you . . . and then think how much contact you are likely to have with your insurers. Why can one live off the interest on the balance in your checking account, while the other needs to take 35 cents—or more—of each dollar you deposit? Could it be that one is vastly more efficient?

It takes 1.9 million people to staff the insurance industry. Would you say it takes twice as many to run the banks? *Five* times as many? (After all, they have all those credit applications to analyze, all those security guards to keep on patrol, all those toaster-ovens to give away.) At the end of 1980 there were actually more Americans employed in the insurance industry than in banking. The banks presided over three times as much money, handled vastly more "transactions"—and yet managed to make do with about a quarter of a million fewer people. And without grabbing off 20 or 40 or 50 cents of each deposited dollar.

Or look at this: In 1950 there were some 7.2 million Americans working in agriculture in the United States and around 800,000 working in insurance. Thirty years later just 3.3 million were required to grow the nation's food, while the number of people required to provide the nation's insurance had more than doubled. Incredibly, these were the *same* thirty years that saw clerical, number-crunching, paper-shuffling businesses like insurance revolutionized by the computer. (Not to mention the pocket calculator.) The average cost of processing 100,000 computations fell during this time from more than a dollar to less than a quarter of a cent, and *still* the ranks of the insurance industry swelled.

The tallest building in the United States is Chicago's Sears Tower. In each year since 1977, Sears has earned more from insurance—Allstate—than from retailing. New York's World Trade Center, second in height, and Chicago's Standard Oil of Indiana Building, fourth, are not creatures of the insurance industry. But number three, the Empire State Building, is owned by the Prudential Insurance Company of America. Prudential owns, in addition, 200 other office buildings, 500 industrial buildings, 75 hotels, 50 shopping centers, 55 residential buildings and 600,000 acres of farmland. The thousands of properties on which it merely holds a mortgage are a whole other category. Fifth tallest is the hundred-story John Hancock Center in Chicago; number six, the Chrysler Building, was recently sold at a nice profit by Massachusetts Mutual; and number seven is New York's American International Building. American International Group (AIG) is a wildly successful global insurance conglomerate most Americans have never heard of. It is valued by Wall Street, as I write this, at more than Merrill Lynch, Safeway and TWA combined.

There follow a few tall bank buildings (the banks would like nothing better than to get into insurance, but are prohibited from doing so by law), San Francisco's Transamerica Pyramid (the bulk of Transamerica revenues come from insurance), New York's Pan Am Building, purchased in 1981 by the Metropolitan Life for $400 million, and so on down the line. Boston's skyscape is dominated by the Prudential Center and the pane-popping John Hancock Tower. Hartford, in financial terms, is little more than thirty-five insurance companies at the intersection of two Interstate highways.

A naive tourist, measuring in terms of plate glass, might gain the impression that ours is a four-pronged power structure of banks, oil companies, insurance companies and the federal bureaucracy. And he might not be altogether wrong. Of these four, the insurers are the ones that have largely escaped public scrutiny—a result, in part, of the skill with which the industry, *alone among major American industries,* has managed to exempt itself from federal regulation.

The head of one small but highly regarded Wall Street investment house describes the industry as "the last vestige of totally obscured power. Invisible, vast power." Particularly the mutual life insurance companies. "The directors of those companies have *no* one to answer to! It's incredible—no one can throw them out of office!"

When the Federal Trade Commission, in 1979, began making real headway in providing life insurance buyers with the information needed to make an informed purchase, such was the clout of the industry that it got the Senate Commerce Committee to vote— unanimously—to ban the F.T.C. from further work in this area.

That same year, President Carter invited the heads of twenty-five leading insurance companies to meet him at the White House. Seven were "unable to attend." Now, I grant you that nothing earthshaking was likely to be accomplished at that meeting. It promised to be a big waste of time. And, as insurance industry thinking tends to be much of one mold, it was hardly necessary to have twenty-five different spokesmen advocating the same point of view. Nor would the chief executives of Allstate, Travelers, Aetna and the others who couldn't make it have any trouble finding out what, if anything, they'd missed. (As it turned out, they missed very little.) But I am nevertheless intrigued by the idea of being too busy to meet with the President of the United States. What else did those fellows have to do that day? A check of their offices turned up the most natural, if somewhat vague, explanations. "A previous engagement." "A scheduling conflict." Where lesser corporate chiefs might kill for the opportunity to break a lunch date this way—"Sorry, but the President has asked to see me"—*these* fellows had met with Presidents before and, in any event, knew that there was more to the true power structure of this country than Jimmy Carter and Hamilton Jordan.

In early 1980, over Carter's protests, the full Senate passed, 77 to 13, a bill banning the F.T.C. from investigating or reporting on "the business of insurance."

Around the same time, the Carter administration announced it would set up an "Office of Insurance Analysis" in the Treasury Department to inform itself about the industry and the issues facing it. What cheek! Imagine, the executive branch of the United States government wanting to peek into this preserve! The industry soon got the government to back down.

Ironically, at a time when federal regulation is widely perceived as excessive, the life insurance industry is one place a measure of it is probably needed.

International Telephone and Telegraph, eleventh of *Fortune's* 500 "industrial" companies, makes more money from insurance than from telecommunications. It owns twenty-five insurance companies. Challenged by the Justice Department on his 1971 acquisition of the Hartford Group, ITT's Harold Geneen cast off the nation's second-largest auto-rental company, one of its larger homebuilders and one of its largest vending and food-service companies rather than give up the Hartford. However else he may be perceived (it may also have been to save the Hartford that he helped underwrite the 1972 Republican National Convention), few have ever disputed Geneen's financial acumen. The same might be said of Gulf + Western's Charlie Bluhdorn (G + W owns eighteen insurance companies), Loew's' Larry Tisch (twelve) or Teledyne's Henry Singleton (fifteen). Insurance is a business canny businessmen like to get into and are loath to abandon. When Transamerica (seventeen) was faced in the mid-1950s with selling off either its banks or its insurance operations, it spun off the banks.

Insurance rivals even the oil business for profitability. Tenneco, owner of 15,000 oil wells, 16,000 miles of pipeline, 860,000 acres of farmland and 150 factories—among other things—exchanged 11.4 million of its shares to acquire Southwestern Life in mid-1980. It already owned Philadelphia Life. In a transaction of about equal size several weeks later, Getty Oil paid $572 million to acquire ERC Corporation, a group of five insurers. "Getty's oil business has never been more profitable," Value Line reported at the time, going on to say, "Profitability of the acquired group of companies is . . . slightly better than Getty's average."

American Express owns Fireman's Fund. Sears owns Allstate. J.C. Penney and Montgomery Ward have little insurance arms too. Citicorp owns Family Guardian Life. Merrill Lynch owns Family Life Insurance. Armco Steel jumped headlong into insurance with its own captive insurer, Bellefonte (proving that even in insurance you can get burned if you don't know what you're doing); then set things right by hiring a pro and acquiring NN Corporation. You or I might never have heard of NN Corporation before, a group of thirteen insurance companies headquartered in Milwaukee, but in the seven years preceding its marriage to Armco in December 1980, NN reportedly was approached by more than twenty-five corporate suitors. Insurance companies are attractive. Everybody wants to own one.

General Motors owns Motors Insurance Group. General Electric owns Puritan Life. Anderson, Clayton, the food-processing company, owns American Founders Life and three other insurers. Cargill, the gargantuan grain dealer, owns three. Beatrice Foods (Clark bars, Samsonite luggage) has four. Control Data—fourteen. Kaufman & Broad, the homebuilder, owns Sun Life. Halliburton, the oil-field outfit, owns Life Insurance Company of the Southwest and a chunk of $180-million-a-year Highlands Insurance. Filmways (*Dressed to Kill, Hollywood Squares*) survived the 1970s by selling cancer insurance. And National Student Marketing Corporation, at its zenith, owed well over half its profit *not* to class rings or emblazoned beer mugs but to a Chicago-based casualty insurer. (The head of National Student Marketing may have been a crook, but he was no fool.)

It is hard to exaggerate just how much of our money goes, one way or another, to insurance. Much of what we pay for insurance we pay indirectly.

Nearly 7 cents of the average American's dollar is spent directly on health, life, auto and property insurance. Something over 3 cents more goes to Social Security, a publicly funded insurance program. Subtotal: a dime.

Another 14 cents or so goes to taxes other than Social Security. Some of this pays the cost of fire and police protection—insurance of a sort. (If ever we need a fire brigade, it comes rushing over "free." We pay on a steady, predictable basis to insure some measure of protection against fire.) Another portion—small, until California's $50 billion earthquake finally hits—goes to provide federal disaster assistance, which is nothing more than a public insurance program. And a large chunk goes to transfer payments to the poor and elderly. What are transfer payments but a way of spreading the risk of hardship over society as a whole? The social contract is in no small measure an *insurance* contract.

And there is more. Beyond the dime of each dollar we pay directly, plus whatever portion of our taxes we choose to think of as "insurance," every product and service we purchase contains in its price a pass-along of insurance premiums. There is liability insurance on the product itself, lest it poison us or explode in our faces; fire insurance on the factory whence it came; insurance on its shipment to the retailer; the *retailer's* insurance premiums; the group health policies of the workers who made it and shipped it and sold it—ad infinitum.

Workers' compensation alone, the insurance system under which practically every worker in America is eligible for swift redress if injured on the job, cost employers some $25 billion in 1981. Like any other cost of business, this one was passed on to customers. In Florida not long ago it accounted for $2,000 of the cost of building a $55,000 house, 5 cents of every dollar's worth of garbage collection, and $1.75 of every $25 bag of groceries.

And then you have unemployment insurance. Because it is funded by a tax on employers, it may be nice to think it's "free"—but of course it's not. The premiums are merely being assessed in a different way. They are paid by employers, but passed on, naturally enough, to us. You will find unemployment insurance premiums figured into the price of lawnmowers, softballs, chili con carne, a telephone call—or anything else. All told: about $200 per household per year.

Employers' contributions to Social Security (which match wage earners' contributions dollar for dollar): another $800 or $900 per household per year.

However many hundreds of billions all of this totals (about five, I'd say)—the Gross National Premium, if you will—it is plainly a very big pool. And, like it or not, we are all in it together. Insurance is just a way of spreading financial risk from individual shoulders to the shoulders of us all as a group. Supertankers collide, gas mains explode, paintings are stolen, autos are totaled, workers are laid off, hotels go up in flames, diseases ravage, tornadoes destroy. And all these losses, or almost all of them, are insured. The costs are spread and spread and spread until they are in some measure borne, financially at least, by practically everyone. There is a famous old bell in the great hall at Lloyd's of London, known as the *Lutine* bell after the eighteenth-century frigate from which it was salvaged, that Lloyd's' "caller" would strike upon receiving word of a ship lost at sea. These days it is rung only rarely. Nonetheless, the symbol is irresistible: When it tolls, it tolls for thee.

Americans are not enamored of the insurance industry. In a survey by *U.S. News* in 1978, people were asked how favorably they felt toward thirty-one industries. Auto insurance ranked thirty-first. Another poll the same year included insurance (not broken down by type) as one of thirty-two industries. It ranked twenty-ninth, followed by the chemical, oil and tobacco industries.

Nor has the industry ever been swamped with talent. The story is told of a public relations survey conducted on behalf of the College of Insurance, an accredited four-year college in lower Manhattan. High school seniors were asked to rank a list of a dozen colleges in order of preference. Supposedly, the College of Insurance came in dead last. The *other* schools on the list were fictional.

"Insurance!" a friend screamed at me. "Insurance is *boring*!"

People do think so—and for reasons that will become evident, nothing could better serve the interests of the insurance industry. They just want us to *think* it's boring.

And yet whatever our feelings about insurance companies, most of us are great believers in the product, more so than in any other country. The U.S., with only 5 percent of the world's people, accounts for over two-fifths of its insurance premiums. Ninety-three percent of all U.S. homeowners are insured against fire; 91 percent of all U.S. car owners carry auto insurance. Some 86 percent of American households are covered by life insurance, at an average of more than $50,000 worth each. This is all the more remarkable when you appreciate that the term "households" includes millions of single persons without dependents, as well as others with no economic need for life insurance. In all, we had better than 400 million life insurance policies in force in 1981 (many of us had more than one). Our lives were insured for more than $3.5 trillion.

WHO BUYS INSURANCE?

Rank	Country	Percentage of Total World Premiums*
1.	**United States**	**44.7**
2.	Japan	11.6
3.	West Germany	10.6
4.	Great Britain	6.3
5.	France	5.6
6.	Canada	2.9
7.	Netherlands	2.2
8.	Italy	1.7
9.	Switzerland	1.6
10.	Australia	1.5

*Includes life, health and property/casualty. Does not include government programs. Data are for 1979, latest available.
Source: North American Reinsurance Corporation

In terms of sales, insurance is arguably the largest industry in the country.

A recent *Playboy* survey asked nearly 2,000 males to distinguish among items they considered "necessities" and items they thought of as "luxuries." Twenty-six percent of the men believed that owning a credit card was a necessity; 16 percent felt that way about dining out at least one evening a week; slightly more than half considered "having new clothes every year" a necessity; 72 percent thought one vacation a year was a necessity; a like proportion thought a savings account was a necessity (and what is that, really, but insurance against a rainy day?); 79 percent considered life insurance a necessity, even though only 60 percent of those surveyed were married. Just three items ranked ahead of life insurance as necessities (food and water, not to mention alcohol and sex, were not on *Playboy*'s list of choices): health insurance (88 percent), a telephone (87 per cent) and a car (91 percent). Owning a car, of course, is not ordinarily possible without insurance.

Insurance digs deeper into our pockets than we realize. Where does all that money go?

A large chunk, to be sure, goes where it should: to the payment of legitimate claims. The rest goes to expenses, profit and the payment of *il*legitimate, or padded, claims. Expenses include such things as those 1.9 million salaries; nearly as many desks and telephones and pension plans; billions of dollars in legal fees; what seems like—and may actually be—billions of dollars in travel and convention expenses (there is not a day of the year—with the possible exception of Christmas, but I doubt it—when an insurance congregation of one sort or another is not in session); and hundreds of millions of dollars, anyway, in the cost of paper. God, the paper! Aetna Life & Casualty produces a billion documents a year. A spokesman for the Equitable* estimates that in a year it generates a stack of 8½-x-11-inch sheets *six miles high*. He is almost proud of it.

Considered broadly, insurance raises questions of justice and equity and social structure.

Should safe drivers who are young pay more for auto insurance than safe drivers who are older?

Should each of us save for his own rainy days, or should we be required to save collectively and share the risks?

Why does a badly beaten mugging victim get nothing, while a shopper who slips on a grape is handsomely compensated?

Should a man who injured his arm striking a vending machine be entitled to workers' compensation?†

---

*Like savings banks, life insurance companies tend to be referred to this way—"the Equitable," "the Prudential"; "the Bowery," "the Dime."

†On August 21, 1975, Rhode Island foundry worker Michael DeNardo was thwarted in pursuit of his coffee break by an uncooperative vending machine. Pounding on the machine, he hurt his arm. A doctor testified that DeNardo had suffered a 10 percent loss of use of his upper right arm. Rhode Island's workers' compensation commission denied the claim—*not* on the grounds that such a disability, to the questionable extent you can even measure or verify it, is just one of life's problems, like the onset of mild arthritis or the growth of an unsightly wart— but on the grounds that vending-machine smacking wasn't part of DeNardo's job, and so not covered by workers' comp. This finding was overruled; DeNardo won his case, and his money, on appeal.

What is a surgically misplaced bellybutton *worth*?*

Such questions defy definitive answers. One's answers depend on one's social philosophy. The question to which I think answers are possible is the question of efficiency. Because—Republican or Democrat, socialist or conservative—*there* is something on which we can all agree: Waste is bad; inefficient systems rob us all.

If two people can comfortably do what previously required seven, by doing it smarter or with better equipment or by cutting out portions of their jobs that accomplish nothing, it is very much in the social interest to have them do so. This is not to say that the other five should be thrown out into the street; they should be assisted in making the transition to work that's needed. That "transition" is likely to be harrowing for the workers and executives involved. But as long as there *are* things that need doing, as there likely always will be, it is a tragedy to have people doing unnecessary work. Poor productivity undermines the success of any economy, any social system. It makes everyone poorer.

But fire half a million insurance workers? Put them on unemployment? What good does that do?

If the same service can be performed with fewer people, it can be sold for less—leaving customers more money to spend on *other* things, the purveyors of which thus experience higher demand and take on new employees. Or else it can be sold for the same price but at a greater profit—and profit, too, leads to added investment and the creation of jobs.

Actually, the number of superfluous insurance industry employees is probably closer to a *million*. One out of every hundred Americans in the work force!

Roots of the industry's inefficiency are manifold. The fire insurance business grew up as a massive exercise in price fixing. The life insurance business is dominated by giant mutual insurers whose managements have no one to answer to but themselves. They are motivated toward growing larger, not leaner. One might expect the marketplace to impose its own economic discipline—it is competition based on price that has always been the surest spur to efficiency—but insurance prices, particularly life insurance prices, are notoriously hard to evaluate, leaving consumers unable to spot the best values and insurers under little pressure to provide them. Fed-

---

*Eight hundred fifty-four thousand two hundred nineteen dollars and sixty-one cents, ruled the jury.

eral regulation and antitrust statutes largely exempt the insurance industry; state regulators are anxious to keep even inefficient companies profitable, lest policyholders be left stranded or claims go unpaid. Then, too, there are the problems of policyholders gleefully defrauding their insurers and of insurers callously chiseling their insureds—an inherently inefficient and seemingly irremediable circle of distrust.

There are ways to improve the system radically. But this is not an industry, by and large, that seeks radical improvement. Inbred and living in comfortable isolation with its state regulators, it has been slow to innovate. A "cash cow" of the first order, it has resisted change.

2

BY POPULAR DEMAND: A *VERY* SHORT CHAPTER ON INSURANCE ACCOUNTING

How to Take in $52 Million, Pay out $6 Million and Report a Loss

*There is evidence to indicate that
during the turbulent years of 1970 to 1976,
the insurance industry actually made sizable profits
on medical malpractice insurance.*
—**American Trial Lawyers Association Spokesperson, 1979**

There are only two things as complicated as insurance accounting and I have no idea what they are. But failure to toil among the footnotes does not prevent one from grasping some notion of the broad outlines.

For example, a great many insurers, while immensely rich, were

26

sort of bankrupt in 1981. Or vulnerable, anyway, because they were sitting with low-interest investments bought years earlier and carried on the books at cost, but worth billions less in the open market. A 7-percent Telephone bond issued for $1,000 and redeemable in the year 2001 fetched just $580 in mid-1981. If such assets had been carried on insurers' books at current market value—as before the Panic of 1907 they were—the insurers' surpluses (the riches that stand behind their promises to pay all valid claims) would have appeared much smaller. If they appeared at all. One large property/casualty insurer calculated that had it to value its bonds at market rather than cost, its capital base would have shrunk by a third. Aetna Life & Casualty at the end of 1980 carried $14.1 billion in bonds on its balance sheet that had a market value of $10.4 billion. The difference, $3.7 billion, exceeded the company's capital base. Aetna was quick to point out that "Great care should be used in evaluating the significance of the estimated market value of bonds since such securities, in the normal course of business, are not intended to be sold prior to maturity." The bonds may pay low interest, but so do the whole life contracts they were bought to secure—so the problem is not as grave as it seems.

Meanwhile, however, policyholders have the right to borrow against their whole life contracts at 5 percent or 6 percent or 8 percent interest. Many, in the last couple of years, have done just that. What if a lot more did? Where would insurers get the money to lend, as contractually they must? Sell off bonds or mortgages "that in the normal course of business are not intended to be sold prior to maturity"? Some big insurers in 1981 were borrowing money at 15 percent and 18 percent to lend to their policyholders at 5 percent.

Even so, the industry is likely to muddle through.

For all of 1979, property/casualty insurers earned $7 billion after taxes. In 1980, they did a little better.

Seven or eight billion dollars is not money you'd walk around with on the street. ("What *is* it, honey?" "I've lost all our *traveler's checks!*" "What kind *were* they?" "Eight billion dollars' worth of American Express." "Oh. Then we're okay.") But such large numbers are really only meaningful in context. Seven or eight billion dollars in relation to what? At the beginning of 1979, property/casualty insurers had a "consolidated policyholders' surplus"—which might roughly translate as "total capital at risk"—of $35.4

billion. To have earned $7 billion on $35.4 billion was to have earned around 20 percent. For 1980, the profit was higher but the capital at risk was, too, which made for an overall return a bit above 18 percent.

Forbes, in 1981, compared the five-year performance of ninety-two industrial subgroups. In terms of "return on total capital," property/casualty insurers headed the list. The insurance industry as a whole—life plus property/casualty—ranked fourth out of forty-nine (behind electrical equipment makers, broadcasters and publishers, and tied with the computer industry).

In terms of sales—which is to say premiums—property/casualty profits, after tax, came to 8.4 cents on the dollar in both 1979 and 1980.

The life insurance industry earned about $5 billion in 1979 and 1980.

Healthy as these profits would seem to be, it's hard to be sure they weren't even healthier. Profits in the insurance industry are a slippery thing.

To begin with, mutual companies do not talk in terms of profit at all. The $272 million a private business would have described in its income statement as "profit," the Prudential, in its 1980 annual report, calls, "Addition to the margin of protection for policyowners." At year-end 1980, the Prudential was holding a total of $2.8 billion in its margin for protection. This was in effect accumulated profit that Prudential had decided not to pay out in dividends. It sat atop $57 billion in other reserves the actuaries had determined were necessary.

Critics argue that mutuals like the Prudential should distribute their surplus funds to the policyholders.

"Better safe than sorry," rejoin the insurers; "this is our margin of safety."

"No, it's not," reply the critics. "Your margin of safety is in being able to reduce or omit dividends some year if you ever have to." For, indeed, the Prudential annually refunds its policyholders more than $1 billion in "dividends."

We will not resolve this dispute, other than to point out that the $2.8 billion Prudential has kept as surplus amounts to a mere $107 for each of the lives it insures. Surely those policyholders don't mind adding $107 worth of concrete to the Rock. What one does wonder is, How accurate are the assumptions that underlie the other

$57 billion in reserves? What if people live a little longer than planned? Or not so long? What if more people drop their policies than originally anticipated? Or fewer? What if interest rates zoom? Or plunge?

Figuring profits in the insurance business is not easy even for an expert. To the not inconsiderable extent the process is subjective, one needn't be too much of a cynic to think that insurance professionals and their bosses are likely, more often than not, to lean toward understatement.

In some lines, profit calculations are reasonably straightforward. Take "burglary and theft." In 1978, property/casualty insurers collected $135 million in premiums on this little line. Of that amount, 28.1 percent went to pay claims, 42.4 percent went to pay sales commissions, overhead and other expenses, and 30.3 percent, around $40 million, was left as profit—*plus* whatever the companies were able to earn by way of interest on those premium dollars during the course of the year. (Nineteen seventy-eight was a good year for this little line of insurance, but the years preceding and following weren't all that bad, either.) There's nothing very mysterious about figuring the profit. Claims are filed shortly after a burglary has occurred and a settlement is reached soon afterward. What's left pays expenses, and what's left after that is profit. Simple.

But how about malpractice insurance? The largest writer of medical malpractice insurance is The St. Paul Companies, Inc. In 1978, the St. Paul took in about $131 million in such premiums—perhaps a few thousand dollars from your own doctor. Line 11 of Part 1C of Schedule P of St. Paul's annual statement to insurance regulators—as I say, insurance is very much a world all its own—showed "total losses and loss expense incurred" for the year of $79 million—roughly 60 percent of the premiums that had been collected.

But malpractice claims are not like burglary claims. A quick and amicable settlement is rarely reached. Indeed, quite some time may elapse before the claimant even realizes what it is the surgeon has accidentally left in his chest cavity.* One study found that of malpractice claims that would eventually be paid, only 13 percent were reported in the year the malpractice allegedly occurred. Nearly a

---

*Among the things recently discovered: hemostats, laparotomy pads, plastic tubing, surgical knife blades, a pair of scissors and a 14-inch Babcock clamp.

third had still not been reported after three years. But that's only part of the story. For, once finally reported, the same study found, 72 percent of these claims took longer than two years to settle, and 17 percent remained unpaid after *five* years.

So, much of the $79 million in "losses and loss expense incurred" by St. Paul in 1978 had not actually been incurred at all. Or at least not paid out. St. Paul's *actual* loss payments and expenses in 1978 totaled—are you paying attention?—$3.9 million. The *other* $75 million of "losses and loss expense incurred" was still in St. Paul's pocket, earning interest.

This is not to say that St. Paul may not eventually have to pay out $75 million in claims and legal fees, or possibly even more. With 40,000 doctors insured, and the occasional multimillion-dollar award, losses could be enormous.* The point is that for lines like malpractice that have a "long tail," where many years may pass before final losses are known (auto liability and product liability being two other prime examples), the "profits" insurers report are little more than guesses; those guesses are often conservative; and the cash that sits around to be invested in the meantime is a gold mine.

In figuring profits—which a company has to do, among other things, to pay taxes—insurers must guess at the "severity" of claims not yet settled. Will they cost, on average, $20,000 or $200,000? Hard enough. But they also must guess at the "frequency" of claims that will be, but have not yet been, made. Will there be 200 claims—or 2,000? By multiplying its guess on the number of claims not yet made by its guess as to how much the average claim will cost, it arrives at an estimate of losses. These "losses"—guesses that you or I might round off to the nearest $10 million, but that the St. Paul and its competitors round off to the nearest dollar—come under the heading "IBNR." Incurred But Not Reported. They are treated like any other cost of doing business, as if the cash were actually out the door. IBNR: as much a part of insurance accounting as RBI is part of baseball.

---

*Take the case of Sacramento anesthesiologist William Miofsky (not insured by the St. Paul) who orally copulated patients as they were undergoing surgery. He was arrested in March 1979 after a nurse peaked behind the curtain that separated him from the rest of the surgical team. Scores of women who believe they may have been assaulted while under anesthesia are suing for what could, in theory, at least, total well over $100 million in damages. Against just one doctor!

If time proves these estimates to have been conservative, an adjustment will be made and additional profit reported. And taxed. But in the meantime, the insurer has use of the money.

From 1975 through 1978, during the early part of which the nation was suffering a crisis in the availability of malpractice insurance because insurers felt they were not being paid adequately for the risk, the St. Paul took in $415 million in malpractice premiums and paid out $27 million in claims and claims-settlement expenses. Even so, in the fall of 1978, a St. Paul executive told the Conference of Insurance Legislators (an association of state legislators) that the St. Paul *had lost money* in medical malpractice throughout 1975, but that the line had been "generally profitable" during 1976 and 1977. All of this was based on estimates and assumptions, presumably made in good faith, that only time could corroborate. (At the time of the speech, $52.7 million in premiums had been collected for 1975 but only about $6 million actually paid out.)

Malpractice suits in the early 1970s were being filed with increasing frequency and being settled ever more generously. That the insurers were genuinely scared, and not just pretending, is evidenced by the fact that some of them actually withdrew from the market. Had they been consciously fabricating a crisis to reap huge profits, fewer would have abandoned the business.

Instead, many saw claims rising at the rate of 20 percent a year, with settlements rising an additional 15 percent a year, which suggested that 100 claims settled for $10,000 each this year—$1 million—would grow to 120 claims settled for $11,500 each next year—$1.4 million—and 619 claims settled for $40,455 each in ten years—$25 million. By the same logic, a 12-year-old growing two inches a year might be expected eventually to attain a height of fourteen feet.

As it happened, after rising at 20 percent a year from 1970 to 1975, the St. Paul experienced an 11 percent *drop* in claims frequency in 1976. On the other hand, the severity of claims did continue to grow from 1976 through 1981 at about a 15 percent rate. (At least this was the experience of one large doctor-owned mutual.) But founded or not, the malpractice panic was real. And it had its repercussions.

Doctors began practicing "defensive medicine." Nearly half of 4,000 doctors polled in one survey said they had begun ordering more diagnostic tests as a result of the malpractice tempest, 44 percent were keeping more detailed patient records, 37 percent were writing fewer refillable prescriptions and 31 percent were less willing to give advice over the phone. (As a result, medical care was a bit safer, a bit more expensive and a bit less convenient.) Some irate doctors even went out on strike. "Feeling Sick?" read one popular bumper sticker of the day. "Call Your Lawyer."

Insurers began lobbying to limit malpractice awards. Fumed the much aggrieved president of the American Association of Trial Lawyers in 1979: "At no time in the history of the United States have state legislatures moved with such unanimity or with greater rapidity. Between 1974 and 1976, every state in the union passed some malpractice law." Some states imposed statutes of limitation; some imposed dollar limits; some imposed greater burdens of proof on the plaintiff. It was an effort to restore sanity to the judicial process and contain medical costs (if you believe the doctors and the insurance industry) or to restrict citizens' legal rights and assure stratospheric insurance industry profits (if you believe the trial lawyers).

By the end of 1980, it had begun to appear that 1975 had not been such a loser, after all. Of the $52.7 million the St. Paul had collected in premiums, $15.5 million had been paid out in losses and legal fees; only an estimated $9.2 million remained to be paid.

Losses and loss expenses actually paid for the years 1975 through 1978—against total premiums of $415 million—had climbed to $78 million. Even after a hefty $87 million in selling and administrative expense, that still left a quarter of a billion dollars.

Plus interest. No listing is given in the annual statement to insurance regulators to show how much interest the St. Paul had earned, tax-free, in municipal bonds, on top of that quarter billion. As of the end of 1980, it must have totaled in the neighborhood of an additional $75 million.

But don't worry if, in hindsight, it seems malpractice premiums—and hence your own medical bills—were too high in the 1970s. Chances are, your health insurance covered the tab.

3

YOU CAN'T TELL THE PLAYERS
Without This Scorecard

Insurance regulation in Florida is a myth, a sham.
We don't have enough information to know whether
or not companies are making too much money.
—Bill Gunter, Florida Insurance Commissioner

I will return to insureds who shoot their hands off (there are actually "nub clubs" in the South, one claims adjuster told me, where folks sit around drinking up the proceeds of their dismemberment benefits), and to how much more your life insurance is likely to cost if you have three or more nipples ("supernumerary nipples," they're called), but first some fundamentals:

• *Actuaries* forecast claims, crank in assumptions about interest rates and, thus armed, set insurance rates. They excel at statistics, probability theory, compound-interest calculations and the extrapolation of trends. They say things like (and I quote), "The adjusted rates were graduated by a Jenkins fifth difference modified osculatory interpolation formula with fourth differences at the end points set equal to zero." They tend to be conservative.

• *Agents* sell insurance. The Prudential has 22,280 of them.

• *Brokers,* also known as *independent agents*, represent several different insurance companies. They may work alone or in packs.

• *Big commercial brokers*, like Marsh & McLennan, Alexander & Alexander, Frank B. Hall, Fred S. James, and Corroon & Black, with thousands of employees each, may not handle your automobile insurance but are very good with the problems of multinational chemical combines.

• *Claims adjusters* scrutinize a lot of dented fenders and gutted pizza parlors and are fibbed to from time to time. Life insurance claims adjusters, called claims "examiners," are mostly deskbound and scrutinize a lot of paperwork.

• *Customers* buy insurance to protect their property, their loved ones or, in the case of corporate managers, their jobs. Some buy insurance not so much to be reimbursed in the event of loss as to keep the loss from occurring in the first place. Not entirely rational, this is our loser complex at work—twice. We believe that if we *fail* to insure, after twenty years of having done so faithfully without a single claim, *this* will be the year the moving-van burglars drive up to our door; but that if we *do* insure, no loss will occur. (When was the last time we ever "won" anything, let alone from an insurance company?)

• *Investment managers* parcel out the loot the rest of the industry labors to amass. They buy bonds and write mortgages. By and large, they do a perfectly adequate job. It's not *their* fault inflation came along and decimated the value of fixed-income securities.

Once acquired, their bonds find a comfortable corner in the vault and go to sleep for decades. The Prudential's list of slumbering securities runs well over a hundred pages. Even so—and despite the fact that state laws tightly restrict their investments alternatives—insurers under pressure from inflation have grown increasingly aggressive and imaginative. Many of their loans now require equity or profit participation on top of interest. The Northwestern Mutual is one of several life insurers heavily involved in oil exploration. The Prudential has become America's largest landlord. Aetna Life & Casualty owns a California homebuilder, part of a hockey team (the New England Whalers) and, with IBM and Comsat, a potential communications behemoth (Satellite Business Systems). Even the staid old Metropolitan Life has begun funneling money into venture capital deals.

• *Lobbyists* hang around all fifty state capitols looking after the insurance industry's interests. Not all work at it full time; many represent other clients as well—but they're there when they're needed. Take Massachusetts. Massachusetts had, in all, 400 men and women registered as "legislative agents" in the first quarter of

1981. There was a man representing the Massachusetts Cosmetologists Association, two representing Common Cause, two for the President and Fellows of Harvard College. The tobacco institute had a man on retainer; Ford, General Motors and General Electric each had one. The state's banks and utilities and labor unions had two or three dozen each. The insurance industry had sixty.

Insurance lobbyists outnumber all others in virtually every state. "Our strength?" pondered one. "[It] comes from having a group of people who tell a story that is logical and reasonable to a group of people who don't have the slightest idea what you're talking about."

It comes, too, at least in some instances, from the assistance lobbyists may occasionally provide in obtaining loans and mortgages and insurance, and (for those legislators who are attorneys) in settling insurance claims. Discussing an upcoming vote, a lobbyist was told to expect a certain legislator to vote against the industry. "Oh no," he replied. "I've helped that one settle too many cases."*

• *Rating clerks* look at the year and model of the car you drive, your accident record—all that (or, in the case of a home, the distance you are from a hydrant and all *that*)—and assign you to the proper rating classification. It is not a matter of judgment, simply a matter of following the book.

• *Regulators*, whom I have deliberately separated from lobbyists lest there be an appearance of impropriety (rating clerks would not ordinarily make it onto a list like this), are appointed or elected in each state to oversee the insurance industry. They vary markedly in the degree to which they are overwhelmed by the task at hand. Some are completely overwhelmed but seem not to care. Others are completely overwhelmed but try hard anyway. There is a National Association of Insurance Commissioners, which periodically suggests model laws and regulations. Its meetings are notable for the ratio of guests in attendance. Industry executives outnumber regulators by around four to one.

Illinois has long been considered one of the more hospitable states from which to operate an insurance company. More property/casualty insurers are domiciled in Illinois—290 of them in 1980—than in any other state.† Why is that? Could it have something to do with the regulatory and legislative climate?

---

*As quoted in Karen Orren's excellent *Corporate Power and Social Change*.

†For life insurers, Illinois ranked fourth, behind Arizona ("the Port Said of insurance regulation"), Texas and Louisiana.

Orren describes a $20-a-plate dinner held at Chicago's Palmer House in 1967 honoring Illinois' then Director of Insurance, John F. Bolton. *Nine hundred insurance executives came*. Hell of a guy, too. Three times decorated for his service in World War II, son of a judge, father of six, member of the American, Illinois and Chicago Bar Associations, the Catholic Lawyers' Guild, Ridge Country Club and the Illinois Athletic Club. But one wonders how many executives would have shown up to honor the chairman of the Federal Trade Commission, in mid-term, or Stanley Sporkin, when he was working at the Securities and Exchange Commission.

During his years as insurance director, Bolton remained active with his law firm, which served several insurance company clients. His executive assistant, James C. Cage, had been chairman of a Dallas insurer that failed and executive vice-president of a Chicago insurer whose officers had been accused of fraud.

Of the nine Illinois insurance directors who preceded Bolton, beginning in 1933, Orren found that seven had been lawyers for large insurance companies, an eighth had been district agent for a large life insurance company, and the ninth had been on the board of a life insurance company. The story has been much the same since: regulation of the industry by the industry.

(As for Illinois' state legislators: From 1961 through 1968, the proportion of insurance committee members who listed their occupation as insurance ranged from 21 percent to 33 percent in the House and from 31 percent to 58 percent in the Senate. Today, the proportions are lower but still significant.)

The industry and its regulators do not always get along, nor have they all the same answers. By no means. (In New Jersey, aggressive regulation has driven several auto insurers to abandon the state altogether.) But isolated in a world all their own and fighting off federal scrutiny, they may sometimes not be asking the right questions. In a later chapter you will meet the insurance regulator who insisted that $23 was more than $66.

• *Risk managers,* employed by most large corporations, decide what insurance to buy, then work with the big commercial brokers to obtain it on the best possible terms. (Someday, as they and their staffs grow more sophisticated, they will routinely deal direct with insurers, eliminating the middle man.) In addition, they attempt to prevent losses. At a plant where workers were lax about wearing safety glasses, the risk manager placed on permanent display a glass eye. At Pacific Power & Light, where meter readers were plagued by dog bites, the risk manager turned to a "dog psychiatrist" for advice. Now when a dog starts to attack, PP&L meter readers merely press the button that snaps open the collapsible umbrellas they've all been issued. The dogs almost always turn away in confusion. And at Levi Strauss—perhaps more typical of a risk manager's work—an analysis was undertaken of the jeans maker's suppliers. It was discovered that the company depended on a single plant for all its indigo dye, and that that plant was none too well fire-protected. Levi Strauss' risk manager proposed sharing the cost of upgrading the supplier's sprinkler system. "I knew we would get a credit on our contingent business interruption coverage," he told *Institutional Investor,* "which would make a very adequate return on our investment." The supplier went ahead with the upgrade all by itself; Levi Strauss got the premium reduction it had hoped for and reduced the risk of ever running short of dye.

• *Underwriters* decide whether to accept or decline applications for insurance. In situations too complicated for a rating clerk to determine the correct premium—for a satellite launch or a life insurance applicant with mild diabetes—they will set the rate as well. Underwriters are not nearly so concerned about turning down good risks as about accepting risks that prove to be bad.

• *Victims* are people a sensible insurance system should be designed to serve.

LIFE COMPANIES VS. PROPERTY/CASUALTY COMPANIES

The life insurance industry is characterized by stability. Its money is long-term bedrock capital. Most importantly, life insurance is a *sales* industry. Its product is one people are not prone to purchase without persuasion.

The property/casualty business is cyclical. Losses can be dramatic. Property/casualty pros are more likely than their life industry counterparts to thrive in an environment of uncertainty, to enjoy a roll of the dice. Because they work on a shorter time horizon, much of their money is kept relatively liquid.

Many insurers own both life *and* property/casualty companies. The Prudential now has a property/casualty arm; Allstate has a life insurance company. But the basic distinction remains: Life insurers sell life and health insurance; property/casualty companies sell everything else.

MUTUAL VS. STOCK COMPANIES

Stock companies are owned by shareholders and run to make a profit. Mutual companies are owned, in theory, at least, by their policyholders and run—again, in theory—purely for their benefit.

Stock companies include the likes of Aetna Life & Casualty and The Travelers Corporation, both of which are traded on the New York Stock Exchange. To buy stock in them you need only pick up the phone and call your broker. (From 1970 through mid-1981, Aetna's stock tripled. Its dividend increased fivefold. In the same period, IBM fell from 74 to 58; GM, from 65 to 49.) You can't buy stock in the Prudential Insurance Company of America, even if your broker is Bache Halsey Stuart Shields (a Prudential subsidiary). The Prudential is owned by its policyholders.

Mutual life insurers were started by entrepreneurs who lacked capital. Property/casualty mutuals usually got started when the established insurers of the time, typically stock companies based in Hartford and New York, refused to write some new coverage or refused to insure a particular industry deemed unduly risky. Liberty Mutual was started because the big stock companies were charging Boston's employers too much for workers' compensation insurance. State Farm, today the nation's leading auto and home insurer, with some 15 percent of the entire market, got its start because Illinois auto insurers were charging farmers the same rates as city dwellers. Recognizing that traffic hazards would be fewer in Pleasant Mound, Illinois, than in Chicago, State Farm was able to undercut the established rates by nearly 40 percent. That was in 1922. More recently, in the mid-1970s, when insurers were charging stratospheric rates for medical malpractice insurance or refusing to write the business at all, doctors and hospitals throughout the country banded together to form their own, mutual insurance companies.

You might think mutuals would provide lower prices and better service than stock companies, inasmuch as they have no one to serve but their policyholders. "Invest your money in a stock insurer but buy your insurance from a mutual," runs the old adage. In fact, this is not always the case. Some mutuals, like State Farm and

Teachers Insurance & Annuity (TIAA)*, do get consistently high marks. Others do not. The same is true of stock companies. It's hard to generalize about insurers, and types of insurers, because their competitiveness may vary from state to state, from year to year, and from policy to policy.

Life insurance in America has traditionally been dominated by mutual insurers. Twelve of the fifteen largest life insurers are mutuals.* Taken together, just five of them—Prudential, Metropolitan, Equitable, John Hancock and New York Life—represent close to two-fifths of the industry's assets.

Mutual ownership should, it's true, make for low prices. Profits are returned to the policyholders. But for a century or so the emphasis has been not on low prices but on high sales; not on rebating high "dividends" (refunds of excess premium) but on building enormous reserves.

There are three reasons mutual insurers have not always felt compelled to deliver low prices and high dividends:

(1) Particularly with whole life (read on), customers cannot tell a low price from a high price.

(2) Dissatisfied customers cannot easily switch to a competitor. Once locked into a life insurance contract, it costs dearly to cancel.

(3) The managements of mutual insurers are in a very real sense responsible to no one but themselves. Ownership of mutual life insurers is so broad, so dispersed, so atomized and anonymous, that for all practical purposes *it doesn't exist*. Technically, the policyholders own the mutuals. Practically speaking, *no one does*. Instead, it is the stewards of these institutions who control them.

(No wonder when Bache Halsey Stuart Shields, Inc., faced a hostile takeover bid from Canada's aggressive Belzberg family in 1981, the management ran headlong into the arms of the Prudential. Under Sam Belzberg—a single, hard-driving owner—management might have developed a bleeding ulcer. Who owns Bache now? *No one* does.)

Imagine yourself one of a hundred local dentists who've formed a mutual insurance scheme. If at the end of the year there appeared to be $100,000 more in the kitty than required, you might well phone a few friends in advance of the annual meeting to urge re-

---

*Strictly speaking, TIAA is a "non-profit stock company." Practically speaking, it is a mutual.

funding that money to its owners. Or if the manager who'd been hired to collect the premiums and administer claims had sent himself and his wife first-class to Hawaii, you might consider junking him.

Executives of the large mutuals operate under no such constraints. Many hold no annual meetings (arguing, reasonably, that practically no one would come) and mail annual reports only to those policyholders who request them (arguing, again reasonably, that to do otherwise would be a waste of policyholders' money). In a recent election for board members of the Prudential, four vacancies were to be filled. Vying for these four spots were a total of four candidates, nominated by the board itself. Eligible to vote were 18.4 million policyholders. Of these, 323 did—virtually all of them employees of Prudential. Later in the same year, policyholders of the Equitable were called upon to choose among a field of eleven nominees to fill eleven board seats. An estimated 3,250,000 policyholders were eligible to vote but were not informed of the election; 6,400, mostly Equitable employees, voted by mail. Seven showed up at the election to vote in person.

Under New York State law, a policyholder who wishes to propose his own slate of nominees need only enlist the signatures of a tenth of 1 percent of his fellows. But in the case of the Metropolitan, this would entail gathering nearly 30,000 valid signatures.

In 1974, the Equitable plunged into the property/casualty business so that its sales force could sell homeowners and auto insurance. It was hoped these easy-to-sell lines would enhance the success of the Equitable agent and thus help slow rapid turnover of the sales force (a major and costly problem for any life insurer). It didn't work. "Professional life insurance people," chief executive Coy Eklund told *Forbes*, "simply don't want to get involved in a business that bothers them over the weekend with telephone calls reporting wrinkled fenders." So it proved a poor strategic move. What's more, it cost the Equitable millions. The company was paying out $1.18 in claims and expenses for every dollar it took in. State Farm, in the same period, was paying out just 91.5 cents. So in 1981 the Equitable dropped the whole thing. Total loss to its policyholders: $100 million. Now listen to how Eklund viewed this mess, at least in his interview with *Forbes:* "I'm not a bit interested in whether it was profitable. Our problem is that we're getting no enjoyment from the operation."

If top management of a mutual insurer does a mediocre job, it has the option and the power to fire itself. No one else does. If it wishes to retain, rather than rebate, an extra several hundred million of its policyholders' dollars to enter the auto insurance business, incurring huge losses along the way, it need merely issue the order. If it prefers not to trim the ranks of its bureaucracy (what general wishes a smaller army?), it need not do so.

As a former president of State Farm once summed it up for *Business Week:* "No one is going to fire me if I don't do a good job."

This is not to say that mutual managements are incompetent or dishonest. Most are dedicated and upright. Theirs is a noble calling, not unlike religious or government service. It just pays better.

WHAT THEY PAID THEMSELVES IN 1980

Prudential	
Robert A. Beck, Chairman	$507,760
Frank J. Hoeneymeyer, Chief Investment	344,020
Officer	
David J. Sherwood, President	323,040
Metropolitan	
Richard R. Shinn	$500,000
Edwin B. Lancaster, E.V.P.	270,000
John J. Creedon, President	246,666
Equitable	
Coy G. Eklund, President, CEO	$445,301
John T. Fey, Chairman	339,470
W.C. Millar, Agency Manager (Ann Arbor)	277,311
New York Life	
R. Manning Brown, Jr., Chairman	$409,516
Robert W. Hartman, General Manager	211,168
(Sioux City)	
Marshall P. Bissell, President	202,500
John Hancock	
J. Edwin Matz, Chairman	$407,417
John C. McElwee, President	298,929
Gordon B. Jones, E.V.P.	248,151

WHAT THEY PAID THEMSELVES IN 1980 *(continued)*

Data above are for the three most highly compensated employees of the five largest (assets) mutual insurance societies. By way of comparison:

<u>What Other Non-Profit Executives Were Paid</u>

President, United States	$200,000
Chairman, Joint Chiefs of Staff	51,112
Archbishop of Canterbury	30,000
President, Harvard University	74,449
President, American Red Cross	85,000
President, World Bank	78,000
President, AFL-CIO	110,000
President, Ford Foundation	135,000
Chairman, Teachers Insurance & Annuities Assoc.	200,729

<u>And For-Profit Executives . . .</u>

Chairman, General Motors	$422,000
Chairman, Citicorp	507,000
Chairman, Travelers	533,000
Chairman, Aetna Life & Casualty	609,000

The broad social advantage of mutual ownership is that an extra charge need not be levied to produce a profit. The broad social advantage of *non*-mutual ownership, ironically, is that pressure for profit *is* brought to bear. Stockholders expect management to perform. This translates into considerable attention to efficiency and cost cutting; to letting people go from time to time; even, when things are not going as well as they might, to bringing in executives "from outside." Asked for a case of a chief executive's having been brought in from outside to run a mutual life insurer—from banking or data processing, for example, or even from another insurance company—a spokesman for the American Council of Life Insurance was not able to come up with a single one.

An impassioned attack on mutual life insurers, *The Billion Dollar Bookies,* by Richard Shulman, was published in 1976. It charged mutuals with wasting policyholders' money (and retaining far more than necessary in reserves and surplus). Fun to read and eminently persuasive, if occasionally overzealous, it was largely ignored. I sent a copy to a senior inner-circle executive at one of the nation's leading stock insurers. Because the book is more than a little anti-establishment in tone, and this executive had served in the Nixon White House and now drew down a very established salary indeed, I feared a somewhat testy reply. Instead came this:

> The view of mutual life insurance companies held by stock managements is in genteel agreement with Shulman's view. One of the reasons there is relatively little interchange between the personnel of the two is the entirely different attitude each has about spending money—suspicion that the mutual guy will spend you blind.

The board of directors of Pacific Mutual Life, responsible, for all practical purposes, only to itself, announced in June 1980 a special increase in the pensions of its retired workers. It was the third such voluntary inflation adjustment in eight years and applied to all retirees who had been with the company for ten years or more, or their beneficiaries.

Unquestionably this was a generous thing to do; except that the funds in question belonged not to the board but to the policyholders—who might have preferred to have been paid an increased dividend. This is not necessarily to say that the board acted badly. The policyholders themselves, had they been asked, might have voted the same way. But no one asked.

In a stock company, for better or worse, this might well not have happened.

Contrast Pacific Mutual's generosity with the parsimony of the late John D. MacArthur, whose own privately held insurance company—anything but a mutual—was headquartered in a pair of cramped, dilapidated Chicago "eyesores." Biographer William Hoffman describes a sales extravaganza that was to have been held in the fall of 1962. Admission was to be awarded to the 300 best-performing salesmen of 1961. All through the year pep notices went out to the 3,500 competing salesmen, reminding them of the "three gala days of sun and fun in glamorous Florida." To keep costs down, the extravaganza was to be held at MacArthur's own hotel. In November, when rooms would otherwise go unfilled. The year drew to a close, the winners were announced, and then, sometime before the gala was to have begun, MacArthur (skunk that he was) called it off. Just like that.

His subordinates were dumbfounded. To keep the winners from

quitting the company, they announced that the gala had been canceled "out of concern for the group's safety." Explains Hoffman: "The reason given was the Cuban missile crisis. The real reason was that John MacArthur was congenitally incapable of footing a tab for three hundred conventioneering salesmen."

It was *his* money. The chief executive of a mutual insurer is not spending his own money. Sales spectaculars are held all the time.

By themselves, sales conventions and first-class airfares add just a few hundred million dollars to the national life insurance tab. What really adds up is the care and feeding of a 250,000-man army of sales personnel, plus their recruitment, training, supervision and support.

DIRECT WRITERS VS. AGENCY COMPANIES

So: an insurer may be a life company or a property/casualty company; a stock company or a mutual. A third way insurers are categorized is by the way they sell their product.

"Direct writers" deal directly with their customers, either through their full-time agents, salaried employees or by mail. "Agency companies" procure their business through brokers, also called "independent" agents, who represent several different insurers. When you call one of these brokers—and in the United States you have 70,000 firms to choose from—he will place your business with the carrier he feels best suits your needs. Or the one that best suits *his* needs, but we will come to that.

Direct writers tend to offer lower prices than agency companies because they are more efficient.

State Farm, GEICO and Allstate are direct writers. Travelers, CNA and Aetna are agency companies.

Now here are just a few other basic concepts that, once mastered, will leave your dinner partners rapt.

PERSONAL LINES VS. COMMERCIAL LINES

One of the easier ones to grasp. Types ("lines") of insurance sold to people are called personal lines. Those sold to businesses are called commercial lines. To say an insurer "writes a big commercial auto line" means simply that it insures a lot of company cars.

PROPERTY VS. CASUALTY

Property insurance covers damage to, or theft of, property. *Your* property. Casualty—or "liability"—insurance protects you in case you damage someone else. As society grows more complex, and legal recourse ever broader, the emphasis in "property/casualty" insurance falls increasingly on "casualty."

What would a pioneer setting out to tame the West, or a 12-year-old turn-of-the-century coal miner, have made of this 1980 news item?

> A Connecticut worker who was asked to give a speech at a training session contended the experience upset him so much he became mentally ill. His doctor agrees the incident disabled him and says the man can never work again.

Occupational stress, the illness with which the timid speaker believed he had been afflicted, and for which he wished to be supported with public funds for the rest of his life, may become epidemic. An ex-personnel manager was recently demanding compensation for the crackup he had suffered under the strain of having to promote people in accordance with affirmative action guidelines.

We have come to expect much more of our social system, needless to say, than our great-grandparents ever did. For insurers, the expanding limits of liability create new opportunities.

FIRST PARTY VS. THIRD PARTY COVERAGE

In an insurance contract, you, the policyholder, are the "first party." First-party insurance pays you. *Third*-party insurance protects you if you hurt some "third party."

Your homeowners policy is primarily a first-party contract: It protects your property. But it provides third-party coverage as well. If your second-story guest bedroom directly overlooks a deceptively shallow wading pool, and your guests enjoy an early morning dip, you could need it.

With first-party insurance, the insurer's obligation is to pay its

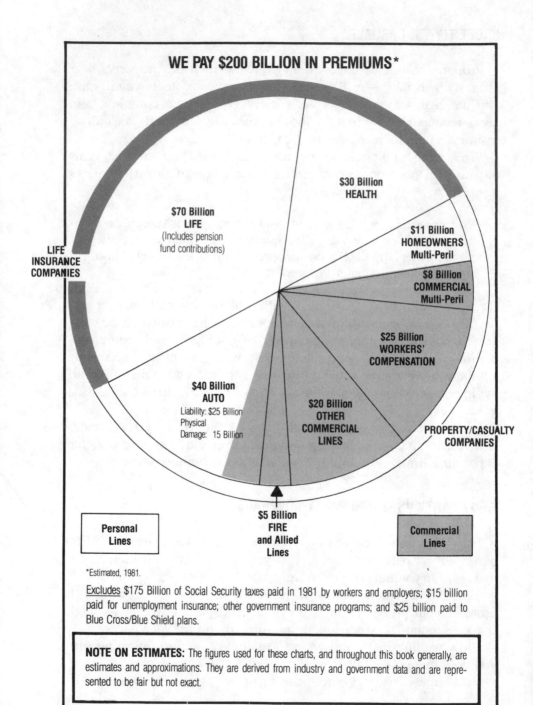

WE PAY $200 BILLION IN PREMIUMS*

$70 Billion
LIFE
(Includes pension
fund contributions)

$30 Billion
HEALTH

$11 Billion
HOMEOWNERS
Multi-Peril

$8 Billion
COMMERCIAL
Multi-Peril

LIFE
INSURANCE
COMPANIES

$25 Billion
WORKERS'
COMPENSATION

$40 Billion
AUTO
Liability: $25 Billion
Physical
Damage: 15 Billion

$20 Billion
OTHER
COMMERCIAL
LINES

PROPERTY/CASUALTY
COMPANIES

Personal
Lines

$5 Billion
FIRE
and Allied
Lines

Commercial
Lines

*Estimated, 1981.

Excludes $175 Billion of Social Security taxes paid in 1981 by workers and employers; $15 billion paid for unemployment insurance; other government insurance programs; and $25 billion paid to Blue Cross/Blue Shield plans.

NOTE ON ESTIMATES: The figures used for these charts, and throughout this book generally, are estimates and approximations. They are derived from industry and government data and are represented to be fair but not exact.

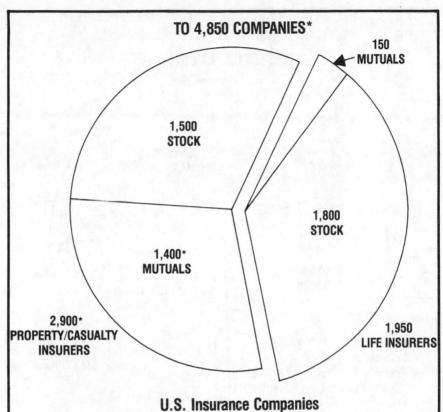

TO 4,850 COMPANIES*

150
MUTUALS

1,500
STOCK

1,800
STOCK

1,400*
MUTUALS

2,900*
PROPERTY/CASUALTY
INSURERS

1,950
LIFE INSURERS

U.S. Insurance Companies

*Approximately 1,000 of these are tiny county mutuals, reciprocals (a type of mutual) and others. The vast bulk of the property/casualty business is written by about 900 companies in all.

LEADING P/C INSURERS	1980 Premiums Written*
1. State Farm	$7.9 Billion
2. Allstate	5.0 Billion
3. Aetna Life & Cas.	4.3 Billion
4. Liberty Mutual	2.7 Billion
5. Continental Ins.	2.7 Billion
6. Travelers	2.7 Billion
7. Hartford Fire	2.7 Billion
8. Farmers Insurance	2.6 Billion
9. INA	2.5 Billion
10. Fireman's Fund	2.3 Billion
11. U.S. Fidelity & Guar.	2.0 Billion
12. Nationwide Mutual	1.8 Billion

*Excludes all life and health premiums.

LEADING LIFE INSURERS	Life Insurance In Force 12/31/80
1. Prudential	$406.6 Billion
2. Metropolitan	349.2 Billion
3. Equitable	197.3 Billion
4. Aetna Life & Cas.	156.6 Billion
5. John Hancock	133.7 Billion
6. New York Life	122.8 Billion
7. Travelers	106.6 Billion
8. Conn. General	80.4 Billion
9. Occidental Life	68.0 Billion
10. Sun Life of Canada	65.0 Billion
11. Northwestern Mut.	61.3 Billion
12. Lincoln Nat'l.	59.9 Billion

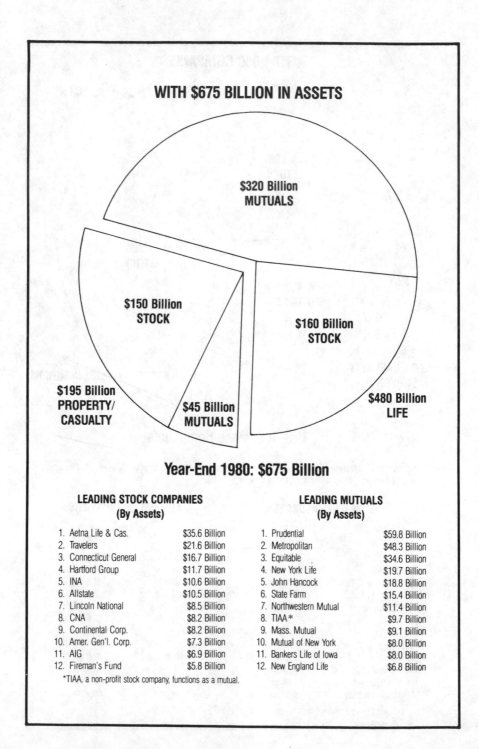

WITH $675 BILLION IN ASSETS

$320 Billion
MUTUALS

$150 Billion
STOCK

$160 Billion
STOCK

$195 Billion
PROPERTY/
CASUALTY

$45 Billion
MUTUALS

$480 Billion
LIFE

Year-End 1980: $675 Billion

LEADING STOCK COMPANIES (By Assets)		LEADING MUTUALS (By Assets)	
1. Aetna Life & Cas.	$35.6 Billion	1. Prudential	$59.8 Billion
2. Travelers	$21.6 Billion	2. Metropolitan	$48.3 Billion
3. Connecticut General	$16.7 Billion	3. Equitable	$34.6 Billion
4. Hartford Group	$11.7 Billion	4. New York Life	$19.7 Billion
5. INA	$10.6 Billion	5. John Hancock	$18.8 Billion
6. Allstate	$10.5 Billion	6. State Farm	$15.4 Billion
7. Lincoln National	$8.5 Billion	7. Northwestern Mutual	$11.4 Billion
8. CNA	$8.2 Billion	8. TIAA*	$9.7 Billion
9. Continental Corp.	$8.2 Billion	9. Mass. Mutual	$9.1 Billion
10. Amer. Gen'l. Corp.	$7.3 Billion	10. Mutual of New York	$8.0 Billion
11. AIG	$6.9 Billion	11. Bankers Life of Iowa	$8.0 Billion
12. Fireman's Fund	$5.8 Billion	12. New England Life	$6.8 Billion

*TIAA, a non-profit stock company, functions as a mutual.

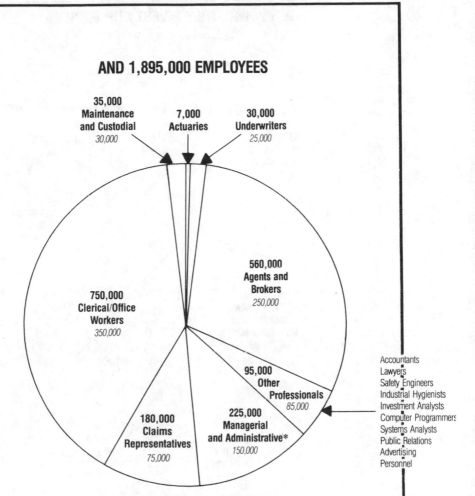

AND 1,895,000 EMPLOYEES

35,000
Maintenance
and Custodial
30,000

7,000
Actuaries

30,000
Underwriters
25,000

750,000
Clerical/Office
Workers
350,000

560,000
Agents and
Brokers
250,000

95,000
Other
Professionals
85,000

Accountants
Lawyers
Safety Engineers
Industrial Hygienists
Investment Analysts
Computer Programmers
Systems Analysts
Public Relations
Advertising
Personnel

180,000
Claims
Representatives
75,000

225,000
Managerial
and Administrative*
150,000

*Includes sales-office managers, who also sell insurance.

SOURCE of aggregate 1980 employment figure: American Council of Life Insurance. Subgroup estimates derived from 1980–81 Occupational Outlook Handbook, U.S. Bureau of Labor Statistics.

Not included here are the risk-management and personnel departments of major corporations, employed in the administration of insurance; state insurance department employees; lawyers (other than in-house) who derive much of their income from the insurance system.

FIGURES IN ITALICS are estimates of the number of employees required if the insurance system were efficient. Total: 975,000.

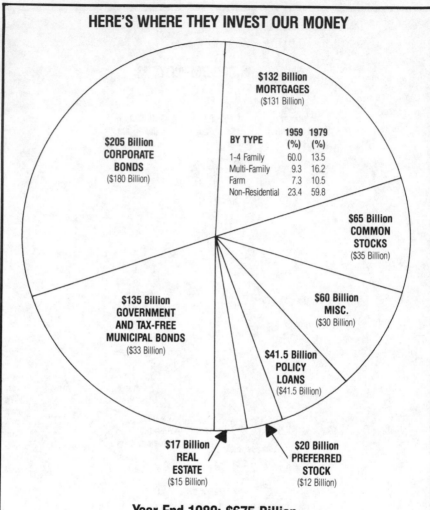

HERE'S WHERE THEY INVEST OUR MONEY

$132 Billion
MORTGAGES
($131 Billion)

BY TYPE	1959 (%)	1979 (%)
1-4 Family	60.0	13.5
Multi-Family	9.3	16.2
Farm	7.3	10.5
Non-Residential	23.4	59.8

$205 Billion
CORPORATE
BONDS
($180 Billion)

$65 Billion
COMMON
STOCKS
($35 Billion)

$135 Billion
GOVERNMENT
AND TAX-FREE
MUNICIPAL BONDS
($33 Billion)

$60 Billion
MISC.
($30 Billion)

$41.5 Billion
POLICY
LOANS
($41.5 Billion)

$17 Billion
REAL
ESTATE
($15 Billion)

$20 Billion
PREFERRED
STOCK
($12 Billion)

Year-End 1980: $675 Billion

FIGURES IN PARENTHESES show life insurance industry assets alone. (Source: American Council of Life Insurance.)

BONDS are carried at cost, MORTGAGES, at unpaid principal, even though their market value was substantially lower. REAL ESTATE, also valued at cost, was appreciably underrstated.

PROPERTY/CASUALTY insurers invest most of their money in government bonds. When the underwriting cycle is with them (and they are making money even before allowing for investment income), they invest heavily in tax-free municipal bonds. When the underwriting cycle is against them (and they are losing money before taking into account investment income), they shift toward higher yielding taxable bonds—shielded from taxes by their underwriting losses.

policyholder's claim. Failure to do so with reasonable good grace risks loss of a customer. With third-party insurance, it is the insurer's job to *fend off* claims that may be brought against the policyholder. There are limits to how hard insurance company lawyers may fend without getting their writs slapped, but the distinction between first-party and third-party insurance is real. Third-party claims on average are much more expensive to process because a finding of "fault" must be made, and perhaps even proved in court. First-party coverage is "no-fault." The policyholder is compensated for his loss no matter who caused it.

(And the second party? What happened to him? The second party—I realized after three years of trying to figure it out—is your insurer.)

WHOLE LIFE VS. TERM INSURANCE

For all the fancy names and combinations, there are really only two kinds of life insurance: whole life and term.

Term insurance is pure insurance. All you pay for in any given year, and all you get, is the insurer's promise to pay if you die. Because the chance of your dying increases as you grow older, so does the cost of term insurance.

Whole life is *two* things. It is term insurance, as just described, plus a savings plan. The premium starts out much higher than with term, but *remains level,* because the extra money you pay in the early years goes to subsidize the later years. What's really happening is that as your savings steadily grow, the amount of *insurance* protection you're buying shrinks. For when you die, the insurer pays out only the face amount of the policy—not the face amount *plus* your savings.*

Whole life was conceived in England in the mid-eighteenth century when James Dodson, a mathematician, was denied life insurance on account of his age. He was 46. It was Dodson's notion that, in contrast with term insurance, premiums should *not* rise with age but rather be set high enough in the early years of the contract to remain level through the whole of a man's life. The very substantial

---

*I keep saying "die." I shouldn't do that. In the euphemistic world of life insurance, people never die, they're just "taken out of the picture." Or "hit by a bus." Or "something happens to them."

"overpayments" in the early years would accrue and earn interest so as to permit equally substantial "underpayments" later in life. Obviously, this is not a good system for someone who fulfills the contract in its early years, overpaying, but drops it before reaping the advantages of "underpayments" in later years. Nor has it merit when, after years of faithful adherence to the plan—at no small scrimp and sacrifice—inflation comes along and destroys its value. Ten thousand dollars was once a lot of money.

Because a whole life policy is so largely a savings plan, the real question is: *What's the interest rate?* For a great many policies the answer is: *Lousy.* Particularly, as I say, if the policy is allowed to lapse after just five or ten years. *(Just?)* But answering the interest rate question—and what question could be more basic?—is complicated by the fact that, in a quaint holdover from the commercial practices of the Middle Ages, insurers *don't tell you.* At least not in any form one could reasonably be expected to understand.

Insurance companies have long prospered pushing whole life, but for a lot of reasons—inflation being the most immediately compelling—most people would have been a lot better off buying term insurance instead.

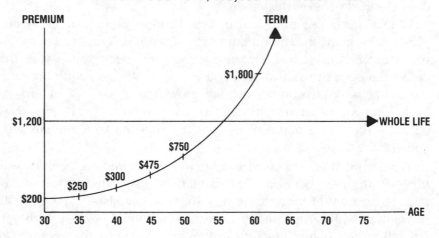

ANNUAL COST OF $100,000 LIFE INSURANCE

PARTICIPATING VS. NON-PARTICIPATING POLICIES

A participating life insurance policy is one that pays dividends. If the insurer manages to invest your savings reasonably well, and if your fellow policyholders don't die off at an unexpectedly rapid clip, dividends will be paid as illustrated. Although not guaranteed, dividends effectively reduce the cost of your premium.

Non-participating ("non-par") policies pay no dividends.

Mutual companies generally offer participating policies; stock companies offer both.

It's okay to buy non-participating term insurance, but non-participating whole life policies are a very poor choice. They are savings plans that lock you in to a low rate of interest.

LOSS RATIO VS. COMBINED RATIO—VS. REALITY

If an insurer pays out 60 cents of every premium dollar to settle claims, its "loss ratio" is 60 percent.

If it spends another 30 cents of each dollar on such things as sales commissions, clerical salaries, postage stamps and overhead, its "expense ratio" is 30 percent.

And its "combined ratio" is—that's right—90 percent. A combined ratio of 90 percent leaves an "underwriting profit" of 10 percent. Ten cents on the dollar. When the combined ratio exceeds 100 percent, as it not infrequently does, the insurer has an underwriting *loss*. But premiums are not an insurer's only source of income.

Besides the money we pay them (premiums), there is the money they *earn* on the money we pay (investment income). One of the things insurance executives like to do most—property/casualty executives in particular—is to downplay the importance of investment income. They prefer to think of it, publicly, at least, as a special little bonus, a happy quirk in the workings of their business, like being able to fly free if you work for an airline—surely not something to get all excited about in, say, the setting of insurance rates. Which may have been true when Treasury bills were yielding less than 2 percent, as they were throughout the 1930s and 1940s, and less than 4 percent throughout the 1950s. In 1981, Treasuries yielded 16 percent.

FIRST-HALF LOSS PUT AT $985 MILLION, declared the lead headline in a 1979 property/casualty issue of *The National Underwriter*. This was the industry-wide underwriting loss. But investment income for the same period was reported in the body of the story to have been $4.3 billion—so the headline might more accurately have read, FIRST-HALF PROFIT PUT AT $3.3 BILLION.

Even the $985 million underwriting loss was grossly overstated. It included as an expense item $629 million in policyholder dividends. (As in, "It was such a lousy year, we decided to declare a dividend.") What kind of expense item is that?

For all of 1980, according to a press release issued by the Insurance Information Institute, property/casualty insurers suffered a $3.04 billion underwriting loss. "What the industry barely made note of," observed the *Journal of Commerce,* "was that despite the underwriting loss there was a $7.51 billion profit."

4

TELL US THE ODDS
A Little Disclosure Would Go a Long Way

*Price competition is so ineffective
in the life insurance industry that companies
paying 20-year rates of return of 2 percent or less
compete successfully against companies paying 4 to 6 percent.
This disparity should be contrasted with the banking industry,
where differences of a quarter of a percent
are considered to be competitively crucial.*
—FTC Staff Report, July 1979

The name of the game is risk. Here is how it's played.

I have in my hand a genuine silver dollar. An "honest coin," as they say. If I offered you two-to-one odds on the flip of this coin—heads you win $10, tails you lose $5—would you take the bet?

Once you decided my proposition was on the level, you would take the bet. Now let's do it again (you lost, incidentally), only this time for higher stakes. Heads you win $800, tails you lose $400. Will you take the bet? No? Yes? You certainly should if you can afford to—the odds are skewed magnificently in your favor.

Now raise the stakes to some real finger-snapping money: heads you win $1 million, tails you lose $500,000. There is a fabulous bet—which many of us would simply have to pass up. Terrific odds, but too much risk.

Too much risk for us, that is, but not for an insurance company. An insurance company has the resources to make hundreds of such bets. And therein, of course, lies its advantage: the outcome of any single coin flip is highly uncertain; the outcome of a long string,

55

much less so. The insurance company might lose the first few tosses (losing just once, let alone twice running, would have wiped *us* out). Conceivably it could lose the first *ten* tosses (the odds of this occurring are fewer than one in a thousand). But over hundreds of coin flips, you can rest assured the company will win just about as often as it loses. Win $100 million, lose $50 million. Win $1 billion, lose $500 million. Win $4 billion, lose $2 billion.

Speaking broadly, again, insurance is the business of taking terrific bets that most people simply cannot *afford* to take. Indeed, it is just the other way around—we do take those bets, but on the wrong end. Almost every time we buy insurance, we are giving the insurance company odds more or less equivalent to two-to-one on the flip of a coin. Heads they win a dollar; tails we win 50 cents. It is the kind of bet one hopes to make only when absolutely necessary. Life being what it is, for most of us it is fairly often necessary.

In theory, the profits in a business that paid off two-to-one on the flip of a coin would be so enormous, so lush, so inviting, that competition would come streaming in to play, offering better and better terms to get our business, until the odds were much narrower—and consequently much better for us. In practice, it has not always happened quite this way. One reason is that in many instances purchasers have no idea what insurance should cost—and so cannot shop for it intelligently. Unlike a simple coin toss, where both parties to the bet know the odds, in an insurance bet it is generally only the insurance company that knows the odds. State regulators have shown little interest in requiring them to pass this exceptionally useful information on to their customers. As a result, some lines of insurance—life insurance prime among them—have tended to compete not so much on price as on elaborate (and inefficient) selling methods.

The best kind of bet is a sure one. The most profitable insurance to sell is insurance against something that doesn't happen (or, conversely, insurance against something that happens with such regularity as to be predictable, like the flip of a coin). Sixty years ago in Chicago, W. Clement Stone began selling low-priced policies that covered things like "loss of a leg while riding on a train, boat, or aeroplane," as one writer put it. You would be amazed how few people lose their legs while on a train, boat or airplane. Now Stone is a conservative philanthropist and professional positive thinker (co-author of such pep-tomes as *Success through a Positive Mental Attitude* and *The Success System That Never Fails*). His initial efforts selling accident insurance door-to-door have grown to be the wildly profitable Combined Insurance Company of America. Not once in the last 28 years has Combined failed to increase its dividend.

(An alternate route to sure profit was taken by Stone's rough contemporary, the late John D. MacArthur, also of Chicago, the man who rescinded his salesmen's Florida gala. John D. started building *his* billion by selling insurance against things that *do* happen—but not paying off when they did.)

The odds of any individual's actually being hit by debris from Skylab were infinitesimal—hence a fine "hazard" against which to write insurance. Some firms actually tried to do so. The problem, from a marketing point of view, was that Skylab was a one-shot deal. Moreover, as no one had ever actually been killed or injured by falling space debris, it was hard to find people adequately frightened to buy coverage. Because just as the marketers of cosmetics are largely selling "hope" and fantasy rather than powders and creams, so the marketers of insurance are in large measure selling "peace of mind." Earthquake insurance sales pick up in California after a rumbling in Alaska; flood insurance sales pick up in Ohio after inundation in New Orleans. It is hard to sell peace of mind to folks who aren't worried in the first place.

If you were selling malpractice insurance to clergymen, for example, you would want your prospects to appreciate its importance. You would want them to worry. You might recount—as a Church Mutual Insurance Company salesman did for the Des Moines *Register*—the now-famous case of the Missouri woman with marital problems who was advised by her clergyman to leave her husband, only to have the husband shoot her when she did.

The woman recovered, patched things up with her mate—and proceeded to sue the clergyman for all his earthly possessions. Not surprisingly, this story was picked up by the wire services and national media. The job of selling clerical malpractice insurance became that much easier. It hardly matters that, as it happens, *no such incident or lawsuit may ever have occurred*. A Church Mutual spokesman told *Business Insurance* in the spring of 1980, "Our position is that we can't verify it. It may exist, but it's not important either way because we don't use it to sell insurance." In fact, Church Mutual admitted, it knew of not a single successful malpractice suit *ever* brought against a clergyman. Another purveyor, Western World Insurance Company of Ramsey, New Jersey, knew of none either. But both firms persist in selling this valuable protection anyway.*

And then there is flight insurance. This line is admittedly minor— a few tens of millions of dollars in premiums a year. But it is instructive. And two very large insurance companies are not above offering it: American Express, which in 1980 derived more than half its total revenues from its subsidiary, Fireman's Fund Insurance; and Mutual of Omaha, the *Wild Kingdom* people.

"Dear Cardmember," begins a letter millions of people have received over the past few years: "An important benefit of American Express® Cardmembership is that you can easily enroll in our Automatic Flight Insurance Plan and have $175,000 Flight Insurance every time you fly.

"Automatic $175,000 Flight Insurance is available only to American Express Cardmembers—and with no age limits or physical requirements. [The life expectancies of all passengers in a crashing plane being about the same, there may be less to this liberal eligibility than meets the eye.] It is an economical, convenient, no-rush way to purchase this vital coverage . . . ."

Now hold it. Convenient such insurance may be—it is automatically tacked on to your American Express bill whenever you charge an airline ticket—but economical? Vital? Why does anyone need, let alone "vitally," extra life insurance when flying in an airplane?

In 1977, there were sixty-four fatalities on scheduled domestic flights—49,500 on streets and highways. Flying, thus, would seem to have presented no extraordinary hazard whatsoever.

In 1978, U.S.-based air carriers made 4,995,000 scheduled flights here and abroad. Of those, only four—fewer than one in a million—were what might politely be called "unsuccessful." (Nonscheduled airlines and private aircraft are substantially less safe, but the insurance American Express offers doesn't cover those.)

Three times as many people died in bathtubs in 1977 as on scheduled domestic flights. Another seventy, according to the Na-

---

*This is not the only apocryphal lawsuit that enlivens actuarial cocktail parties. Another much touted case involved a man who allegedly picked up his lawn mower to trim a hedge, trimmed himself instead, and successfully sued the manufacturer for the unsafety of its product. Much was made of this by the insurance industry to show the ridiculous lengths to which product liability awards were being taken. But so far as anyone can tell, it never happened.

tional Safety Council, drowned in "wells, cisterns, and cesspools." You are more likely to be *kidnapped* than to be killed in a plane crash. And, perhaps most telling of all, life insurers themselves rate commercial airline pilots—who do more flying than any of us—"standard" risks, no more likely than anyone else to die young. It's bartenders they worry about.

So it is hard to see why American Express considers it so vital that you obtain special coverage when you take to the safety of the skies. The answer, of course, is that it's not vital at all—it's salable. And it's salable because people are still nervous about flying. (And because it can be charged to their expense accounts.)

The fact is that, need it or not, you *already* have $75,000 worth of extra life insurance protection when you fly on a ticket charged to American Express or Diners Club.* That much automatic flight insurance comes "free," just for being a dues-paying cardholder. Then there is the ordinary life insurance coverage 86 percent of us carry; and the "bonus" for accidental death many of those policies include. And if all that weren't enough, there is the likelihood that your heirs would collect something from the operator or manufacturer of the aircraft in which you were incinerated. The average settlement for the 644 passengers and crew killed or injured on the runway at Tenerife in 1977, for example, approached $120,000.

Net net: the coverage American Express professes to think it vital that you buy is something far from vital that in all likelihood you have plenty of already. And all it costs you is an extra $3 per ticket. Traveling with the kids? No problem! "You can easily extend this coverage to your spouse and dependent children . . . by charging their tickets *separately and individually* to your Card account." At an extra $3 each. (It's not clear who would need such lavish extra protection if the whole family perished on the way to Disney World at $175,000 apiece, but some grateful and astonished beneficiary could doubtless be found.) Indeed, so concerned is American Express with airline safety that, for a while anyway, even pets and packages were being covered with $175,000 of flight insurance, automatically, whenever their fares were charged by American Express cardholders signed up for this plan. "Each time the mutt was

---

*Diners Club, until Citicorp bought it in 1981, was a subsidiary of Continental Insurance. Despite the extraordinary hazards insurers like Continental bravely subject themselves to on our behalf, Continental has managed to pay dividends without interruption since 1853. Insurance may be less a risky business than, simply, the highly profitable business of risk.

weighed in," complains a woman of the world, "I was charged insurance. It took six months to get a credit and almost a year before Amex finally canceled the policy." But not before charging her $3 for life insurance on some luggage she air-freighted home.

Actually, flight insurance itself is nothing more than a limited form of term life insurance—for terms like three or four hours. Paying $3 for four hours of life insurance is not unlike buying toothpaste one brushful at a time. The premium comes to $6,574.50 a year; hardly economical, especially when you understand that these policies do *not* cover you if you simply die during an otherwise uneventful flight. ("Wake up, sir; we've landed. Sir?")

Every million times you fly on a scheduled airline you are likely to die about once. Those are the odds. So for every $3 million you and your fellow cardholders lay out, you are likely to get back $175,000. Six cents on each dollar. Or, assuming that all tickets are purchased in round trips, two at a time, then for every $3 million collected in premiums, Amex would have to pay out for two deaths—$350,000. Twelve cents on the dollar. Even state lotteries give you 50 cents (with most of the remainder going to support some ostensibly worthwhile cause). And you don't have to die to win.

Admittedly, in addition to covering you on board the aircraft, this policy also protects you "while traveling to and from the airport by taxi, bus, or limousine." (The presumption here must be that, late for a flight and careening along in your *own* car, you might easily end up splattered against an abutment—but that in the hands of a pro, who cares not a zit whether you make your flight or not, the risk is slight.) And, yes, the policy also covers loss of sight (as in the case of a stewardess accidentally ramming a plastic fork into your eye). Still, the skies would have to be fairly raining aircraft before Amex's payout on $3 million in premiums approached even $1 million in benefits, let alone more.

So there's the bet: heads you win 10 or 15 cents; tails you lose $1. The other 85 or 90 cents of your premium goes to expenses, overhead and profit. This may be an efficient, computer-driven way for American Express to sell insurance—*approximately a million and a half American Express cardholders have enrolled in this plan*—but it is hardly an efficient way for us to buy it. Analogous would be the charity that spends 85 or 90 percent of your contribution on fundraising and overhead, only 10 or 15 percent on its mission.

Mutual of Omaha's charges for flight insurance are even higher (and their airport-counter selling methods far less efficient), with the odds skewed even more heavily out of your favor.

But how is one to know this?

When you go to buy sugar at the supermarket you are not required to try to guess the weight of the bag. It's printed right on the front. When you buy a car, you don't have to try to guess its fuel efficiency. When you buy processed foods, you are actually told what's in them. Indeed, in most cases you are supplied a breakdown of the nutritional content as well. When you go to borrow money from a bank, or finance a department store purchase, you are told, in bold type, the effective annual rate of interest you will pay. When you purchase newly issued securities, you are issued a detailed prospectus replete with warnings. So why is it that when you go to buy insurance (of any type) you are not advised of the odds? A simple standardized disclosure statement along the following lines would in many cases be all it would take:

> Based on Past Loss Experience, It Is Expected That
> LESS THAN *15* PERCENT
> Of Your Premium Dollar Will Be Used to Pay Claims.
> The Remainder Is Used to Cover Expenses, Overhead and Profit.

Simple disclosure, prominently displayed, in a standard format. It might not do wonders for flight insurance sales, nor for sales of many of the health and accident insurance offers that are mailed out en masse, printed on parchment by a computer obsessed with calling us by name in every sentence. But why shouldn't consumers have this information? You can be sure the insurance companies have it.

(To recoup any premiums it might lose as a result of this reform, American Express could begin offering Automatic Restaurant Insurance®. Yes! You could choke! Or be poisoned! Really, in these days of botulism and exploding champagne bottles, people all too often underestimate the hazards of eating out. For only 75 cents, automatically added to your American Express bill whenever you charge a meal, this vital protection will be yours . . . *regardless* of your age or physical condition. Put each of your guests on a separate tab, and they, too, will be covered! Die before having had a chance to settle your bill? No problem! You're covered, provided only that you've charged at least one meal to your card within six weeks prior to your demise.)

This one reform—simple, meaningful disclosure—would go a long way toward "rationalizing" the insurance industry. If people had an easier time understanding and comparing values, they could shop for insurance more wisely. That, in turn, would force the industry to compete more on the quality of its offers, less on the quality of the parchment they are printed on. By promoting price competition, meaningful disclosure would help to cut out waste.

Insurers should be free to offer grossly overpriced protection and customers, to buy it. But customers also have a right to know what it is they are getting. Tell us the odds!

"Sections of the main cabin were found as far as two and a half miles apart," writes free-lance claims adjuster John J. Healy; "bodies were discovered in excess of five miles from each other. Actually, it was the fact that the wreckage had been strewn over such an expanse of ground that told the authorities some kind of explosion had occurred in the air. Also, there had been no Mayday call from the pilot.

"Checking the passengers against the amounts of flight insurance they had taken out, one name stood out clearly. Joseph Stevens of Salt Lake City, Utah, had taken out over four hundred thousand dollars' worth of insurance, most of it covering him for that specific flight only."*

Healy found it equally suspicious that this same Joseph Stevens had several weeks earlier checked out from the library a book on explosives.

It is little wonder that the Air Line Pilots Association has never been happy with flight insurance. As with many kinds of insurance, flight insurance has an impact not only on the individuals who buy it, but on the citizenry as a whole. (Fire insurance policies, for example, as currently written, have been directly responsible for the

---

*John J. Healy, *A Game of Wits*.

torching of tens of thousands of buildings, the loss of hundreds of lives.)

The question of how best to provide flight insurance—How God Would Restructure the Flight Insurance Business, if you will—thus has two possible aims. How do you lessen the psychopath's financial incentive to blow up his fellow passengers? (On November 1, 1955, Jack Graham, 23, packed a bomb in his mom's suitcase, drove her to the Denver airport, got her to sign several vending-machine flight insurance policies, and kissed her good-bye.) And, or, how do you provide flight insurance more efficiently?

Plan #1. At one extreme, you could ban flight insurance altogether. This might encourage potential suicides to choose some vehicle other than a 747 as they went about their estate planning.

Plan #2. Somewhat less draconian would be to ban single-flight policies of the type now sold at airports but allow open-ended arrangements a la American Express. At the same time, some sort of 60- or 90-day waiting period might be required before flight insurance policies went into effect. This would foil your more impulsive financial aerocides.

Plan #3 would have the airlines themselves quietly provide insurance to *everyone* on the plane ($100,000 in economy, say, $200,000 in first class), just as they now provide flotation cushions, almonds and piped-in music. If airlines simply added life insurance to the price of each ticket, the cost would be more like 25 cents than $3. It would be a far more efficient way to provide the coverage.

It's true, such a charge would be foisted on people who might not wish to buy flight insurance, even for a quarter, but this is no different from the charge for the "free" soft drink that is built into the ticket price for people who might not be thirsty.

If American Express believes flight insurance is vital coverage to have, then surely we should all have it—for a dime or a quarter instead of $3. (Actually, it need not cost us *anything,* as I will demonstrate in a moment.)

The trade-off—as it so frequently is—is between efficiency and individual choice. (If cars came in only one color they would be cheaper.) Presumably, insurance coverage that "everyone should have" is best provided automatically, while coverage only some need is best sold one policy at a time. But this is sometimes an easier distinction to draw than to implement. Not surprisingly, the insurance lobby recoils in horror at the prospect of automatic coverage (including, when it was first proposed, Social Security), no matter how efficient it may be. Automatic coverage eliminates sales commissions and profit. Imagine how expensive Social Security or unemployment insurance would be if they had to be sold door-to-door, one policy at a time. The Social Security system may be in deep trouble, but not because it is inefficient. Ninety-eight cents of every dollar contributed to the system gets paid back out in benefits.

What might be very much in everyone's interest—*Plan #3a*—would be to provide insurance to passengers automatically, but with a clause *voiding* it if the deceased's heirs chose to file suit. Heirs would thus have a choice: they could sue, as they do now—a process of uncertain duration and outcome. Or they could accept an immediate $100,000 or $200,000 death benefit, undiluted by legal fees.*

Airlines *already* buy liability insurance—in large, efficient chunks— the cost of which is *already* added to our fares. It would cost no more if that insurance were written to cover specific, automatic death benefits instead of uncertain jury awards. Thus we could all have $100,000 or $200,000 of automatic flight insurance at *no* additional cost! Just by restructuring the system!

The millions of solicitations American Express prints and mails each year—unnecessary. The flight-insurance counters at airports—unnecessary. The people who man those counters, the people who empty airport insurance vending machines and repair them, the people who mollify passengers whose dogs have been charged for life insurance—unnecessary. The lawyers and their assistants who work so hard for their 30 percent contingency fees plus expenses when a plane crashes—unnecessary. The delays in collecting those settlements—unnecessary. Here, in sum, is a line of insurance that wastes 80 or 90 cents of each premium dollar—unnecessarily.

(Meanwhile, removing flight insurance counters and machines from airports might also remove the reminder that passengers too ill or poor to obtain insurance any other way can, even so, leave loved ones an enormous estate.)

---

*All but eight of the 644 claims arising out of the 1977 Tenerife disaster were settled out of court, although not without delay and expense. Only two of the eight claims that did go to court resulted in awards higher than had been offered in the first place: an extra $5,000 in one case, $20,000 more in the other. A third plaintiff turned down an $80,000 settlement offer, only to be awarded *nothing* by the jury.

LETTERS TO THE EDITOR

An article I wrote along these lines elicited responses from American Express and Mutual of Omaha. American Express pointed out that the accident rate abroad is "three or four times" what it is in the United States. Thus, for policyholders who fly primarily abroad, the ratio of claims paid to premiums collected might rise to 30 or 40 cents on the dollar—still not a great bet. But U.S. cardholders do most of their flying domestically.*

Mutual of Omaha wrote: "We firmly believe that our Company is fairly and effectively providing an important and necessary service to consumers through its marketing of travel insurance. We are proud of our record."

The insurance industry is filled with good people who believe in their work and their companies, but who may never have challenged the assumptions underlying their efforts. There are, for example, thousands of near messianic life insurance salesmen who would be astonished to know what a poor value they are selling relative to other policies available. (Comparing insurance policies is often not just beyond the ability of consumers, but beyond the ability of salespeople, as well.) W. Clement Stone never doubted the value of his products. No sir! He trained his legions to rise every morning chanting—"I feel happy, I feel healthy, I feel terrific"—and to go out selling their "Little Giant" accident policies with a Positive Mental Attitude. It is the sort of approach that leaves little room for soul searching or analysis.

The Mutual of Omaha spokesman went on to point to the *unpredictability* of airline crashes as a justification for requiring high premiums relative to claims paid. Actually, however, annual airline safety statistics follow a clear trend: toward fewer and fewer fatalities. This is only to be expected when you consider the ever increasing technological sophistication of the safety equipment available.

It's true, air crashes are not as predictable as more common accidents. More common accidents conform to statistical expectations with almost frightening, fatalistic reliability. We may not know

---

*In 1980, there were a total of eleven passenger deaths on scheduled domestic flights. American Express raised its coverage from $175,000 to $250,000 and, in 1981, began offering $500,000 coverage for $5.50.

in advance *who* will choke to death in any given month—but we sure know how many. Here are the month-by-month totals for a recent year as compiled by the National Safety Council:

January	274
February	267
March	278
April	229
May	234
June	229
July	234
August	240
September	240
October	284
November	252
December	272

For any given household, death by "ingested food or object," as choking is called, is a freak accident. But for the nation as a whole, given the law of averages, it could hardly be more predictable. The same is true of deaths by poison—350 a month, like clockwork. Some routine accidents follow seasonal patterns: fires take the heaviest toll in the winter months, drownings in the summer. But the tolls, even so, are predictable. Lightning bolts? About a hundred fatalities a year. Less spectacular electrocutions? Eleven hundred a year. People struck and killed by falling objects? A thousand to twelve hundred a year. Fatalities with respect to air carriers are more erratic, but upper limits may nonetheless be estimated. In not one year in the last 25 have fatalities on scheduled domestic flights reached 300. It is not as though every once in a while there is a year when 5,000 or 10,000 fatalities occur. It just doesn't happen.

"With the ever greater use of the wide-body jet capable of carrying hundreds of passengers," the Mutual of Omaha spokesman continued, "the likelihood of catastrophic losses increases substantially. If, for example, a single fully loaded wide-bodied jet, which typically can carry at least 340 persons originated at a New York City airport and crashed with no survivors, and all passengers had purchased our maximum limit $300,000 flight policy for $6.00 each, Mutual of Omaha Companies would be liable for a staggering $102 million. The premium would be *only* $2,040."

True. What this staggering example neglects to acknowledge, however, is that 100 percent of airline passengers do *not* buy coverage. If they did, then the company would take in well over $1 billion of premiums in the course of the year, leaving it an underwriting profit after *three* such crashes well in excess of $700 million.

Barring a conspiratorial kamikaze-type insurance fraud involving a cultist suicidal tour group (whose beneficiaries I presume would be disqualified from any death benefits at all), there is no reason to expect that the proportion of insurance buyers will be significantly greater on flights that crash than on flights that don't. And all but a handful each year don't. The odds favor the insurer overwhelmingly, no matter how large or small a proportion of the flying public chooses to take the bet.

Actually, insurers do not particularly care to have their transactions likened to bets, nor their business to gambling. And it is true that buying insurance is in a sense just the opposite of gambling. When you bet on a horse, you actively seek risk. (So-called "speculative" or "dynamic" risk.) When you buy insurance, you are acting to limit or *avoid* risk. ("Static" or "pure" risk, that offers no corresponding reward.) Alfred Jaffe, associate professor at the College of Insurance, writing in the *National Underwriter,* put it this way: "The buyer of insurance is taking a small, certain and manageable loss—payment of the premium—in return for which he has removed the terrifying uncertainty of the possibility of sustaining a huge loss which could utterly destroy him financially."

Of course, often we insure against such "terrifying" losses as a dented fender or a stolen stereo—losses we might be able to manage without buying insurance. But Jaffe continues:

"He has thus bought peace of mind, the charge for which is the premium. He has eliminated the risk by buying insurance. Thus insurance is the exact opposite of gambling, wherein the risk is created by the act."

Jaffe goes on in the very next sentence to say that "insurance remains a gamble—but for the insurer, not the insured." You see? The insurance companies are making bets, but we, the other parties to each transaction, are not. We are buying peace of mind. (So don't worry your little head trying to figure out the odds.) Concludes the author:

"It seems to me that with a clear understanding of this very sharp difference between gambling and insurance, one can effectively squelch and straighten out the know-it-all at the Saturday night party who disparages people in the insurance business by equating them with bookmakers."*

With a copy of *Accident Facts,* issued each year by the National Safety Council, it's not all that difficult to do a little bookmaking, or handicapping, anyway, of one's own. Take the case of the thick envelope that arrives in your mailbox offering $50,000 if you die accidentally or are doubly dismembered. The cost is only $48 a year, to be tacked onto your MasterCard bill in quarterly installments. What are the odds?

Well, accidents account for some 105,000 American deaths a year, or one for every 2,000 of us. At first blush, then, it would seem that for every 2,000 annual premiums the insurer takes in— $96,000—it can expect to pay, on average, one claim—$50,000. To this estimate would be added a few dollars for the occasional dismemberment, but dismemberments are rare. (You say you broke both legs, lost half your left foot, all your fingers, one ear, and need a metal pelvis? Sorry—you have not been dismembered. To qualify, feet must be severed at the ankle or above, hands at the wrist.) In all likelihood, these are about the odds the insurer has built into its offer: paying out 50 or 60 cents for every dollar it takes in. Of course, the insurer also has expenses to pay—principally the cost of the mass mailing to sign us up in the first place; but so has it a second source of revenue—the income it earns investing our premium dollars until claims must be paid.

Or here is a mass mailing from Ford—yes, Ford has a life insurance subsidiary (but, no, "Here's more good news: You don't have to be a Ford customer to own our policy")—headlined, THE CLOSER YOU LOOK, THE BETTER WE LOOK. No matter how closely you look, you can't find the loss ratio of the accident insurance they're offering. But rest assured: "In Every Way—Ford Means Value."

Asked about the loss ratios on its policy, a spokesman for Ford Life was forthright. "We as a rule don't provide this information for obvious reasons," he said, "but generally speaking our term life

---

*Even so, the purchase of life insurance is forbidden under Islamic law as a form of gambling against the will of Allah.

product is in the vicinity of 50 percent. The loss ratio has been as low as 35 to 40 percent; this year [1980] it's actually running above 50 percent." The loss ratios on Ford's accident-and-sickness policies, he said, run considerably higher—60 to 70 cents of each premium dollar paid out to settle claims—so much so as to be "almost unprofitable."

Gulf Oil runs virtually the identical offer as Ford, down to the very same business-reply permit number on the return envelope. The marketing details of both plans, it turns out, are handled by a common subcontractor. Gulf's spokesman was *not* forthright and would not reveal any figures. "We file all required information with the state insurance departments," a Gulf spokesman said. "We do not care to go beyond that." I called the California department to see whether loss ratios on policies registered for sale in that state were available, but Gulf's secret was safe. (Inasmuch as its offer is identical, Gulf's loss experience is presumably about the same as Ford's.)

If you were an insurance company, one of the things you might consider before making such mailings is "anti-selection." Anti-, or "adverse," selection occurs when you make an offer to a group of potential customers and a preponderance of the worst risks sign up. (In the jargon of the insurance business, death and destruction are "hazards," people and property are "risks.") For example, you wouldn't want to offer life insurance without regard to health or age, other than at an extraordinarily high rate, lest you receive as customers a preponderance of aging arteriosclerotic alcoholics. In the case of accident insurance, a preponderance of coal miners, circus performers and window washers might sign up (which is why some of these policies exclude accidents that occur on the job). That, too, would be anti-selection. *Or* you might find that, by and large, the people prudent enough to sign up for accident insurance are just those prudent enough to drive carefully and look both ways crossing streets. (Window washers are actually very careful people.) Your "loss experience"—the number of claims you wound up having to pay—could prove benign indeed.

In either case, as an insurer there would be ways you could skew the odds in your favor. You could, for example, choose mailing lists weighted away from the accident-prone ages (15 to 24; over 65)— or toward women. Women are only half as likely to die accidentally as men. You could, furthermore, purge your list of Alaska, Montana, Nevada, New Mexico and Wyoming zip codes, among others, where the accidental death rate runs consistently above the national average; or even limit your mailing to such states as Connecticut, New York, New Jersey, Illinois, Hawaii, Rhode Island, Maryland, Ohio, Pennsylvania, Massachusetts and a few others where the death rate runs consistently and substantially *below* the national average. Alaskans are three times as likely to die accidentally as Hawaiians or New Yorkers. You might favor *Business Week* subscribers over subscribers to *Playboy,* on the not unreasonable assumption that they will have safer jobs, on average, and more conservative driving and recreational habits.

(The Ford Life executive said that about the only underwriting they did on most of their accident policies was to try to avoid mailing to lists of motorcyclists.)

You might thus be able to do a certain amount of your underwriting—your risk selection—en masse, rather than analyzing each application as it came in. Those life insurance policies advertised on the radio with the line "You cannot be turned down for this coverage!" are actually saying, "For policies this small, it would cost us more to decide whom to turn down than simply to accept everybody—and make them pay through the nose."

W. Clement Stone never turned down a potential customer. From selling newspapers at the age of six on the streets of Chicago and, later (after dropping out of high school), accident policies door-to-door, Stone built a small empire. Indeed, in his lifetime he has *given away* several tens of millions of dollars. Bow-tied, with a pencil mustache, he became a well-recognized "civic leader" and, among other things, Richard Nixon's biggest financial backer. In 1980, Stone had 3,000 employees working to provide the world with accident (and health and life) insurance. His holding company, Combined International Corp. (New York Stock Exchange symbol: PMA—"Positive Mental Attitude"), collects premiums well in excess of half a billion dollars annually. The policies are still sold one-on-one, door-to-door, smile-to-frown.

Here is what the Little Giant accident policy—mainstay and motive force of the company even throughout the 1960s (during which decade Combined's premiums quadrupled)—offered. For a mere $3 every six months you could count on:

- TWO THOUSAND DOLLARS ($2,000) if killed or doubly dismembered while riding on a "surface or elevated railroad, subway car, streetcar or passenger boat," or while riding in an elevator or on a scheduled airline.

• FIVE HUNDRED DOLLARS ($500) if, while on one of these public conveyances, you lost just one hand or one foot. (We all know people, I think, who, rushing for a closing elevator door, have thrust out, and had chopped off, a hand or a foot.)

• TWO HUNDRED DOLLARS ($200) if you merely lost an eye.

• FIVE HUNDRED DOLLARS ($500) if you were killed in or by an "automobile, bus, trolley-bus, taxicab or truck" or "at the hands of a burglar, highwayman or robber when robbing the Insured" or "by drowning" or "while within any burning building," provided you didn't rush in after the fire started to save someone.

• FIFTEEN DOLLARS ($15) a week up to a maximum of $225 if through one of the accidents described above you were not killed or dismembered, but were "continuously, necessarily and wholly" disabled from "performing each and every duty pertaining to [your] usual business or occupation." PLUS! Up to $4 a day in hospital expenses (not to exceed $56).

For policyholders under 14 or over 70, the premium was the same, but all benefits were cut in half.

No wonder they called it the Little Giant! And no wonder thousands of salesmen have over the years been able to sell hundreds of millions of dollars worth of this policy!

The policy, retired from service in 1972, did not include any sort of statement as to the odds of this bet, but if it had, the disclosure statement, according to calculations based on accident statistics from the period, would have looked about as follows:

It Is Expected That
APPROXIMATELY *10* CENTS
Of Your Premium Dollar Will Be Used To Pay Claims.
The Remainder, Plus the Interest We Earn on Your Money,
Is Used to Cover Expenses, Overhead and Profit.

Which prompts the question: Was it *insurance* that was being sold—or simply a harmless illusion? Is Stone to be commended for having sold so much low-cost peace of mind to so many? Or condemned for having scared them in the first place, the better to sell

60 cents' worth of protection for $6?

The question would be moot if Combined, and all other insurance companies, routinely had to disclose—clearly and prominently—the anticipated loss ratios of their contracts.

THE ODDS

A TABLE

That, While Very Rough in Its Approximations, Is Sort of Basic to the Whole Ball Game

For Every Dollar We Collectively Deposit in:	This Is How Much, *Roughly,* We Collectively Get to Withdraw:
A SAVINGS BANK	$1.05
A COMMERCIAL BANK	$1.00
SOCIAL SECURITY[1]	$0.98
UNEMPLOYMENT INSURANCE	$0.93
BLUE CROSS	$0.93
GROUP LIFE INSURANCE	$0.90*
GROUP HEALTH INSURANCE	$0.87*
INDIVIDUAL HEALTH INSURANCE	$0.50
WORKERS' COMPENSATION	$0.75
AUTO INSURANCE[2]	$0.62
HOMEOWNERS INSURANCE[2]	$0.58
FIRE INSURANCE[2]	$0.54
BURGLARY & THEFT INSURANCE[2]	$0.38
TERM LIFE INSURANCE[3]	$0.40 to $0.90
WHOLE LIFE INSURANCE[4]	—
CREDIT LIFE INSURANCE[5]	$0.48
INDUSTRIAL LIFE INSURANCE[6]	$0.20
CANCER INSURANCE[7]	$0.41
PRODUCT LIABILITY INSURANCE[8]	$0.27
MEDICAL MALPRACTICE INSURANCE[9]	$0.18
RENTAL CAR INSURANCE[10]	$0.20
TITLE INSURANCE[11] (an exception—see note)	$0.15
FLIGHT INSURANCE	$0.10

*Returns are lower for "group" plans sold by mail, one customer at a time.

1. **Social Security.** The cost of administering Social Security is less than 2 cents per dollar collected. There are no selling costs.

2. **Fire/Auto/Theft.** Estimates based on Best's *Aggregates & Averages,* for the years 1970–1980. These figures include the billions of dollars paid in settlement of fraudulent and inflated claims. Honest policyholders get

to withdraw, collectively, even less of each premium dollar. (See pages 94-95.)

3. **Term Life Insurance.** A range is shown for this coverage because its cost varies so widely from insurer to insurer. The *amount* of coverage you buy also makes an enormous difference. Purchasing relatively small amounts can be terribly expensive.

4. **Whole Life.** The bulk of your premium goes to fund a savings plan. Added to it is, in essence, a term insurance policy. The longer you keep your policy in force, the better the rate of return on your savings; cancel your policy after a year or two and you will lose almost the entire amount. Any figure shown here would involve so many assumptions as to be meaningless. The only things to be said for sure are that in most cases we don't get to withdraw as much as we should; and that with one of the new universal life plans (page 265) we would likely withdraw more.

5. **Credit Life.** This coverage, offered and sometimes required by a lending institution, cancels your debt if you die while a balance remains outstanding. It is written without regard to health or age, and so is a terrible deal for young healthy people, not bad for the elderly and infirm. The National Association of Insurance Commissioners recommended in 1959 and 1966 that the payout on credit life insurance be at least 50 cents on each premium dollar. (Why not 80 or 90 cents?) But as recently as 1979, when U.S. life insurers had 106 *million* credit life insurance contracts in force, in a state like North Carolina they were paying out a mere 29 cents of each premium dollar. One of the reasons for credit life's low payout is that insurers generally pay the lending institution a portion of your premium as its "commission." Thus much of the competition to sell credit life insurance revolves *not* around offering consumers a low price but around offering banks, auto dealers and others a high commission. Lenders will frequently sign up with the insurer that charges the highest rate in order to get the highest commission. This is what's known as "reverse competition."

6. **Industrial Life.** Still sold in some poverty pockets, particularly in the South, industrial (or "debit" or "home service") life insurance once dominated the industry. These policies are for very low face amounts, intended primarily to cover burial expenses. In the old days, the company "debit man" would visit his policyholders weekly, collecting three cents or a nickel or a dime from each. In 1980, the premiums were a bit higher, but debit men were still making the rounds, weekly or monthly. It is a ludicrously expensive way to provide insurance. In 1980, there were 62 million such policies still in force, at an average face value of $620. Many families had been sold more than one.

7. **Cancer Insurance.** This estimate comes from an embargoed F.T.C. staff report. In many cases, salesmen are paid half the first year's premium in commission ("Well, ma'am, if you can't afford $5 a month, you certainly can't afford cancer"), plus 10 percent of each subsequent year's commission. Other expenses include salaries of executives of the offering companies, most conspicuously the $1.1 million (1979) compensation of American Family Life's chairman, John B. Amos. At the beginning of

1981, there were some 20 million such policies in force, even though their sale had been banned or severely restricted in New York, New Jersey, New Hampshire, Connecticut and Massachusetts. Although cancer is admittedly the most financially devastating of the primary diseases afflicting Americans, cancer policies pay only a small portion of the expenses likely to be incurred. *It is inherently inefficient to sell health insurance one disease at a time.*

8. **Product Liability.** This is an estimate of the portion of the product liability premium dollar that gets paid to victims (before splitting same with their lawyers).

9. **Malpractice.** This is an estimate of what the victims get after paying their lawyers. (Other estimates range as high as 30 cents.) But it is doctors, not victims, who buy malpractice insurance. For them, the insurance not only pays claims, it provides a legal defense.

10. **Rental Car.** When you rent a car, you are automatically covered by insurance for all but the first few hundred dollars of damage. "Free." When you accept the *optional* insurance, which then covers you down to the last penny, you make Hertz et al very happy.

11. **Title Insurance.** This line is an exception. Most of the cost of title insurance goes toward researching the property in question to be sure the title is clear. If the insurer does his research well, he eliminates the risk and thus will have little or nothing to pay out in claims. So you are paying primarily for a legal search, not insurance, and should not be put off by the low loss ratio.

Please Note: Low loss ratios do not always mean huge profits. Some lines of insurance are so expensive to provide, or provided so inefficiently, that even paying very low benefits there may be little or nothing left, after expenses and overhead, for profit.

5

NOT INVENTED HERE
Bonds Against the Common Peril

*Assurances among Merchants . . . [have] been of use
time out of mind in Trade; tho perhaps never so much . . . as now.*
—Daniel Defoe, 1697

Five thousand years ago, Chinese transporting goods on the Yangtze River adopted the practice of distributing their cargoes among many different boats as they approached the rapids. They distributed the risk. Today even the largest insurers—even nations, the Soviet Union included—lay off *their* largest risks in a global weave of shared financial responsibility.

A British merchant with little aptitude for punctuation, Daniel Defoe, traced the evolution of insurance this way: "'Tis a Compact among Merchants," he wrote, "Its beginning being an Accident to Trade, and arose from the *Disease of Mens Tempers,* who having run larger Adventures in a single Bottom than afterwards they found convenient, grew fearful and uneasy; and discovering their uneasiness to others, who, perhaps, had no Effects in the same Vessel, they offer to bear part of the Hazard for part of the Profit; Convenience made this a Custom, and Custom brought it into a Method, till at last it becomes a Trade."

Hammurabi's Code, thirty-seven centuries ago, included provisions to encourage commerce and investment. If a Babylonian traveler was robbed, the local government was obliged to "render back to him whatsoever was lost." (Travel insurance.) If a farmer owed a debt but natural disaster struck, that season's payment was forgiven. (Crop insurance.) And if a merchant's goods failed to arrive safely, the debts incurred to finance his caravan were forgiven. (Cargo insurance.) There was even a provision for social security: If a man adopted a son, the son was obligated to provide for the father in his old age. Failure to do so was punishable by death.

A thousand years later, the caravans of Babylon had given way to the ocean commerce of Rhodes—but the insurance mechanism remained the same. Rhodian merchants would borrow funds to finance their voyages, pledging their ships and cargo as security. If the voyage was successful, the loans were repaid with interest; if ship or cargo was lost at sea, the loan and interest would be forgiven. The interest charge was set high enough to compensate for the risk of loss. *In large part it was thus not interest at all but an insurance premium.* Wealthy Rhodians were acting not just as bankers when they financed these voyages but as insurers, too. So long as they spread their risks over a large number of vessels (or "bottoms"—such loans are known as "bottomry bonds"), they were likely to come out ahead even after suffering occasional losses.

Rhodian law also established the principle of contributorship. "If, in order to lighten a ship, merchandise is thrown overboard, that which has been given for all shall be replaced by the contribution of all." In other words, no one merchant would be made to suffer disproportionately just because it happened to have been his goods that the crew, desperate to save the ship and their lives, pitched overboard.

The Rhodian practices were shared by the Phoenicians and Greeks (duly chronicled by Demosthenes) and helped to finance the commerce of the Roman Empire. In A.D. 533 the Emperor Justinian fixed the rate of interest that could be charged on loans at a maximum of 6 percent—but at 12 percent on bottomry bonds, in recognition of the special risk involved. Half the rate was thus interest, half an insurance premium.

The Romans had burial societies—*collegia*—organized to defray the costs of elaborate funerals. Roman soldiers contributed to a fund for the survivors of their felled comrades. Medieval guilds attempted to provide their members fire insurance and some form of support in old age, sickness or poverty. (In 1288 the English Guild of Blessed Mary, we are told, withheld fire insurance benefits from persons guilty of "lust, dice-playing, and gluttony.") In *any* civilized pocket of the globe, at *any* time, there will have been formal or informal arrangements to share risks. But the modern insurance industry may be said to have had its beginnings in late-seventeenth-century London. There, in the wake of a five-day blaze (1666) so devastating it would be officially remembered each September 2nd for more than a hundred years, fire insurance companies began to appear. And there, too, in the 1680s, Edward Lloyd established a coffeehouse. Lloyd's' largely spontaneous evolution is a remarkable case study of the way a free market can profitably respond to economic needs.

Coffee was introduced to England in the late seventeenth century from the eastern Mediterranean. People were not of one mind how to spell it ("kauphy," "kauffee"), but they were nearly unanimous in their enthusiasm. Advertisements of the day credited the stuff with curing gout, dropsy and scurvy, for being "a most excellent remedy against the spleen, hypochondriac winds, and the like." Not only that: "It will prevent drowsiness, and make one fit for business."* London was soon a city of 300 or more coffeehouses, each catering to a particular clientele.

Edward Lloyd's establishment, being close to the docks, attracted the seafaring crowd. It became a focus for business dealings, just as a hundred years later a certain buttonwood tree on Wall Street would become the place to go to trade stocks. That was the marvel of Lloyd's—to be able to transact all one's business under a single roof. Today, satellite communications have brought the entire world under a single roof, but the value of a central marketplace remains. Office space on the "fringe" of Lloyd's is so highly coveted by competitors that it rents for double the price of good space just a few hundred yards away. Why? "Because," explained an old hand, "brokers don't like to walk very far—particularly in the rain."

Seventeenth-century shipowners gathered at Lloyd's and, seeking insurance, would write out the particulars of a proposed voyage—the name of the vessel, its captain, the ports of call—specifying the amount for which hull and cargo were to be insured and the premium rate. Other prosperous coffeehouse denizens, many of them shipowners themselves, could then accept as much or as little of the premium, and risk, as they liked by writing their names underneath. *Underwriters.* A brief voyage to a single port under the command of a respected captain might rate a modest 2 percent premium—£2

---

*As quoted in the highly readable *Lloyd's of London*, by Antony Brown.

for every £100 insured; the most dangerous voyages, as much as 15 percent.*

Lloyd himself insured nothing. He sold coffee. But he quickly became one of London's best-known commercial figures. "All coffee houses saw it as their duty to supply their customers with pens and ink," Antony Brown relates, "but Edward Lloyd went one further. He supplied them with news." Lloyd's runners would shuttle to and from the wharves; important news was read to the assemblage from a pulpit. Then in 1696 came *Lloyd's News,* a periodical "Printed for Edward Lloyd (Coffee Man) in Lombard Street." Business boomed. The number of men available to underwrite risks steadily increased (it would be nearly three centuries before women were admitted as Lloyd's underwriters); and gradually their mix shifted from those, like merchant Daniel Defoe, for whom underwriting was a sideline, to those who focused upon it their full attention and resources.

This is not to say that the road to institutional renown was all profits and propriety. Defoe himself went bankrupt in 1692 insuring ships that France had the discourtesy to sink, and eighteen other British merchants went down with him. ("Ensurers fail much," William Penn lamented in a letter to Pennsylvanian James Logan in 1704.) Best-known for his *Life and Strange Surprising Adventures of Robinson Crusoe,* and for *Moll Flanders,* published in 1719 and 1722, respectively, Defoe was a strong advocate of insurance—notwithstanding his own misfortune. "If God Almighty ha[s] Commanded us to Relieve and Help one another in Distress," he wrote in 1697, "sure it must be commendable to bind our selves by Agreement to Obey that Command; nay, it seems to be a project that we are led to by the Divine Rule." Specifically, he had in mind a variety of mutual insurance societies. "All the Contingencies of Life might be fenc'd against by this Method, (as Fire is already) as Thieves, Floods by Land, Storms by Sea, Losses of all Sorts, and Death itself, in a manner, by making it up to the Survivor."

He offered particulars. For example, lamenting the way merchant seamen, when assailed by pirates, would not resist—and noting that they were right not to do so, as there was no provision for them or their families if in the course of repulsing attack they be maimed or killed—he proposed a plan of workers' compensation. It was to

---

*In 1981, rates for cargo insurance ran just two- to three-*tenths* of 1 percent. Hull insurance, written annually rather than by the voyage, was comparably inexpensive.

be a *"Friendly-Society* Erected for Seamen,'' who would pay one shilling per quarter to belong, thereafter to receive benefits if ''either in Fight, or by any other Accident at Sea,'' they should become disabled. As follows:

For the loss of:

An Eye	£ 25		
Both Eyes	100		
One Leg	50		
Both Legs	80		8 percent thereof
Right Hand	80	*or*	*per annum*
Left Hand	50		for life
Right Arm	100		
Left Arm	80		
Both Hands	160		
Both Arms	200		

And Broken Arm, or Leg, or Thigh, towards the cure—£10. If taken by the *Turks,* £50 towards his Ransom. If he become Infirm and Unable to go to Sea, or Maintain himself, by Age or Sickness, £6 *per ann.* To their Wives if they are Kill'd or Drown'd, £50.

Defoe then runs through an example of 4,000 seamen so associating, engages some of their number in hypothetical battle, enumerates their hypothetical casualties (one ''had a Great Shot took off his Arm''; another ''With a Splinter had an Eye struck out''), sums up their losses, divides by 4,000, and arrives at an assessment of one shilling three pence per seaman. '''Tis but a small matter for a Man to Contribute,'' concludes Defoe, ''to Relieve Five Wounded Men of his own Fraternity, but at the same time to be assured that if *he* is Hurt or Maim'd he shall have the same Relief.''

He proposed like societies for wives, lest they become widows; developed a social security scheme (whereby, ''I doubt not but Poverty might easily be prevented and Begging wholly suppres'd''); noted the potential for embezzlement (to foil which he proposed ''a great Chest, lockt up with 11 Locks,'' each member of the governing committee to have one key); and for each of his schemes provided budgets and performed rudimentary actuarial calculations to project expenses, claims and premiums.

His plans were not immediately adopted.

"As an insurer of other men's property," wrote biographer John Moore, "Defoe [failed]. But in his own contribution to the theory and the practice of insurance he served a purpose not unlike that of the coral. The wreck of his personal fortunes lies near the base of one of the most stable business undertakings in the modern world."

Meanwhile, other imaginative souls were hatching schemes of their own.

There was the larcenous Lloyd's broker who wrote fictitious names at the bottom of an underwriting slip, pocketing the premiums himself; a fine scheme so long as the insured voyage went uneventfully, but the ship sank. When the time came for the fictitious underwriters to pay up, the fraud was revealed. (Even today it is not uncommon for agents or brokers to issue bogus policies, pocketing the full premium for themselves without ever intending to bear any portion of the risk.)

And there was the speculative binge that gripped the City of London early in the eighteenth century. The stock market mania known as the South Sea Bubble has been much chronicled. Nearly as well known are some of the associated speculations that thrived in its wake, like the public issue of stock in "A company for carrying on an undertaking of great advantage, but nobody to know what it is." According to Charles Mackay, author of the classic *Extraordinary Popular Delusions and the Madness of Crowds,* the issuer of this stock was deluged with buyers the very first day, whereupon he took the proceeds, departed for the Continent and was never heard from again. Less well known, however, are the "insurance policies" sold to an eager public during this financially demented period. "You could get policies against death from gin-drinking, against being lied to by your business competitors, even a policy on what was delicately described as Female Chastity," recounts Antony Brown. (I am not the first to wonder how the latter "insurance" was verified, nor how it was possible to keep parties to the contract from attempting forcibly to violate it.).

To restore sanity, the government in 1720 abolished all but two for-profit insurance companies. But the individuals who constituted the market at Lloyd's—not themselves being "companies"—were left untouched.

Then, fifty years later, the gambling fever returned—to the point, writes Brown, that it was threatening Lloyd's good name. "You could get a policy on whether there would be a war with France or Spain, whether John Wilkes would be arrested or die in jail [he was arrested but, far from dying in jail, became mayor of London], or whether some Parliamentary candidate would be elected. Underwriters offered premiums of 25 percent on George II's safe return from Dettingen; there were policies on whether this or that mistress of Louis XV would continue in favoₗ ᴐr not.''

Lloyd's' more sober-minded underwriters decided to splinter off from the rest, moving to new quarters and, in 1771, entering into a formal association. Seventy-nine in number, they were the *new* Lloyd's. Others would collect hundreds of thousands of pounds sterling in "insurance premiums" in the years that followed over such matters as the Chevalier d'Eon's sex—was he a man or a woman?—but the new Lloyd's underwriters would have none of it. (On the basis of sworn medical testimony, a British magistrate in the early 1770s ruled that the Chevalier, a former lieutenant of the dragoons, was in fact a woman. Others were not so sure—including, it would seem, the Chevalier himself. In 1792, he turned up as "Madame d'Eon," petitioning unsuccessfully to serve in the French army. At his widely attended autopsy, years later, it was determined that Madame d'Eon was most definitely a man.)

And old Edward Lloyd? In a spectacularly poor endorsement of the aforesaid healthful properties of coffee, it transpired that Lloyd's wife died in October 1712; that Lloyd himself died the following March; and that Lloyd's headwaiter, who had had the presence of mind to marry Lloyd's daughter (thereby to inherit the establishment), soon died too. But Lloyd's was too firmly entrenched for any of this to matter. Even fifty-five years after his death, and in its new quarters, Lloyd's remained Lloyd's—as it does today.

Looking down from the gallery of Lloyd's, the world's oldest and largest insurance market (for Lloyd's of London is *not* an insurance company but a marketplace, like the New York Stock Exchange), one sees some 4,000 conservatively tailored underwriters, brokers and clerks in a skylighted area the size of a football field ("The Room"), quietly but purposefully writing insurance that produces premiums of $5 billion a year.

And, given the proper credentials, you could become a part of it. Some of that $5 billion could be yours.

As a member of Lloyd's—a "name," as Lloyd's calls its silent ("sleeping") partners—you would join thousands of others whose collective personal fortunes stand behind the association. "Individually we are underwriters," runs the classic explanation, "collectively we are Lloyd's." You would take tiny pieces of a great many different risks, ranging from a riding stable in Kent or a 19-year-old's Porsche to an oil rig in the North Sea or a dam under construction in Pakistan; from the mundane (a cargo of tuna en route from Japan, a factory in Dayton) to the sensational (NASA's lunar lander, Marlene Dietrich's legs). You would be insuring others against all manner of plague and disaster: the possibility of race horses going berserk in air cargo planes, of lottery-ticket printers accidentally printing 5,000 winning tickets instead of 500, of Cutty Sark drinkers actually *finding* the Loch Ness monster and presenting it for the advertised $1 million reward. And you would hope that your share of the premiums (plus interest) in any given year exceeded your share of the claims, in which event you would have a profit. Should it go the other way round—should losses exceed premiums plus interest, as occasionally they do—you would be called upon for your share, *no matter how great*. It's almost that simple.

The wooden "boxes" at which the underwriters at Lloyd's sit today are much like the booths at which they sat sipping coffee and initialing risks 300 years ago: two facing high-backed teak benches with a long teak table running between. Brokers, bringing risks that have been funneled from all over the world, but more than half from America, go from box to box in search first of a lead underwriter with whom to work out the basic terms and premium. (Twenty-five hundred pounds, in the case of the million-dollar Loch Ness monster reward; an eighth of 1 percent of the insured value in the case of the berserk clause for flying race horses.) Once the premium rate is set, other underwriters add their initials to the "slip," taking 2 percent of the risk, 5 percent, 3 percent, and so on, until it is fully subscribed. (Sub-scribed: under-written.)

Those 500-odd underwriters are the front men for 430 syndicates, each consisting of anywhere from a handful of names up to several hundred. Each underwriter has his own areas of expertise. Collectively, they represent the greatest concentration of insurance brainpower in the world. Many specialize in the risks Lloyd's has traditionally insured, ships and cargo, representing about 40 percent of Lloyd's business. But in the last hundred years the underwriters have branched out to provide just about every other conceivable coverage as well. By accepting risks other insurers lacked the imagination or the nerve to handle, Lloyd's has facilitated high-risk, high-reward projects that might otherwise have been delayed or scaled down or perhaps not even attempted at all. Only recently has competition for the difficult but lucrative risks been heating up. Two American firms in particular, the American International Group (AIG) and the Insurance Company of North America (INA) have aggressively pursued Lloyd's-type risks. And insurance exchanges like Lloyd's, thus far all but ignored, have been spawned in New York, Illinois and elsewhere.

Meanwhile, Lloyd's membership has grown steadily—the natural result of people wanting to get in on a good thing, but also in response to Lloyd's dignified efforts to attract new members among whom to spread the ever-growing volume of risks.

The insurance industry's ability to accept risks is known as its "capacity." At times when capacity is short, premium rates rise. Profits follow. And that attracts more players, new capacity. Gradually, the capacity shortage turns into a capacity glut. Insurers begin competing aggressively for risks to insure, lest they lose market share. They lower their premiums. Losses, or at least slimmer profits, follow. Much wailing pervades the industry, both in the U.S. and abroad, which discourages the addition of new capacity. Some may even be withdrawn. So that, with time, capacity again becomes scarce and prices rise. And around it goes. This swinging every few years from undercapacity to overcapacity and back again is called the "underwriting cycle." It is little different from the cycles in any number of industries, from sugar to cattle to cement. In 1981, the underwriting cycle appeared to be approaching its nadir. Profits among property/casualty insurers, despite unprecedented income from investments, were slipping. But over the long haul, global demand for insurance—and global insurance profits—have risen right along with world trade and world economic development.

In 1948, Lloyd's claimed 2,422 members, all Englishmen. Membership had climbed to 6,042 by 1969, the first year foreigners were admitted. (Women were admitted the year after.) At December 31, 1980, there were 18,552 names, of whom 3,479 were women and 1,191 American (with 108 more about to join). There were, as well, Italians (16), West Germans (29), Irish (166), South Africans

(192), Kenyans (19), Saudis (6), Israelis (10), Iranians (9), Swedes (10), Swiss (17), Greeks (15), Japanese (2), an Abu Dhabian, an Argentinian, a Romanian and assorted others, including one woman of no citizenship at all (but considerable means).

To become a member of Lloyd's, one must come personally recommended by another member and satisfy the admissions committee that he has readily realizable assets in excess of $300,000 or so. Upon election, he would join the likes of the Duke and Duchess of Kent, the Duke of Norfolk, Sir Freddie Laker, tennis star Virginia Wade and members of the "Pink Floyd" rock group. A letter of credit from his bank, drawn against the value of his securities, would be posted in an amount geared to the volume of annual premiums he wished to write. Thus the new member's initial investment would be next to nil (if you consider a $5,000 initiation fee and similar trifles "nil"), and on that investment after three years he would begin receiving his return; unless the syndicates he joined lost money, in which event he would be called upon to pony up his share. It takes three years to close accounts on a year's business because claims take time to settle.

It is a nifty business, for if the syndicates one chooses to join have a reasonable measure of luck—or at least not an unreasonable measure of bad luck—then one may never have to part with a dime and yet reap a profit of some tens of thousands of dollars each year. Just for being wealthy and for putting that wealth at risk. The rich get richer.

Although individual syndicates have fared worse, Lloyd's as a whole has lost money in only three of the years between 1948, the first year for which aggregate figures were compiled, and 1978, the last year on which the books have been closed. Even including "the lean years," as they are known around the Room—1965, 1966 and 1967—profit from 1948 through 1978 totaled well over a billion pounds.

The record, in other words, is reassuring. But in recent years there have been problems. "Lloyd's is going through a rough patch," Lambert Coles, chairman of C.T. Bowring (Underwriting Agencies) Limited, told 350 of its assembled names at lunch in November 1980. There was the meltdown of "butter mountain," a warehouseful of the stuff in Holland. What rankled was not the trifling loss, $14 million, but that Lloyd's had not realized the butter it was insuring was all in one place. There was, too, some "prime

U.S. real estate" one Lloyd's syndicate thought it was insuring that turned out to be a package of properties largely in the South Bronx. Thirty Lloyd's members could have faced personal bankruptcy over that one had a settlement not been reached. And there was a computer-leasing fiasco that exposed Lloyd's to an estimated $400-million loss. (When IBM brought out its new model, lessees of the old one opted to terminate their leases. Had no one at Lloyd's foreseen this possibility?) The informal but highly effective structure of Lloyd's that had served well enough when membership was relatively small showed signs of stress as, through the 1970s, Lloyd's membership exploded and risks grew ever larger and more sophisticated. In consequence, 1980 brought the 198-page Fisher Report, calling for a tightened structure and more effective disciplinary procedures.

Lloyd's has had rough patches before. The San Francisco earthquake cost Lloyd's members $100 million. In 1906, $100 million was a lot of money. Losses from the *Titanic*, six years later ($5 million), were relatively slight by comparison. What's interesting about the *Titanic* is the drubbing it gave Lloyd's "overdue brokers."

When a ship had not arrived as scheduled, the underwriters who had insured her would try to hedge their bet by themselves purchasing insurance. The underwriters who specialized in accepting such risks were called overdue brokers. The more precarious the situation, the steeper the rate they would charge—25 percent of the potential loss, 50 percent, or even more. "Once the *Titanic* was known to have hit the iceberg, of course the rate was very high," H.G. Chester, three-time Lloyd's deputy chairman, has recalled. "There was one man who wrote a lot of reinsurance on her all the same—that was Sir Percy MacKinnon, who afterwards became Chairman of Lloyd's. . . . Sir Percy believed the *Titanic* wouldn't sink, she was such a marvellous ship and there'd been so much publicity about her. So he wrote the reinsurance on her. . . . He must have lost a lot of money."

There will always be dramatic losses, and not only for Lloyd's. Just when the directors of a large Hartford insurer were meeting to congratulate themselves on the good year they were having (1835), and on the prospect of being able to resume dividend payments at last, word arrived by stagecoach that fire had razed much of New York's financial district.

For members of Lloyd's, 1979 was among the worst years ever.

African swine fever devastated Spain's pig population; NBC's plans to televise the Olympics were canceled ($78 million); the satellite that would have relayed those broadcasts went floating off into space ($77 million); nineteen airliners crashed; marine results were awful (including the collision of two supertankers); hurricane Frederic broke all records; and computer-leasing losses kept flooding in. Plus your usual fires, floods and freak accidents. "Not since the Napoleonic Wars," reported *Business Week* in February 1980, with a bit of classic American overstatement, "have so many Lloyd's members faced the prospect of financial ruin."

Lloyd's members assume unlimited liability for their proportionate share of a syndicate's losses. Unlimited liability. It is a sobering concept that Peter Green, Lloyd's' chairman since 1980, used to have difficulty making applicants fully appreciate. Then he hit on a way to do it. He began asking prospective members to sign a stack of blank checks. "I'll keep them in my safe," he would say to them, "to fill in from time to time if need be." Those who calmly reached for their checkbooks were told not to bother. Green was satisfied they understood the concept of unlimited liability.

In fact, it is rare for members to be called upon for cash. Oh, $10,000 or $20,000 on infrequent occasion, perhaps, but nothing truly serious. Still, one might wish, if one were a member of Lloyd's, to obtain a little insurance oneself. To limit one's risk.

And where would one go to get protection like that?

But of course! To Lloyd's.

The market for "stop-loss" policies is irregular and volatile. After bad years, there is little enthusiasm for writing them. In 1981, coverage could have been had for £650 that would pay up to £75,000 of a member's losses beyond the first £50,000. Should the member's losses exceed £125,000—highly unlikely—the insured member would once again face unlimited liability for the balance.

And if everyone is insuring everyone else, might not the whole house of cards come shuffling down some terrible year? "I had the same question," says a bright young member, "and they assured me that the syndicates that take on such risks are *very* well heeled."

This is Lloyd's strength. Even an *enormous* loss some year—say $2 billion—would amount to "only" $100,000 per member, which for many would be less than $50,000 after tax. There is no way to know the ultimate resources of Lloyd's, the collective net worths of nearly 20,000 members, but few members would stand or fall on $50,000. If the average net worth were $2 million (even the tiniest castle these days is worth more), then nearly $40 billion stands behind Lloyd's. In its worst year ever, 1965, Lloyd's collective loss was a mere $105 million, or about $17,500 per member. The problem, so far as any individual member is concerned, is that losses are not spread over the entire membership, except as a last resort; they are borne by the syndicates that wrote them.

Lloyd's second strength is the expertise and motivation of its underwriters. As much as anyone can—and more than most others do—they know the odds. Further, unlike the employees of large insurers, who at best can get raises and at worst lose their jobs, Lloyd's underwriters stand to lose everything, or to gain nearly as much, by their judgments. It is an arrangement that keeps a man's mind focused on his business.

Finally, if the game were not already heavily weighted in Lloyd's' favor, the Internal Revenue Service provides an added incentive. Simplifying a bit: Losses, should an American member suffer any, are deductible dollar for dollar from his other income (because they are operating losses, not capital losses). Profits, however, are only partly taxed. This is because part of the profit takes the form of untaxed interest, earned on premium dollars that will eventually be paid out but that are in the meantime invested in tax-free municipal bonds. Also, because profits are held for three years before the final accounting is made, they are sheltered from taxes for that long, earning interest all the while.

Oh, yes. Neither food nor drink, including coffee, is permitted in the Room today. The members' restaurant, on the other hand, reports annual coffee consumption of about 28,000 gallons.

The first *American* insurance company was the Friendly Society for the Mutual Insurance of Houses Against Fire, founded in Charles Town, South Carolina, in 1735. Charleston (as it's now known) was thus poised to become the insurance capital of America—and might have, too, had half the city not burned to the ground shortly before Thanksgiving 1740. The Society went broke.

In Philadelphia, meanwhile, Benjamin Franklin, inventor of the lightning rod, was busy forming a volunteer firefighting association. "An ounce of prevention is worth a pound of cure," he explained at the time. His Union Fire Company, limited to thirty members, set an example for a score of others. Later—shortly after establishing the University of Pennsylvania and just prior to reorganizing the postal system—Franklin persuaded his fellow firefighters to contribute $1,000 to "a fund for an Insurance Office to make up the damage that may arise by fire among this Company." This became the Philadelphia Contributionship for the Insurance of Houses from Loss by Fire.

The Contributionship developed along what were, to say the least, conservative lines. Wooden houses at first were charged nearly triple the premiums of brick. Later, the Contributionship would stop insuring wooden structures altogether. To be insurable, a house had to have a way up to the roof from the inside, so that firemen could quickly reach the chimney—and some sort of railing on the roof, so they wouldn't fall off.

By 1763, the number of structures insured had risen to 801. Rather than accumulate the interest earned on subscriber premiums, the Contributionship had been returning it all each year in the form of dividends. Now it was decided to let such interest remain in the Contributionship to build a reserve against unexpectedly large losses.

The year 1777 found the Contributionship flush with cash ($47,500) and the British on their way to Philadelphia. Many Contributionship members were on their way someplace else. When the British occupied Philadelphia, they burned twenty-seven houses, two of which belonged to policyholders. *The Contributionship refused to pay their claims,* arguing that the fires had been deliberately set. This was one mutual insurance society that was not about to part with its members' money easily. (Others would follow.)

A few years later the membership went so far as to resolve "that no Houses having a Tree or Trees planted before them shall be Insured." Trees, it was thought, hampered the proper fighting of fires. So prudent did this measure at first seem that the Pennsylvania legislature went a step further. It ordered *all* trees removed from the streets of Philadelphia. That struck the populace as so preposterous it was soon repealed. Nevertheless, the Philadelphia Contributionship would not budge: even homeowners willing to pay extra for their hazardous foliage were denied insurance.

Such inflexibility had all the markings of a monopoly. Into the breach marched competition. On September 29, 1784, a group of sixty-one homeowners "who liked trees," as one writer put it, established America's second property insurer, the Mutual Assurance Company for Insuring Houses from Loss by Fire. Ye gods! Only two insurance companies in the entire nation and already their names were stupefyingly unmemorable. Today the confusion is hopeless.*

To simplify things, the Mutual Assurance Company for Insuring Houses from Loss by Fire became known as the Green Tree company; the Contributionship, as the Hand-in-Hand. Two hundred years later, both may be found in the Philadelphia phone book. They are perhaps best known for the "perpetual" policies they offer, instituted in the days of Thomas Jefferson. Under such policies, a single large deposit is paid—today it might be $7,200 for homeowners insurance on a $100,000 frame house—the interest from which funds the insurance ever after. If the policy is dropped, the deposit is returned in full. The plan proved popular with Philadelphia homeowners, but not with the nation's fire insurance agents, who saw themselves being denied their annual commissions for renewal. Neither the Green Tree nor the Hand-in-Hand became a large insurer. The big insurance company in Philadelphia, and the first stock company in the United States, is the Insurance Company of North America—the INA.

What can you say about a $9 billion insurance giant one of whose founding fathers, in 1792, was named Ebenezer Hazard? (Was one of the founders of Procter & Gamble Silas Suds?) And yet there was old Hazard, wealthy Philadelphia merchant and Postmaster General of the United States until 1789, helping to sell 60,000 shares of stock in a new enterprise called the Insurance Company of North America.

It was a hot issue, and it filled a need. Not so much for fire insurance, which was already available, nor for life insurance, which until 1957 the INA did not write, but for the very same line that had so enriched the underwriters at Lloyd's—marine insur-

---

*Aetna Life & Casualty, of Hartford, Connecticut, owns Aetna Casualty & Surety and Aetna Life & Annuity; but the Aetna Insurance Company, also of Hartford, is owned by Connecticut General. If someone says he works for "the Aetna," the only intelligent response is "Which one?" Meanwhile, The Life Insurance Company of Virginia is part of Continental Financial Services, a subsidiary of the $5 billion (sales) Continental Group—but is in no way related to the Continental Insurance Company, one of twenty-nine insurance affiliates of $9 billion (assets) Continental Corporation. The Phoenix Mutual is located in Hartford.

ance. The American underwriters who gathered at a coffeehouse down by Philadelphia's wharves, in imitation of Lloyd's (it was even called The London Coffee House), had only just begun to accumulate capital. Risks that the British could write with the stroke of a pen strained American resources. The INA changed that. Six hundred thousand dollars had poured into the company treasury, a vast pool of risk capital.

One could easily lose oneself in the history of a company like the INA—which just weeks after its launching realized it had forgotten to exclude "War Risques" from its standard policy (and so added: "It is mutually agreed that this Insurance is not made against any Risque or Loss occasioned by War; but only against such Risques & Losses as are usually insured against in Time of profound Peace"), but which 189 years later would be writing as much in annual premiums as all of Lloyd's 18,552 members combined. Suffice it to say that in its first year of operation the INA collected $213,464 in premiums and another $15,000 or so in interest, against just $23,990 in losses (a dividend was declared); that soon fire policies were being offered on structures not just in Philadelphia but anywhere in the United States, which sowed the seeds of the American agency system. Wars and financial panics did occasionally set back the fortunes of the INA. (The Gold Rush of 1848 hurt, too. When ships reached San Francisco, they were frequently abandoned by their gold-crazed crews; at one point 500 such ships were bobbing helplessly in the bay.) But by 1981, shareholder equity in the company—which had in the meantime moved to larger headquarters and taken on an additional 35,000 employees—had grown from the initial $600,000 to $2 billion. And it appeared, in November 1981, that the INA would be merging with the Connecticut General, roughly its equal in size.

The history of fire insurance in America, precursor of today's property/casualty industry, is a history of insurers themselves learning the odds (not a few going broke in the process) and then fixing prices by cartel to be sure the odds were stacked amply in their favor. Nor was this altogether a bad thing, even if at first it was illegal. The public wanted low rates, to be sure; but even more than that it wanted insurers sufficiently rich to be able to pay off in case of loss. What good were low premiums, which any fly-by-nighter could, and many did, offer, if when the neighborhood went up in smoke the insurer did, too? "The stock fire insurance companies were somewhat in advance of the state in appreciating [this]," wrote William Wandell. "They sought the answer, even in contravention of state laws, in combination and agreement on the price to be charged for their insurance."*

It was a Sunday evening in the fall of 1871 when the cow in Mrs. Jeremiah O'Leary's stable on the West Side of Chicago kicked over a kerosene lamp. At least they think it was the cow. By Monday night, 2,124 acres of the city had been destroyed. Sparks from the fire went on to ignite a million acres of Michigan and Wisconsin timberland, as well. Two hundred two insurance companies received claims totaling just over $100 million. Only fifty-one were able to settle their claims in full. No fewer than sixty-eight, from as far off as Philadelphia, were bankrupted by the fire.

Thus the paradox: We do not greatly love insurers, yet, so that they may withstand disaster and pay our claims, we want them to be rich. They are eager to oblige. To build financial strength, fire insurance executives from the Civil War period straight through to 1944 "turned again and again to the technique of agreement. In time," writes industry consultant and former New York State insurance superintendent Richard E. Stewart, "the agreements and the machinery for their enforcement grew into powerful engines of conformity—the bureaus and the boards and fire insurance exchanges, the eastern and western unions, the adherence compacts, in-and-out agreements and acquisition cost conferences—all private law policed by private governments caught up in the romance of self-regulation. It all made for a dependable and rather clubby business environment. . . . There [was] plenty to go around."

In 1944, the fire insurance cartel was struck down by the Supreme Court. The Court ruled that insurance was "interstate commerce," after all, and so subject to federal antitrust laws. Appalled, the industry quickly prevailed upon Congress to pass the McCarran-Ferguson Act, leaving regulation of the insurance industry to the states. The industry has been fiercely independent of federal meddling and exempt from antitrust statutes ever since. The purchase of cash-value life insurance may be the largest investment many families ever make, but the Securities and Exchange Commission has no jurisdiction. Door-to-door health insurance salesmen may perpetrate

---

*William H. Wandell, *The Control of Competition in Fire Insurance*.

heinous frauds upon the elderly, but their sales practices are out of bounds to the Federal Trade Commission.

To be sure, property/casualty insurance has become a good deal more competitive since the golden age of the cartels, but this is its heritage.

The heritage of the life insurance industry, not a great deal more savory, we will encounter further on. But this is not a history book, and even as you read it shots are being fired in one of the world's longest-running, most costly battles.

6

THE BATTLE
It's Almost Enough to Make You Feel Sorry for Insurance Companies

*I don't care if they get a hundred doctors to
examine you. If you say that your back is killing
you, they can't prove it isn't. That's what we
call pain and suffering. And the money you get
for that is tax free.*
—**Walter Matthau to Jack Lemmon in** *The Fortune Cookie*

The Reverend Roland Gray, pastor—and owner—of the Bethel
Missionary Baptist Church in South Chicago, collected $85,400 in
settlement of no fewer than seventy-six insurance claims over a
four-year period. He claimed to have slipped and fallen on numerous occasions, to have been injured in thirty automobile accidents,
four fires, to have been twice burglarized and even to have been
poisoned in a restaurant (I told you it could happen). All the while
he was receiving welfare and Social Security disability benefits.
When finally confronted, the Reverend pleaded guilty to fraud—
committed, he said, to help support his church. It was subsequently
discovered that he owned a Cadillac, two houses, two apartment
buildings and had $46,000 in the bank. In 1979, he was sentenced
to two years in jail.

But then he decided his confession had been in error, that it had
been given under the influence of medication, and that he was not
guilty after all. The appellate court, in its wisdom, ordered Gray
free on bail pending appeal—perhaps those seventy-six insurance
claims had been legitimate, after all.

If one prime cause of insurance industry inefficiency is lack of adequate disclosure, which prevents us from shopping intelligently, an even more fundamental cause lies in the very nature of the business itself. It is a business based largely on trust between potential adversaries—insurer and insured—who have come increasingly to *dis*trust one another; between the heartless insurance company that will cover you for any loss except the one you actually incur (like the banker who will lend money to anyone who doesn't need it), and the conniving insured who will, in concert with his conniving auto mechanic and their conniving attorney, crucify the insurance company. It is a relationship fraught with friction.

When you go to withdraw funds from your bank account, it is done efficiently, in a matter of seconds. When you go to withdraw funds from your "insurance account," a substantial bureaucratic effort ensues. Paperwork, negotiation, investigation—sometimes even litigation. Much of it is necessary; none of it is cheap. The cost of settling claims ("loss adjustment expense") runs anywhere from a penny or two per premium dollar in those lines where claims are infrequent and hard to dispute, like earthquake insurance, to as much as 20 cents in a few, like malpractice, where claims frequently involve litigation.

It cost one company, years ago, four days of legal fees just to fend off a woman who claimed some huge amount for the loss of her late husband's false teeth. The mortuary had lost or discarded the dentures, which had cost a great deal to fashion, and now—despite their total lack of value absent the jaw they were designed to fit—she was demanding either the money or the teeth.

The INA alone pays out more than $50 million a year in legal fees, in addition to maintaining 130 in-house lawyers of its own.

But even more costly than settling claims is paying those that are inflated or fraudulent. This runs high into the billions and makes the odds for *honest* policyholders even worse than they appear. An insurer may pay out 65 cents of each premium dollar in claims; but if, say, 20 percent of that goes to pay the cost of fraud and padding, there is that much less to pay unpadded, legitimate claims. Dishonest claimants get a disproportionate share of the pot.

Here's how the table at the end of Chapter 4 might be modified in a few lines of insurance particularly prone to exaggeration and fraud:

ANOTHER TABLE
Even Rougher in Its Estimates Than the First

For Every Premium Dollar *Honest* Policyholders Deposit In:	This Is How Much, Collectively, They Get To Withdraw:
A SAVINGS BANK	$1.05
AUTO INSURANCE	$0.47
HOMEOWNERS INSURANCE	$0.44
COMMERCIAL FIRE INSURANCE	$0.26

To an extent, insurer and insured are natural allies. Neither wants the insured event to occur. A policyholder is no more eager to have his life insurance pay off than the Prudential or the Connecticut General is to write the check.

Large corporations work with their insurers to devise safety programs that prevent losses from occurring. Nor are they likely to fabricate or seriously inflate their claims. One does not picture Corning Glass torching an outmoded facility to get the money to modernize. But homeowners do set fire to rooms they wish to redecorate. And small-business fires always increase during recessions. Burglaries are invented, damages inflated. Jewelry disappears when money is tight; is "found" again when conditions improve. (Net result: an interest-free loan. The invisible bankers, indeed!) It is an age-old battle between insurer and insured, and it has tended to escalate, for two reasons. One, as society has become more complex and impersonal there is ever more room for dispute and deception. Two, what each side does to combat the abuses, or perceived abuses, of the other only aggravates the grievances of the first. A spiral of fraud.

"By the end of the sixties," wrote the Insurance Crime Prevention Institute in 1979, "fraudulent claims were milking the insurance industry of an estimated two billion dollars a year. Organized fraud rings were running rampant on automobile claims. Body shops were raking in unprecedented profits by arranging accidents and collecting on previously-damaged automobiles; unscrupulous doctors and lawyers were doubling their incomes by inflating the bodily injury claims of legitimate accident victims. But as fraud rose, so did losses, and therefore rates . . . And as rates rose, so did public resentment, and therefore fraud, as otherwise honest policyholders began to pad their claims to get a 'little of their own back' from the insurance companies."

A study conducted in Florida not long ago found a clear correlation between people's attitudes toward insurance companies and their willingness to cheat them. Faced with a hypothetical opportunity to defraud their auto insurers, 14 percent of those polled—and fully a quarter of those under 25—said they would do so. But where 90 percent of the survey group as a whole believed their insurance companies to be "very fair" or "somewhat fair" in settling claims, only 30 percent of those willing to cheat thought so. Implication: If more people trusted their insurers, fewer would cheat.

There's really no way to tell with any kind of accuracy the proportion of insurance claims that are fraudulent, and to what degree. Just 14 percent of this particular sample *said* they would cheat; but how many, given an opportunity to do so, actually would? And under what circumstances? The hypothetical example used in the Florida study involved collusion with a body shop mechanic. Might a policyholder be even more likely to pad a claim in a situation where no one else need participate?

An erstwhile friend of mine with a chic little Manhattan office and a secretary had his IBM Selectric typewriter stolen. Actual value at the time: about $600. Loss claimed: $3,000—for his typewriter, but also for inventory he alleged to have had in the office. The insurance company paid. How could it possibly prove, if it even suspected, that inventory *hadn't* been stolen? And what would such a fight have cost?

Needless to say, had my friend gone into a bank and stolen the same $2,400—for it is clearly that: theft—he would have run a considerable risk of going to jail. Instead, he went to Southampton.

People who defraud insurance companies do occasionally go to jail. The Insurance Crime Prevention Institute (ICPI), for one, has assisted in obtaining more than 3,000 convictions since its founding in 1971. *But it's so much easier to rob an insurance company than a bank.* And, truth to tell, it seems so much less . . . criminal. One act conjures up visions of gunfire and penitentiaries; the other, titillated laughter at cocktail parties or in movie theaters.

Consider Dick and Jane (George Segal and Jane Fonda), a lovely upper-middle-class couple squeezed by recession. They have just borrowed $1,000 from a finance company. As they are getting ready to leave, the place is robbed. Everyone in the office is wiped clean. When the dust settles and the police have finished taking statements, Ned, the loan officer, buttonholes Dick.

NED (confidentially): "How much did you tell 'em you lost?"

DICK (puzzled): "A thousand dollars. What do you mean?"

NED: "Schmuck! You couldn't have told 'em two thousand? The insurance would have paid, and I'd have split the extra grand with you."

Later it develops that *Jane,* sort-of-accidentally, in the heat of things, fell on top of $2,000 that the robbers dropped in their hurried exit and—a little to her own amazement—put it in her purse. When they get home and Jane confesses, Dick is thrilled. Jane can't believe he actually thinks they should keep the money. She's going to give it back, she says. To whom? asks Dick—the robbers?

JANE: "Of course not. The money belongs to the loan company. (Pause as she reflects.) Of course, they're insured . . ."

It is as if there had been no robbery at all! That stolen $2,000, because of insurance, *doesn't belong to anybody!* Jane has qualms about stealing from a loan company (even), but not from an insurance company. Still, she is not entirely convinced.

JANE: "God, suddenly I'm thinking like a criminal."

DICK: "No you're not, Jane." (Yes she is, Dick.)

JANE: "We've always done things the straight way, Dick."

DICK: "And I'm getting tired of belonging to a minority group."

JANE: "All right. I won't give it back!" (Attagirl, Jane.)

Most people are basically honest. Even claims adjusters think so. But even basically honest people weaken when it comes to stealing from an insurance company. The rationales are familiar:

• "I've been paying premiums all these years—it's about time I got a little back." Unfortunately, all those years when *you* had no claims others did. Your premiums went toward covering their sometimes huge losses. It's not the insurance company's fault you were not "lucky" enough to have a loss. If some are to withdraw much more than they deposit, it follows that many will have to withdraw much less—particularly when so much of everyone's deposits must go to feed the insurance company.

• "The insurance companies are richer than God—and they've been ripping us off for years." While it would be a mistake to underestimate God's net worth, it would be equally foolish to deny that, in the case of some companies, anyway, there is a grain of truth here. But you know what Bobby Fischer's mother told him about two pawns not making a knight. And in any event, padded claims, in the aggregate, just lead to higher insurance rates and profits. The thing to do is not to cheat the companies but (Chapter 9) to buy less of their product.

- "The adjuster is going to chisel me, so by padding my claim I'll merely wind up with what I'm owed." If he should actually *accept* your padded claim, you would, of course, repent and return the excess. Sure you would.
- "It did have sentimental value, no matter what any cold-blooded insurance company thinks—not to mention all my pain and suffering, and the time this has taken. What's a few hundred bucks extra to an insurance company?"
- "Everyone else does it."

Such rationalizations (easily adapted, I need hardly tell you, to the preparation of income tax returns and expense accounts) would be no problem if everyone did cheat—equally and just a little—and if to everyone there befell approximately the same amount of insured misfortune. Then we would all be paying a little extra in premiums, all be getting a little extra in benefits. It would be analogous to the way many counties assess property taxes. Homes are assessed at ridiculously low values—but as long as the assessments are more or less equally ridiculous, no one is treated unfairly. The hitch: All homeowners have homes to be underassessed, but not all policyholders have claims to inflate. In any event, it would hardly be practical to write into insurance contracts that it was okay to cheat "a little."

So what is an insurer to do? It knows that a considerable proportion of the claims it receives are inflated, and not a few—total fictions. But it's often impossible to tell honest claims from dishonest ones. If the insurer contests the claim or, equally infuriating, cancels the insured's policy after paying it, it increases the perception that it treats its policyholders unfairly. And so invites cheating. But if the insurer simply pays off, as in the case of the $3,000 Selectric typewriter, it must lose money (which insurers are loath to do) or else—more to the point—spread the cost over all its other policyholders. Again that *Lutine* bell starts clanging.

There may well be no acceptable solution to this problem.* As long as there are insurance contracts there will be hefty expenses in

---

*Lie detector tests, even if reliable, would not likely be acceptable—although an inventive insurer might someday offer a 10 or 15 percent premium reduction to those willing to agree in advance to their use, at the option of the insurer, in the event of a claim.

verifying and settling claims, and substantial fraud. Which suggests that insurance works best where it is really needed: not to protect against losses we could bear ourselves, which are relatively expensive to process, investigate or challenge, but for the big losses we could *not* shoulder individually. As things stand now, people with small losses tend to be *over*compensated—and promptly— because it's cheaper to pay the claims than to scrutinize them, while people with large losses tend to get less than they deserve, and only after long and costly delays.

As a practical matter, it is of little import "who started" this escalating fracas between insurers and insureds. In the earlier years of this century, the companies were doubtless guilty of the lowest blows. The citizenry then were burdened with an old-fashioned morality, coupled with a greater fear of the wrath of large institutions. But even as insurers have tended to mend their ways, policyholders seem to have moved in the opposite direction, increasingly prone to exploit a vulnerable system.

There is an easy cynicism that "justifies" such theft. Indeed, there is a sort of 1960s-spawned *idealism* that has been twisted into little more than a rationale for selfishness. Some years ago I went to look at a loft that was up for rent in a marginal area of town (my finances being then somewhat marginal as well). The place was decorated in power-to-the-people purple, with Vladimir Ilyich much in evidence on the bookshelves and in the choice of wall hangings. The loft was heated electrically, my revolutionary tour guides explained; but every so often, before Consolidated Edison came to read their meter, they vacuumed it. They had a way of sucking their meter reading down to any level they wished, leaving a little something to avoid arousing suspicion.

In their minds, this was a selfless act—ripping off the capitalist-pig utility. Instead, of course, the cost of the electricity they stole from Con Ed was simply added to the price everyone else had to pay. They were robbing their neighbors. Power *from* the people. And yet there is the widespread feeling that all large institutions— businesses, government and certainly insurance companies—"rip us off." Therefore, runs the argument, we need hardly be bound by anything so trite as honesty in our dealings with them. The dishonesty and incompetence that do exist in these large institutions are taken as justification for shoplifting, tax fraud, insurance fraud, welfare fraud, unemployment-insurance fraud. Such selfishness in the name of idealism may be charming (for about ten minutes) in a college student exploring alternative ideologies; but under any ideology it is simply theft.

Look at Raymond Mungo, a most talented writer who not so long ago detailed for *Mother Jones* how he managed to rack up tens of thousands of dollars in credit card charges—and then blithely go bankrupt. (It is, of course, perfectly legal to go bankrupt.) Far from contrition or embarrassment—the man had, after all, gotten all of these goods and services "free," for which the rest of us would now have to pay—his story brimmed with a sort of mirth. He was *laughing* at those people so foolish as to have extended him credit. Why, he wondered, should his word be his bond when it came to large, impersonal creditors? As for the banks he stuck for foolishly honoring his promise to repay their loans, he wrote, "I was raised by working-class parents who talked bitterly about the banks' repossession of homes during the Depression; and I think it made me despise all banks ever after."

(Bankruptcy, I might point out at the risk of being truly tedious, is itself, in a sense, a form of insurance. We have passed laws to spread the risk and costs of financial disaster from the bankrupt's shoulders to the shoulders of society as a whole. Most of the bad debts a bankrupt incurs are passed on to the rest of us as just one more cost of doing business.)

Simultaneous with their publication of Mungo's story, the editors of *Mother Jones*—circulation in excess of 240,000—made him their *religion* editor! A marvelous touch. And these are the same folks who are outraged by, and often commendably effective in exposing, dishonesty in the corporate suite and in government.

Before proceeding further to criticize the big bad insurance companies, therefore (all in good time), it may be appropriate to explore some of the ways we rip *them* off—and, in turn, ourselves.

In Dade County, Florida, according to an outstanding series of articles the Miami *Herald* ran in 1979, "half a dozen private-eye firms do nothing but investigate suspicious [workers' compensation] claims." One involved a Miami police officer who was unable to work for eight months, he said, because of a bad back. Surveillance films showed the disabled law enforcement officer "lifting the transmission out of his jeep, lugging a heavy floor jack, lifting an automobile wheel, repairing a flat tire, lifting engine parts . . . and roughhousing with three large dogs—all without apparent pain and without the back brace he said he needed." As of the time of the story, the city of Miami had paid the man $1,861 in medical and disability benefits. The cost of the surveillance was extra.

Ronald Dunwoody, a CETA worker for the city of Miami, filed a workers' comp claim on May 1, 1978, the day he was told his CETA program would expire. According to his boss, his injury had been sustained when he deliberately dove out of a moving car.

Maria Campuzano claimed to have hurt her shoulder folding towels at Miami's Doral Hotel. (Imagine how bad the injury might have been if she had been folding blankets!) She withdrew the claim when management reminded her she had been complaining about her shoulder "for years."

Not so Willie Pollack, who hurt his hand so badly in a Disney World tram accident, he claimed, that he could no longer drive a bus. He received $3,810 for his disability. Yet he reportedly managed to play pinball right after the tragedy, then to drive a bus back to West Palm Beach.

You read of cases like these and you wonder, *Gee,* what about the state insurance regulators—can't they do anything to tighten up the system?

"Former Florida Insurance Commissioner Tom O'Malley," reports the *Herald's* Patrick Riordan, "recently convicted of 21 counts of extortion and mail fraud, filed a workmen's compensation claim for a heart attack he suffered after running to catch a plane in Atlanta. He was on state business, he said, on his way to a Las Vegas convention." He subsequently expanded his claim to include arthritis, ulcers and depression. He had received $19,000 by the time Florida courts ruled that his claim was indeed compensable.

Jack Lemmon, the nice-guy TV cameraman, has had an accident—but don't worry; he's okay.

Enter his brother-in-law, Walter Matthau, the attorney.

> "I hate to break it to you, kid," says Matthau in this marvelous script by Billy Wilder and I.A.L. Diamond (*The Fortune Cookie,* 1966), "but you got a spinal injury."
>
> *"What?"*
>
> "Your left leg is numb, and you got no feeling in the first three fingers of your right hand."
>
> "You're crazy," says Lemmon (checking). "I can move my hand . . . *and* my leg."

"Sure you can—if you want to blow a million bucks."

"A million—? What are you talking about?"

"That's what we're suing for. They'll offer a hundred thousand, and we'll settle for a quarter of a million."

Lemmon protests. Matthau won't listen—and adds double vision to the list.

"Double vision?"

"How many of me do you see?"

"*One*. One cheap, chiseling shyster lawyer who, of all people, had to marry my sister."

"Nice talk! I'm handing you a quarter of a million dollars on a silver platter—" (Matthau holds out a bedpan.)

"I don't want the money—and I don't want the silver platter."

MATTHAU: *"What's the matter—you feel sorry for insurance companies?"*

Few people do.

Of course, Walter Matthau's portrayal of a personal injury attorney can hardly be taken as representative. Here is how Professor Jeffrey O'Connell describes the breed in his book, *The Lawsuit Lottery:* "Personal injury lawyers . . . are usually extremely self-confident, a self-confidence generally enhanced . . . by *passionate* belief in their function. As they view it, gigantic and heartless insurance companies will grind down helpless victims unless modern gladiators—they themselves—intervene to protect the injured party. Many plaintiffs' lawyers hate insurance companies. 'I'd represent *anybody* in *any* kind of case,' says one of the best of them, 'but *never* an insurance company for *anything*.' They scorn insurance companies' large and posh buildings, erected, as they see it, by bloodless, massive institutions that at the same time would deny the weak and helpless their due. Only trial lawyers, as they see it, stand between the accident victim and harsh destitution."

Says Matthau, as "Whiplash Willie," of insurance companies: "They've got so much money they don't know what to do with it—they've run out of storage space—they have to microfilm it. What's a quarter of a million to them? They take it out of petty cash. So don't give me with the scruples."

It would be a gross injustice to judge the attorneys who battle insurance companies by the caricature Matthau so deftly etches. Better to judge them on their own etchings.

Taking off from a 1977 Gallup poll that showed only 26 percent

of the populace felt lawyers had "high" or "very high" standards
of honesty—"a rating far below medical doctors and exactly even
with undertakers"—an editor of *American Lawyer* magazine, Jane
Berentson, chose thirteen New York attorneys at random and put
them to a test. Posing as a recent arrival to New York, she told each
attorney the identical story.

She had been walking home one brisk autumn evening, day-
dreaming, she told them, when she stepped off a curb in the vicinity
of some Consolidated Edison construction and fell flat on her back.
In each interview she stressed that she hadn't fallen because of the
Con Ed construction. However, in telling her story, she emphasized
its proximity "and strongly implied that I was willing to shift the
location of the fall slightly."

Result: Eight of the thirteen lawyers explained that Berentson
simply had no case. They sympathized, but said that legally no one
was liable for her accident but herself. The remaining five lawyers
told her she should shift the scene of the accident slightly and sue
the bejeezus out of Con Ed.

"My experiment yielded no gray areas," she reported. "The
dishonest lawyers picked up on my suggestion immediately; the
honest ones couldn't be tempted no matter how hard I tried."

Summarized one of the five, a Columbia Law graduate, offering
to take the case for a $1,000 retainer, expenses, and 30 percent of
whatever was won: "Basically it's up to you—whether you're up
to, well, quite frankly, lying."

Another, whose contingency fee was 35 percent plus expenses,
soothed: "You don't have to *lie*. All you have to do is shade the
facts a bit. Just a little *shading* about where you fell. Everything else
is fine."

Only a fraction of the lawyers in America do personal injury
work (the American Trial Lawyers Association boasts a membership
of 34,000); and there is no telling whether Berentson's five-out-of-
thirteen ratio was representative. It may have been too high. But
clearly, one need not look too far to find attorneys willing to play
dirty. Indeed, if they smell a good case, they'll come to you. "A
study conducted during the 1950s," reported the U.S. Department
of Commerce two decades later *(Crime in Service Industries)*, "indicated that 85 percent of all accident victims were contacted by an
unethical attorney. This percentage probably has remained constant
in the years elapsed since that survey was taken."

But the tactics have grown somewhat more sophisticated. Ambulance-chasing attorneys risk disbarment and criminal prosecution if caught. Rather than go racing to the scene of an accident themselves, therefore, some now employ "runners." Police, doctors, auto mechanics—perhaps even ambulance drivers themselves—will not infrequently receive kickbacks for helping to secure accident cases. With nearly two million motor vehicle accidents each year alone, you can fairly hear the whiplash cracking.

One attorney sent Christmas hams to the relatives of victims of a plane crash, hoping to get their business. Others have reportedly gone so far as to climb hospital fire escapes. Just how a sedated accident victim is to assess the talent and integrity of an attorney who has dived through his hospital-room window it is hard to know. But he had best beware. Many is the case in which, after expenses and fees, the attorney has walked away with more than half the settlement. O'Connell offers the example of a Los Angeles attorney, since disbarred, who managed to process *thousands* of personal injury cases a year, referred to him and his fifty employees by an aggressive network of chasers. According to the 1977 testimony of a former chief investigator for the Los Angeles District Attorney's Insurance Fraud Division, "He'd tell the client he'd be handling him on a percentage or contingent fee basis . . . yet somehow in the typical case, involving a settlement of about $1,800, the client would end up with only [$200 or $300]."

"Now tell me, Mr. Cimoli," asks Matthau of an accident victim who has stumbled into his office, "exactly how did you break your hip?"

"I was coming out of this store," Cimoli says, taking a banana peel out of his pocket . . .

"You were coming out of *what* store?" demands Matthau.

"Nat's Delicatessen, on Euclid Avenue."

Matthau moans. "Too bad."

Yes, agrees Cimoli—"such pain!"

No, explains Matthau, "I mean too bad it didn't happen further down the street, in front of the May Company. From them you can *collect!*" And then, with real exasperation, almost scolding: "Couldn't you have dragged yourself another twenty feet?!"

Lawyers—in astonishing numbers—are not the only ones who

supplement, or multiply, their incomes at the expense of insurance companies. The medical establishment is paid primarily through insurance. This provides it with a population of patients who are, when it comes to medical care, almost all rich. Can hospitals, strapped for funds and eager for the newest life-saving equipment, be blamed for jiggering their accounting a bit to play the insurance game to best advantage?* There is the temptation in dealing with rich customers to sell them more than they need, or to charge them premium prices. Sometimes the temptation goes even further: four Los Angeles chiropractors indicted in early 1981 for bilking insurers out of more than $1 million, a Tucson osteopath indicted the same month for Medicare fraud, medical doctors and pharmacists—yes, even your friendly local pharmacist!—being indicted by the dozen. And claims adjusters! When portions of a corporate jet flying over McLean, Virginia, crashed through the roof of the $130,000 Clarke home in the spring of 1977, exploding in flames, the Clarkes were deluged with independent adjusters and appraisers offering to inflate the estimate to be used in filing their claim. At a fee, of course. Some company adjusters, meanwhile, routinely cooperate with auto mechanics, padding repair bills and splitting the excess.

But let us assume most attorneys (and doctors and pharmacists and claims adjusters) are honest, as I believe they are. Let us assume that attorney Stephen J. Johnson, Jr., who filed a claim of his own, really did injure his back while "stretching over his . . . desk to procure a pen," as apparently he did.† What about clients? Might they not on occasion go to an honest lawyer with a set of facts they've managed to fabricate, or exaggerate, all by themselves?

SIMPLE FRAUDS YOU CAN PERPETRATE CLOSE TO HOME, IN YOUR SPARE TIME (AND THOUSANDS OF PEOPLE DO)

• Break a pane of glass in your front door and go through the house looking for valuables as if you were a burglar. Go out to the party you were invited to and return home only to discover *you've been burglarized!* Call the police and give them a careful list of

---

*For details, see Dr. George Ross Fisher's excellent *The Hospital That Ate Chicago*.

†In bed for ninety days with his (quite real) injury, Johnson recovered. By 1981, he had himself become a deputy commissioner of Florida's workers' compensation system, charged with ruling on the compensability of other people's claims.

what you lost, complete with serial numbers. Such as the RCA SelectaVision you just bought and for which you have a receipt (but which actually was sent as a Christmas gift to your children in Pago Pago). Call your agent, and hope the company—those bastards—doesn't cancel your policy just because you filed a claim.

• Quit your job but persuade your employer to say you were laid off. File for unemployment insurance.

• Park your car on the street in Boston, but, to get the lower rate, tell your insurer it is garaged at your sister-in-law's in Newton and rarely driven.

• Take your gas guzzler to a really bad area of town. Wait half a day and report it stolen. By the time the cops find it, it will have been stripped of all working and non-working parts. File your claim and buy a car you can live with.

• *Sell* the car to a crooked junk dealer. Let *him* strip its valuable parts, then squish it like a beer can. Report it stolen and collect from the insurance company. In 1977, 94,420 automobiles were reported stolen in New York City. At least 25 percent of these claims, authorities believe, were phony.

• Having first obtained medical, accident and disability policies from ten or twenty different carriers, pile all your friends and relatives into the station wagon, wait for a Cadillac or Mercedes to crowd your tail—and stop short. Whiplash! Collect, ten or twenty times over, for your medical costs and lost time at work. And don't forget to sue for pain and suffering. If you are hit from behind—never mind why—it's the other guy's fault.

Or, simply drive into a ditch or a tree. Bring along an ex-prize-fighter to bruise and batter you appropriately around the head before the police arrive to make their report. One fraud ring actually did that. Now you are ready to have a friendly osteopath bill you for twenty weekly heat treatments—not that you need ever show up for the treatments, it's the bill you're after—and to have a lawyer press your claim.

Staging accidents has been particularly popular among certain Hungarians in California and among altruistic foreign students eager to send a little money to the terrorists back home:

> LOS ANGELES—Insurance investigators believe that as much as $5 million in fraudulent insurance claims have been collected by Middle Eastern students in this country since 1971 and fun-

neled to the Palestinian Liberation Organization. [*The New York Times,* February 20, 1977.]

One Hungarian immigrant, part of a ring of 300 estimated to have bilked insurers of tens of millions of dollars *annually*, actually went so far as to publish a manual detailing the fine points of the business. The book, *They've Got You Covered,* not available in stores, was written by a former insurance agent and Hungarian freedom fighter. Los Angeles County Deputy District Attorney Fred Stewart told *New West*: "Some of the Hungarians in this ring came here with nothing. Their skills wouldn't permit them to lead the kind of life they wanted. They found insurance and it has proved to be a bonanza. Some are earning six-figure incomes and living in areas like Mt. Olympus in $200,000 homes with swimming pools . . . driving Rolls Royces, Mercedes, Ferraris and Porsches—all paid for by insurance companies."

• Hire a torch to burn down your overinsured slum properties.

The late father of a woman I know would never have been party to such a thing, but did once suffer a small fire in his dress factory. While half the company was racing for fire extinguishers and buckets of water, he was rushing for racks of last year's fashions, hoping to expose them to smoke damage.

• If you're having trouble obtaining inflated coverage on your property (because insurers recognize the temptation created by covering a flammable property for more than it's worth), sell it back and forth a few times among friends and co-conspirators. What better proof of a property's market value than the price you paid?

• Make your suicide appear accidental. If you opted for the accidental-death rider, your policy will pay double.

• Shoot off your foot.

Claims adjusters were not born yesterday; and there are a variety of information banks, such as the National Automobile Theft Bureau and the Property Insurance Loss Register, maintained by the industry to perform cross-checks and to watch out for claimants, doctors and lawyers whose names tend to crop up in patterns. *Thus the very real problem with most of the schemes suggested above, other than the glaring moral one, is that one runs the real risk of ruining his life for the sake of a lousy few thousand dollars.*

But there are still loads of people reckless enough to do so, or whose lives weren't so great to begin with; and it's not easy to prove an accident or a fire was deliberate, or that a man's back *doesn't* ache.

And yet it should be noted, if only for the sake of irony, that a high general level of fraud is not *entirely* contrary to the industry's interests, even though any given insurer will do its best to avoid it. A rising tide of arson, for example, means high fire insurance rates. And high rates mean extra tens of millions of dollars in insurance premiums for the companies to invest.

A little arson joke:

These two older fellas are walking down the beach in Miami. "My factory burned down," says the first, "and I retired on the insurance."

"*That's* funny," says the second. "*My* factory got washed away in a flood, and I retired on the insurance, too!"

"Really?" asks the first, incredulous—"How do you start a flood?"

Most of the insurance fraud that occurs undoubtedly goes undetected. But here and there perpetrators are caught and prosecuted.

Small businessman Wolfgang Kuepper, 31, and his young wife, Sheryl, claimed burglars robbed their Cleveland apartment of $16,675 in jewelry in June 1978. The items, including a Patek Philippe watch and a wedding ring, were all well documented. The claim was paid. Five months later, now insured by a different carrier, they claimed to have been robbed of the same items while walking on the beach in Florida. This time they collected $18,167. The following spring, visiting Toronto (it's not hard to see where they got the money to travel), they managed to get themselves handcuffed to the steering wheel of their car in a dark parking lot. When help arrived, they claimed to have been robbed once more, and collected $18,715 from yet a third insurance company. Only this time the robbery made the news. The story was picked up by a radio station within earshot of the claims adjuster who had processed the second claim. He managed to find his counterpart at the third insurer, compared notes (and serial numbers), then referred the case to ICPI, which in turn found the first insurer and referred the case to the Cuyahoga County prosecutor. The day Wolfgang Kuepper was to have begun serving a light sentence (that would have allowed him to attend school), he killed himself.

ABILENE, TX [*ICPI Report*]—On the afternoon of March 17, 1978, a bricklayer hired to "train" a racehorse named Ed led the five-year-old thoroughbred out to the yard behind his mother's house, stood the animal in a puddle of water, wrapped electrical wire around his neck and legs and plugged him into the house current. Ed fell to the ground, lunged back to his feet, was knocked down again, lunged up once more and finally died on the third or fourth jolt.

In addition to being unspeakably cruel, this bricklayer, Larry Mataska, was unusually dumb. He performed this murder under the eyes of a teenager watching from a neighboring building, who called the Humane Society. Mataska was charged with and pleaded guilty to the class A misdemeanor of cruelty to animals. (He could have *shot* the horse with impunity under Texas law, but Ed's insurance carried no provision for being gunned down. It did contain an endorsement covering death by "artificial electricity.") The horse's owner, Eugene I. Patton, mailed in his $3,000 claim. Mail fraud. The following year, a federal grand jury indicted Patton on two counts, suggesting that he had offered Mataska $250 to electrocute Ed to collect the insurance. Patton pleaded guilty and was sentenced to three years in federal prison.

They shoot people, too. Four Boston men—an attorney, a physician, an insurance agent and a businessman—arranged for an $800,000 insurance policy on the life of George S. Hamilton. Hamilton ran a furniture mart in Braintree, Massachusetts, and this policy—on top of a $1 million policy already in force—was ostensibly to protect the firm's investors should anything happen to its founder and president. No one mentioned to George that an extra $800,000 had been put on his head. A few weeks later, Hamilton, 33, answered his doorbell in the middle of the night and was gunned down by an unknown assailant. To date, no one has been charged with the murder, but a jury did convict the four of obtaining Hamilton's policy fraudulently, forging his signature and filling out his application erroneously.

In Cleveland, delicatessen owner William J. Bourjaily, 25, took out $100,000 of insurance on his manager, then hired two men for $7,500 to murder him and burn down the business. Instead of dying, the young manager struggled out of the burning building, bleeding from eight stab wounds. He recovered and identified his assailants.

And in Florida, in the summer of 1981, insurance investigators were trying to crack what they believed to be a wholesale murder-for-profit ring.

Also:

• Hurley B. Bowers, a Summit Park, West Virginia, heavy equipment mechanic, filed claims totaling $90,000 for the loss by fire of three antique cars. The cars had come from a junk heap. Bowers got a five-year prison sentence.

• The proprietress of a San Francisco fortune-telling salon and her husband claimed a set of golf clubs was stolen from their car. Sixteen times. They got caught when they accidentally submitted the identical claim to the same insurance company twice.

• A young Pennsylvanian was charged with six counts of mail fraud for claiming his motorcycle had been stolen when in fact he had buried it.

• A former insurance man, aged 79, no less, was sentenced to 135 years in jail and fined $54,000 for staging accidents with rented trucks.

• The author of a sweeping plan to reform the Pennsylvania criminal justice system, a state legislator, was among a ring of professionals convicted of staging fake accidents and inflating claims from real ones.

• Minneapolis pediatrician, allergist and landlord Robert Coifman specialized in billing insurance companies for treatments he did not provide—and for providing treatments patients did not need. Even tenants who came by about their rent were given blood tests. Convicted of fraud, he was sentenced to a year in the workhouse and placed on ten years' probation.

And so it goes. Obviously, some progress is being made in tracking down and prosecuting the blatant and repeated frauds. Headquartered in Westport, Connecticut, with regional offices in New York, Chicago and Los Angeles, the Insurance Crime Prevention Institute has the cooperation of 2,000 postal inspectors around the country, as well as other law enforcement officials. It has managed better than a 90 percent conviction rate of those it helps to indict. Among the thousands whom ICPI has helped to collar since its founding in 1971 are more than 400 doctors and lawyers.

Just as the I.R.S. attempts to strike the fear of God into the broadest possible range of taxpayers, so ICPI attempts to multiply the effect of its efforts with well publicized arrests, indictments and convictions. The leading Baltimore-area auto insurer ran an analysis for the years 1973 through 1978 comparing its bodily injury payments nationwide with those in Baltimore alone. Before the spring of 1974, Baltimore bodily injury payments were right in line with the national average—around $2,000 each. But then insurance fraud became big news in Baltimore, thanks to ICPI, with more than two dozen doctors and lawyers variously pleading guilty, losing their licenses, being disbarred, convicted, fined and in some cases sent to jail—*and Baltimore's average bodily injury payment dropped significantly.* After a year or so it did begin to rise again—but not nearly so fast as for the nation as a whole. The average payment in Baltimore by the end of the study, in the spring of 1978, was around $2,700, while the average national payment had reached almost $4,000.

It would appear that crime fighting does pay. Even the aforementioned Reverend Gray, of the seventy-six insurance claims, eventually wound up in Joliet prison. But what this study really suggests is that bodily injury payments for the nation as a whole are grossly inflated.

Fraud (like the supertanker *Salem* that authorities suspect was scuttled *after* surreptitiously unloading its $57 million cargo, but for which a $57 million cargo loss was claimed) . . . padded claims (like my friend's $3,000 Selectric typewriter) . . . vindictive juries hot to stick it to insurance companies (like the jury in San Bernardino, in 1975, that awarded $2.5 million to a 52-year-old woman who had been denied disability benefits for a bad back, or the jury that awarded $182,000 to a man in 1979 for "loss of consortium" with his wife due to a fractured toe, or the one in Tennessee that awarded $1,500,000 to an 84-year-old woman who suffered mercury poisoning from the use of a skin creme)—it's almost enough to make you feel sorry for insurance companies.

7

THE BATTLE II
I Said, "Almost"

*Prompt fair settlement of all just claims,
with courtesy and consideration for all.*
—The Allstate Claims Philosophy*

But perhaps not quite.

The first known life insurance contract was written in 1536 on the life of a British merchant, William Gybbons, for a term of one year. Gybbons died shortly before the policy was to expire, but the insurers refused the claim. They held that Gybbons had indeed survived "twelve months"—twelve *lunar* months (of 28 days). The insurers were taken to court and ordered to pay.

More recently, in the summer of 1977, when New York's lights went out and enterprising residents gave new meaning to the term "window shopping," insurers were reluctant to chip in for the losses. "Insurance companies shouldn't have had to be ordered to pay damages," opined Malcolm Forbes. "Trying to avoid shelling out on the technicality that no one officially branded the sickening pillage a 'riot' is just the sort of thing that puts the insurance industry behind the public opinion eight ball."

In the settlement of insurance claims, the opposite of customer fraud is insurer bad faith.

Ten or twenty times larger, even, than the fortune amassed by W. Clement Stone was that of another high school drop-out, John D. MacArthur. An atheist, MacArthur was the son of an iron-willed,

---

*In 1970 and 1977, *Consumer Reports* polled subscribers with regard to auto insurers' claims-handling practices. Both times, Allstate landed near the bottom in the ratings.

self-ordained evangelist whose own father and grandfather had been self-ordained evangelists as well. John MacArthur had the fervor, but it was directed toward the service of himself. When he died, on January 6, 1978, at the age of 80, MacArthur owned Bankers Life and Casualty Company, the ninth-largest life insurer in the country (among stock companies, second only to Aetna). All of it. He was the largest landowner in Florida, with a hundred thousand acres in areas like Palm Beach and Orlando. He owned banks, oil wells, office buildings (including New York's Gulf + Western Building), ranches, resorts, restaurants and airplanes. He flew tourist, dressed poorly, and in later years conducted his affairs from a corner table in the coffee shop of his own hotel, the Colonnades, in Palm Beach. MacArthur was a certified billionaire who had inherited not a dime. He made it all himself. In insurance.

"They see all that money," he once remarked, "and figure I've got to be crooked. Of course they're right."*

In 1928, John was 31 and unemployed. Older brother Charles had written a play that year called *The Front Page,* and would marry Helen Hayes three days after the raves poured in; older brother Telfer was a successful Chicago newspaper publisher; and older brother Alfred, nearly as evangelical as his father, had attained a lofty executive position at Central Life, a small Chicago life and health insurer. John had earned handsome commissions working for Alfred in earlier years as Central Life's number-one salesman, but had squandered much of his capital in two failed entrepreneurial attempts—first a gas station, then a bakery. Now, at 31, he plunked down $7,500 to acquire his third business, this one even shakier than the first two. It was the Marquette Life Insurance Company, consisting of nine salesmen and 600 aging, aching policyholders (most of them rejects from other companies). Marquette was likely to go bankrupt or to be shut down by the Illinois Insurance Department at any moment. MacArthur set about adding new policyholders to his pool—young healthy ones—and terminating the poorer risks whenever possible. But it takes time to sell life insurance and for reserves to mount. Not all Marquette's 600 clients were able to wait. One particularly bad week MacArthur was hit with five deaths, totaling $65,000 in claims. To stay afloat, he began finding excuses to deny claims. Others he simply ignored. And then—you know

---

*William Hoffman, *The Stockholder.*

the wonderful cliché about its always being darkest before the dawn?—things got worse. The stock market crashed. Policyholders who had not already died began terminating their policies voluntarily and demanding the cash values they had been building. On December 31, 1929, MacArthur's accountant drew up a balance sheet showing Marquette's net worth at $15.31. Only this accounting conveniently failed to include more than $50,000 in unpaid claims.

MacArthur was himself now on the verge of bankruptcy and could have gone to jail. But policyholders hadn't the money to sue, and investigators from the Illinois Insurance Department could be made to look the other way. A $5 bill was usually all it took. (There are those who say some of the nation's state insurance inspectors are still not above being shown a good time.)

One such investigator finally did come to padlock the doors. Enough was enough. Marquette was showing assets of only $1,000, against liabilities of $3,000. Bankrupt companies have no business selling people insurance. MacArthur begged for a day's grace, during which time, as biographer William Hoffman tells it, the investigator assumed he would solicit friends and relatives for $3,000 in new capital. Instead, MacArthur simply trumped up grounds upon which to deny an additional $3,000 in claims.

And so it went. Seeing the importance of not paying claims—a crime that, for cruelty, might be likened to a savings bank stealing its depositors' life savings—MacArthur devised his own special policy, with a highly restrictive clause buried amid pages of fine print. When the Illinois Insurance Department spotted the atrocity, MacArthur was ordered—at the very least—to print it in ten-point type. He complied by setting the entire policy in ten-point type.

Said brother Alfred, who by then had become president of Central Life: "The darkest day in insurance history was when my brother entered the business."

Maybe so. But there have been dark days from time to time since.

Anne Wetherbee, a Eureka, California, widow, bought a disability policy from the United Insurance Company of America that was to pay her $150 a month for life if she suffered a "confining disability." She subsequently suffered a stroke, but was denied payment because "with crutches, a foot brace and an attendant," according to one report, she could leave the house to visit her doctor. (A jury in 1971 slapped United with $500,000, later trimmed to

$200,000, in punitive damages.)

In another case, a company denied benefits to policyholders who had been mangled by an uninsured motorist on grounds that the uninsured car had not itself hurt the bleeding policyholders, but had merely slammed another car into them. In some ultra-literal way this may even have been true, just as a quadriplegic may not literally have suffered a confining disability if he can be wheeled out onto the porch. (Remember those charming childhood playmates who would make deals, then welsh on them with the excuse that their fingers had been crossed? They have grown up and may now be reached in the legal departments of certain insurance companies.) Such interpretations have not stood up well in court. The courts have held with regard to disability insurance, for example, that the strict definitions of "disability" in the policies are meant to prevent people from collecting benefits fraudulently—not to prevent legitimately disabled people from collecting benefits.

In fact, because of the way disability policies are written and interpreted, here is what sometimes happens: There is an accident; a claim is filed; it is denied. The unsophisticated policyholders, furious, hire lawyers, go to court and win. The sophisticated policyholders, nearly as furious but feeling a little foolish for not having read the policy more carefully in the first place, go back and read it. Sure enough, they see that, according to the contract, their claim doesn't qualify. Grumbling, they shelve the claim.

Bad-faith cases that make headlines are extreme. (One judge stated that punitive damage awards *should* be large enough to make headlines, because where insurance companies are concerned headlines are an even more effective deterrent to bad faith than money damages.) For every instance of insurer bad faith that results in a lawsuit, let alone substantial punitive damages and a headline, thousands result in nothing more than the birth of a bitter anecdote to be passed on from barbecue to barbecue, from generation to generation—like curses in a blood feud that will not die.

Most insurance claims are made, and paid, with reasonable good will. This chapter is not about those.

"A case which I handled from its inception," says Phoenix attorney Robert G. Begam, past president of the American Trial Lawyers Association and in the forefront of the fight to preserve a victim's right to sue for damages (and an attorney's right to collect 35 percent of the award), "is entitled *Jones* v. *Fidelity General.*

"Otto Jones was struck down at a crosswalk, sustaining multiple compound comminuted fractures of the leg and hip. At the time we were retained he was in intensive care, having already incurred many thousands of dollars of medical bills and permanent disabling injuries. We learned in an initial conference with his daughter, a schoolteacher, that Otto was in his early sixties and had been an ordinary laborer, very healthy and hardworking. It was apparent that he would never recover sufficiently to continue with that kind of work, and he had no education which would enable him to pursue any other.

"One of the first things we learned in our investigation was that the driver [who hit Otto] only had minimum insurance—$10,000. We told the Jones family we were sure the insurance company would pay its full policy limits. But, as the driver had no appreciable assets against which we could execute, this was a case where the maximum recovery was going to be $10,000—inadequate, but all there was.

"Much to our surprise, Fidelity General declined to pay the policy limits. We sent all sorts of medical bills and hospital reports, but they kept asking for more. Finally we gave them a deadline, advising them that we were working on a minimum hourly fee basis, but that if they showed bad faith and refused to pay what they owed, we would then convert the case to a contingent fee basis, go to trial, get a verdict for the full damages—not just $10,000—and do our best to collect the full amount from Fidelity General."

Fidelity nonetheless ignored the deadline and refused to pay.

Begam sued the minimally insured driver and won all he asked— $100,000. The jury took all of forty minutes to make up its mind.

The driver, of course, had no way of coming up with the additional $90,000. "We then went to the defendant, through his lawyer, of course, and told him that he owed the excess, but that we would forgo executing against him if he would assign to us his claim against Fidelity General for breaching their obligation to act in good faith."

"I might add that before the trial they had tried to negotiate a settlement on several occasions, first offering $5,000, then $9,000, then $9,500 and ultimately $10,000—but at that point we told them we had already spent a great deal of time and money getting ready for trial and we would no longer settle for the policy limits."

The driver, as you might expect, was thrilled to turn his claim over to Begam to get off the hook for $90,000 he didn't have, and Begam sued Fidelity General for its breach of faith. "We engaged in extensive discovery proceedings and found inter-office correspondence between the home office of Fidelity General in Chicago and their Phoenix adjuster in which it became clear to us that Fidelity General *never* paid full policy limits regardless of the injuries. Most of their policies were for minimum $10,000 limits, but they adopted the philosophy that if someone wanted to settle a claim with them they would have to permit Fidelity General to save a little from the full policy limits. This 'save a little' philosophy is well known to all lawyers in this field. Fidelity General just happened to make the mistake of putting it in writing."

The jury took an hour and a half to return a verdict of $90,000—the balance owing Otto Jones—against Fidelity General.

"This is a fairly typical story," says Begam. "The lawbooks are replete with additional examples."

Fifty years after John MacArthur took on his first 600 policyholders and began denying their claims, Standard Life of Indiana was held to have wrongfully refused payment of a $1,000 death benefit. In granting $25,000 in punitive damages, the court noted: "If an insurance company could not be subjected to punitive damages it could intentionally and unreasonably refuse payment of a legitimate claim with veritable impunity."

In other words, why pay claims at all if by not paying them you risk, at most, having to pay them, after all?

(But you *do* risk more: There are the legal fees, which can easily dwarf the actual claim; and even without punitive damages, there are the extra damages that may be awarded for "emotional distress." Even those who see the value of punitive damages in cases against insurers, as many do, question whether much or all of said damages oughtn't to be paid to the premium-paying public at large rather than to one policyholder on top of the other damages awarded him.)

A laborer named Fletcher wrecked his back lifting a 361-pound bale of rubber. His disability insurer, Western National, was obliged to pay $150 a month—for up to two years if the disability resulted from illness, *thirty* years if the result of accident. The company decided that Fletcher's back injury was the result not of lifting a 361-pound bale, but of illness (an illness, no less, they alleged he had contracted from a horse), and so undertook to make payments for only two years. Virtually all the medical opinions concurred that Fletcher's disability was legitimate, and caused by his accident. But, in the words of the appeals judge, Western National "embarked upon a concerted course of conduct to induce plaintiff to surrender his insurance policy or enter into a disadvantageous 'settlement' . . . by means of false and threatening letters and the employment of economic pressure based upon his disabled and, therefore impecunious, condition (the very thing insured against), exacerbated by Western National's malicious and bad faith refusal to pay plaintiff's legitimate claim." All this had been done with the express knowledge of the then president of the company and the company's claims supervisor, who said at the trial that, faced with the same situation again, he would follow the same course of action. "Defendants concede that their conduct was 'deplorable' and 'outrageous,' " the judge continued, noting, however, that at the time of the trial the claims supervisor was still in his post.

The jury split nine to three on the verdict—but in a California civil action nine votes suffice. Fletcher was awarded $700,000 in compensatory and punitive damages. The three dissenting jurors? They wanted to award a *million* dollars.

The jury award was cut by the trial judge to $180,000 and upheld on appeal. Western National's attorneys argued that even $180,000 was excessive. The appeals judge pointed out that, as the company had stood to save $50,000 in benefits over a period of years by bullying Fletcher into relinquishing his legitimate claim, the award did not seem unduly harsh. (What would have happened to Fletcher had he attempted to steal $50,000 from Western National?)

As long as insurers think they can get away with murder, some, at least, will try. Well-publicized suits and large awards have led to a review of and, frequently, improvements in insurance company claims-handling practices.

Egan v. *Mutual of Omaha*, because of the size of the award, is perhaps the bad-faith case that has drawn the most attention of all. Listen to Begam:

"I would say *Egan* has to be one of my real favorites. You have to be one of those greedy trial lawyers that we see in the full-page ads placed by Travelers and the Hartford and INA to really appreciate the *Egan* case. It is a chronicle of insurance company avarice and rascality."

It seems that Egan, a 60-year-old roofer, took out a disability policy in 1962 providing for $200 in monthly benefits—for *life* if disability was total and caused by an accident; for just three months if, though total, it was caused by illness.

In 1970, after having on three separate occasions made claims under the policy and received payment, Egan fell off a roof. He underwent surgery and nine months of physical therapy. But Mutual of Omaha—"The People Who Pay"—decided, without making a full investigation, that the disability was the result not of accident but of illness—"osteo-arthritis." Accordingly, his payments soon ceased. When he complained, an adjuster came to his home, accused him of faking, and offered him a small settlement to surrender his policy. ("When plaintiff expressed his concern regarding the need for money during the approaching Christmas season and offered to submit to examination by a physician of Mutual's choice, [the adjuster] only laughed, reducing plaintiff to tears in the presence of his wife and child.")

Egan got a lawyer. A suit was filed, during the discovery phase of which Mutual of Omaha was asked for their full file on Egan. The company produced it, maintaining that the whole case had at worst been nothing more than a low-level error in judgment. During the trial—in a break of the sort ordinarily seen only on TV—a witness innocently mentioned something about "file jackets." Egan's lawyer perked up. File jackets? It developed that every Mutual claim file had a jacket showing its route through the company. The judge, indignant, ordered that the jacket be produced the next day. It showed that Mutual's "low-level error" had been approved by a variety of higher-ups.

"On the issue of punitive damages,"—Begam picks up the story—" the plaintiff was permitted to prove that Mutual of Omaha had a surplus of something in excess of two hundred million dollars, that they had declared no cash dividends to the accident and health policyholders for ten years (this is some mutual!) and that the president of the company was drawing a salary of $440,000 a year."

(Actually, he was probably drawing rather less than this. What's interesting is that Mutual of Omaha, owned by its umpty-ump million policyholders and run for their benefit, will not reveal the salary of its chief executive, other than to state regulators, as required by law. I say "umpty-ump" policyholders because Mutual will not reveal that number, either. In 1974, Mutual's chairman earned

$125,000 plus $31,250 in deferred compensation. But he was also chairman of United Benefit Life, a Mutual of Omaha subsidiary, which paid him $70,000 more. And Companion Life of New York ($6,000). And perhaps one or two others. "I suspect you've got part of the story on the compensation of the big shots at Mutual of Omaha," says a onetime state insurance commissioner, "but by no means all of it. When dealing with a mutual, always watch out for a management company, a managing general agent, a law firm or some other vendor of services that may be owned by, or paying, the mutual's top management.")

"The jury decided to declare a dividend. The award was $45,600 in compensatory damages, an additional $78,000 for emotional distress, $1,500 in punitive damages against the claims superintendent and $900 punitive damages against the adjuster who went to Egan's home to harass him." Plus $5 million in punitive damages against Mutual of Omaha.

(It was only after his case reached the California Supreme Court, nearly a decade after his fall from the roof, that Egan actually received any cash—about $170,000 in compensatory damages. A jury trial ordered by the Court to reassess the level of punitive damages was scheduled for January 1982.)

Punitive damages take on an odd twist when levied against a mutual insurer. A mutual company is owned by its policyholders. There are no fat-cat shareholders (even if there may be a fat-cat executive or two). Profits are poured into "surplus." When the surplus is considered more than adequate, the excess may be returned to policyholders as a "dividend." Thus, far from the jury's "declaring a dividend," it voted to take $5 million from Mutual's other policyholders and give it to Egan. Meanwhile, the adjusters who did Egan dirt—for it was they, rather than Mutual's policyholders, who were most directly at fault—were fined a total of $2,400, later thrown out on appeal.

Mutual of Omaha maintains that "99.8 percent of all [its] claims transactions are handled without complaint." In 1979, that came to 4.7 *million* claims transactions. If this is accurate, and if the relatively few claims that do generate complaints involve honest differences or errors that are corrected, then Mutual's claims handling, the Egan claim notwithstanding, is either very good indeed—or else overgenerous. Cases like *Egan* tend not only to prod insurers to pay legitimate claims promptly, but also to pay padded and fraudulent claims rather than risk lawsuits.

No one has brought and won more insurance "bad faith" suits than William M. Shernoff, forty-three, who, despite his success and the inevitable national publicity, has managed to avoid falling in love with himself in the manner of, say, an F. Lee Bailey or Marvin Mitchelson. Shernoff's small Claremont, California, firm has won in excess of $35 million in jury verdicts and settlements from 150 insurers over the last six years—more than half of it in punitive damages. It was he who represented Egan in the suit against Mutual of Omaha.

Shernoff won $300,000 in punitive damages, on top of $1,116.05 compensatory damages and $12,000 for "mental and emotional stress," from Blue Shield of California for a client whose $1,116.05 hospital bill had been declined for reimbursement. Blue Shield held that the visit—although ordered by his physician and seconded by the hospital staff—was not necessary. The award will either lead to improved claims-handling practices (if you believe Shernoff), or else to higher insurance rates to pay unworthy claims (if you believe Blue Shield)—or (most likely) to some combination of both.

"People with unquestioned claims, and that's about 95 percent," an Occidental Life attorney told *Time,* "are not benefitted by Shernoff's activities. He should not be pounding the table claiming he's helping the consumer. He's hurting most of them."

Even some insurance men disagree with that view. "There's no doubt that the fact that some large punitive damages have been awarded has caused men in my profession to be doubly sure that we're right," Travelers senior vice president Ray Stahl told the Los Angeles *Times.* "When these cases started, we reviewed how we do things, how claims are to be investigated, what action to take for a doubtful case, how to decline a claim. If you proceed professionally there should be no grounds for a suit." Nor does he think this need be more expensive. "If you do things right the first time round," he says, "it saves time and energy."

Whatever the cost, Shernoff's lawsuits may be worth it simply for the vicarious thrill they give consumers who are ordinarily near powerless in the face of massive bureaucracy. He won $175,000 from Pennsylvania Life for a Mississippi man who, having hurt his back carrying a bathtub, was denied benefits because, on doctor's orders, he managed to take a walk each day. (The jury grew sympathetic when they heard one of the company's former adjusters testify that the company had a quota aimed at denying half its disability claims.) He obtained $50,000 in another back-injury case for a woman who was denied benefits for failing to disclose on her application that she suffered from rhinitis and amenorrhea. (Runny nose and irregularity of the menstrual cycle, respectively.) And he filed a class action suit against Allstate, "The Good Hands People," on behalf of the parents of a boy who was killed in an auto crash, "and all other [Allstate policyholders] similarly situated." Allstate's policy stated that "funeral expenses are covered." But when, in September 1979, the parents submitted their $1,698.40 claim, Allstate promptly paid only $1,441.90, indicating that it was their practice with regard to funeral expenses not to pay for the cemetery plot, clergyman or flowers. Believing these items to be very much a part of what a reasonable man would take to be funeral expenses, Shernoff sought redress and, to set an example, punitive damages. The judicial process may be slow, but not Shernoff. The suit reached Tulare County Courthouse just three working days after Allstate's check was received and within two weeks of the funeral! In an out-of-court settlement, Allstate agreed to pay the remainder of the parents' claim, to do likewise for all other death claims processed in the preceeding three years, and to pay Shernoff $100,000 for his trouble.

It used to be that the only damages a party could recover for the breach of a "contract to pay money," such as an insurance contract, were the monies due under that contract, plus interest. Certainly that was true in John MacArthur's day. But in recent years—and particularly in states like California—the courts have been extending the types of damages recoverable to include damages for emotional distress, for attorney's fees, for economic loss resulting from the breach of contract—even, as illustrated, punitive damages.

A 1979 California decision against Royal Globe Insurance took all this yet another step. It said that one need not even be a *party* to the insurance contract to collect for an insurer's bad faith. In a four-to-three decision that hung in part on the interpretation of two omitted commas, third parties were granted the right, in California, to sue insurance companies for failing to make settlements in good faith. Previously, if your insurer refused to make a fair settlement with a man you injured, he would sue *you*. You could then turn around and sue your insurer for not settling the matter in good faith. Now, in California, the injured man can move directly against your insurer.

Says one California insurance adjuster: "It's really made a big change. Plaintiffs' attorneys all the time are screaming 'Royal Globe! Royal Globe!' And people's premiums are going to sky-rocket as a result, because insurance companies are getting scared and are paying more on their claims. It's affected our attitude immensely—no one wants to be responsible for exposing his company to a bad faith action."

Where a plaintiff's lawyer in a personal-injury case is likely to be a gunslinging entrepreneurial type, and principal member of a small firm, an insurance company is likely to be represented by a more patient, less passionate man or woman from a larger firm. One reason for the plaintiff's attorney's relatively greater level of passion is that he tries fully to appreciate the pain and suffering and outrage felt by his client; opposing counsel would prefer to keep things "in perspective." Another reason: the insurance company attorney is paid a steady, soothing hourly fee, win or lose. The stakes for the personal-injury man are a blood-rushing bonanza if he wins, *nothing* if he loses.

But just as you have personal-injury attorneys who are caricatures of themselves—Walter Matthau's "Whiplash Willie"—so have the insurers a caricature or two of their own.

John Bower—the Vince Lombardi of defense attorneys—is every bit as passionate in defending his clients from the suits of malpractice victims as any victim's attorney is in pressing them. He's glad that his 64-lawyer New York firm, Bower & Gardner, has a reputation for being hard-nosed and tough. "If we are known as bastards who never settle," he told *American Lawyer,* "then plaintiffs' lawyers will look to sue others." Sure, some people are dreadfully damaged by doctors and hospitals. It is Bower's contention that "professional men have the right to be wrong."

Bower told *American Lawyer,* in effect, that his greatest challenge was to win those cases in which badly injured plaintiffs—the blind, the brain-damaged, the maimed—had very strong grounds for their suits. Which prompted reporter Connie Bruck to ask whether he ever felt a surge of sympathy for these plaintiffs.

"Absolutely not," Bower replied. "My sympathies are not wasted on the enemy—it's that simple. My sympathies are reserved for the people who pay my fees."

On one side of the battlefield, then, viewed in stereotype, you have an infantry of clever policyholders scheming with Whiplash Willie to defraud insurers. Sometimes they get caught in a burst of criminal prosecution and go to jail. And on the other side, the uncaring, greedy insurance companies—picture the impregnable Imperial Snow-Walkers in *The Empire Strikes Back*—that will do practically anything to keep from fully paying a claim. Sometimes they get walloped with a punitive-damages bombshell.

LITTLE TRUCES
A Few Tips from the Claims Manual

*A desk job. Is that all you can see in it? Just a hard chair to
park your pants on from nine to five? Just a pile of papers to
shuffle around, and sharp pencils and a scratch pad to make
figures on, with maybe a little doodling on the side? That's not
the way I see it, Walter. To me a claims man is a surgeon, and
that desk is an operating table, and those pencils are scalpels
and bone chisels. And those papers are not just forms and
statistics and claims for compensation. They're alive! They're
packed with drama, with twisted hopes and crooked dreams. A
claims man, Walter, is a doctor and a bloodhound and a cop
and a judge and a jury and a father confessor, all in one.*
—Edward G. Robinson to Fred MacMurray
from the 1944 film *Double Indemnity* ("From
the moment they met it was murder . . .")

If insurance companies are banks, then claims adjusters are tellers.
They count out the money. Only theirs is a great deal more challeng-
ing, responsible and time-consuming job. Each transaction is a potential skirmish in the general conflict, each settlement a little truce.

Even in life insurance, where claims are not easily inflated or
invented and thus relatively easy to assess, interpretations can get
pretty hairy (as in: splitting them). An amateur pilot with a $40,000
life insurance policy piloted his plane into a thick bank of topsoil.
Fearing just such a mishap, the underwriter had required a clause in
his policy specifically to exclude death resulting from accident in a
private plane. The claim, accordingly, was denied. The widow's
attorney, clever fellow, said, "Now wait just a minute. Our man did

125

not die from an aircraft accident; he died of a heart attack! The crash came second.'' The attorney had no way of knowing this was true; but the insurer had no conclusive way to prove it wasn't. The insurer thus found itself in the odd position of having to go around trying to prove that the relatively young man had been in excellent health; ordinarily, to deny a claim, the insurer has to prove the insured was in *worse* health than had been admitted.

Improbable though the claim was, the insurer wound up compromising for about half the policy's $40,000 face value.

Suicidal death is not covered until two years have passed from the time of issuance. Otherwise, any sensible suicide (which, I grant you, limits the field) would buy life insurance just before pulling the trigger. In Missouri there is no waiting period, unless it can be proven that the policy was taken out specifically in contemplation of suicide.

After two years (one year in North Dakota and Colorado), whether for suicide or any other cause of death, the policy becomes incontestable. Even medical and non-medical misrepresentations made in obtaining the policy, no matter how blatant, become incontestable.* A short statute of limitations. On the other hand, if the insured should die within two years, the claim *is* contestable, even if his or her death was totally unrelated to the nature of the misrepresentation—as in the case of a man who concealed his heart condition but died in a fire. The reasoning here is that had the application been honest, the policy would never have been written in the first place.

Meanwhile, many policies include an accidental-death-and-dismemberment feature—''double indemnity''—which doubles the value of the policy if death is caused accidentally.

So it sometimes becomes important to establish the cause of death. Was it murder or suicide? (Murder, for the purposes of insurance, is considered an accident.) Does the aggrieved widow collect double? Or nothing? Or did *she* do it? And *if* she did it, can she still collect? (Not if she was convicted of the murder; but yes if she is found not guilty by reason of insanity. A California woman pulled out a gun and shot her husband for refusing to change a flat tire.

---

*If it can be proven the applicant lied about his age, the policy will pay off in the amount of coverage that the premiums he paid would have bought had he stated his age correctly. Also, if the applicant never existed, other than on paper (such as the recently deceased fourth child of a family that really had had only three children), the policy would be voided.

Acquitted by a jury of her peers, she collected $22,000 from the insurance company.)

Even after the two-year period of contestability, the cause of death is important. Did the insured fall asleep at the wheel—or head for the tree on purpose? If the former, his heirs may receive double payment for accidental death; if the latter, just the face value of the policy.

Is it an accident if a man, trying to extricate his car from a ditch, suffers a heart attack? Or if the insured "punctured a pimple on his lip, causing death"? Or if he died of sunstroke? Or if death resulted from a reaction to novocaine? These are all real, if very old, cases (see "Liability Cannot Be Determined by Just Reading the Life, Health and Accident Policy," by Leon Wasserman, *The Insurance Law Journal*, December 1977)—and they were all decided in the affirmative. All qualified as accidental deaths.

What do you make of this extraordinary case? The insured tried to hang himself; but as he jumped off his stool, the rope snapped. He banged his head badly as he fell, and subsequently died. He died not of strangulation, but from an accidental fall. The court ruled that, based on intent, it was nonetheless a suicide.

An Alabama man swallowed a fistful of sleeping pills, drove to the middle of a bridge, got out, and, just as the pills were beginning to rob him of his consciousness, jumped. It was fifty feet to the water. The fall did not kill him, the cold water, after a time, revived him, and, after floating for quite a long time, he finally managed to pull himself out of the current and drag himself out of the water. He suffered a heart attack from the exertion; and, while lying there, some wild dogs came along and chewed on him awhile. He died. Was it suicide? After all, he had pulled himself out of the water. No, said the state toxicologist, it was "not suicide but the strain and stress of the situation" that killed him.

More bizarre still—you may wish to send young children from the room before reading this—are the *fantasy* hangings that sometimes backfire. In the magnificently diverse sexual galaxy, it develops, there is a small subset of people who hang themselves in front of mirrors, working themselves up into ecstasy as they watch. Executed properly, if you will, this maneuver calls for an escape cord to be released at the moment of, well, release, the practitioner thereupon to slump blissfully to the mattress below (his wife and kids, downstairs, to wonder what Daddy keeps dropping up in the attic with such a thud). In any event, several times a year life insurers are confronted with claims from the embarrassed heirs of policyholders whose rites have gone awry. The courts have ruled that, so long as an escape mechanism is in evidence, however unreliable, such deaths are not suicides.

Nor, on the other hand, need they qualify for accidental death benefits, because such benefits do not apply when an insured voluntarily puts himself into a situation—such as leaping between two buildings on a dare—that could reasonably be expected to carry a high risk of fatality.

Far from paying double indemnity in the case of these fantasies come true, some insurers—knowing full well that suicide was not the motive—have contested the claims. They offer to settle for some lesser amount, confident that few beneficiaries would be willing to submit to the embarrassment of a lawsuit.

THE CLARKE CLAIM

Tens of millions of insurance claims—literally—are handled fairly and promptly each year. To take but a single dramatic example, here is what happened after a wingful of jet fuel fell from the sky over McLean, Virginia, and crashed through the roof of patent attorney Dennis Clarke, his wife Shirley, and their four children. (They were watching TV at the time.)

Step One: The Clarkes race from the house, having no notion what's happened.

Step Two: The house explodes in flames and burns to the ground.

Step Three: A reporter from *Money* magazine, Rachel Lavoie, arrives on the scene to record the ins and outs of one family's ordeal. She files this instructive account:

> Though it left the Clarkes virtually unscathed, the fire also left them with not much more than the clothes they were wearing— and only Jody [aged 7] had shoes on at the time. The two cars in the garage—a '77 VW Scirocco and a '72 Pinto—were demolished. Their third, a '72 Chrysler station wagon parked on the street, was intact, but it was locked and the keys were somewhere in the rubble.
>
> Along with their possessions, the Clarkes in effect lost their identities: birth certificates, driver's licenses, credit cards, bank

books, checks. They had no safe-deposit box and so also lost the
deed to their house, their marriage certificate, their insurance
policies and so forth. . . .

That night neighbors besieged the Clarkes with offers of help
. . . but no one could give Clarke the answer to the one question
that had been haunting him ever since he saw the flames engulf
the house: "Do we have enough insurance?"

Mrs. Clarke spent 15 minutes flipping through the Yellow
Pages at a neighbor's the next morning, hoping to recognize the
name of their insurance company. It finally occurred to her to
ask the bank that held their mortgage. The answer was Travelers,
so an unshaven Dennis Clarke—wearing sweat pants, T shirt,
bathrobe and slippers—set off in a borrowed car to meet with
the company's claim adjuster.

Basically, Clarke learned, he had enough insurance: $109,000
on a house that can probably be rebuilt for that even though it
would sell for considerably more. They had paid $74,000 for it
in 1971, but their homeowners policy had an inflation guard that
automatically increased their coverage over the years.

They were probably underinsured on the contents of the house,
however, as are many people who have accumulated a lot of
possessions over the years. Their standard Homeowners 2 policy
allows half of the policy limit—$54,500—for "unscheduled
personal property." The Clarkes' policy also reimburses them—
up to $21,000—for reasonable "additional living expenses,"
such as temporary lodging and the difference between the cost
of restaurant meals and what they ordinarily spend on food. The
Clarkes think the $21,000 will adequately cover their expenses
for the 10 months or so it will take to rebuild their house.

The Travelers adjuster suggested Clarke take a $5,000 advance
and wrote him a check. Clarke started to take it, then realized he
couldn't cash it because he had no identification. The adjuster
accompanied him to the bank. . . .

In the meantime, the Red Cross had keys made for the Clarkes'
station wagon, arranged temporary lodging for the family at a
Holiday Inn and gave them $740 in credit at a nearby clothing
store.

Their car insurer, Geico, soon made what [the Clarkes] felt
was a generous settlement—$1,040 for his "beat up" Pinto and
$5,848 for her Scirocco, only $130 less than she'd paid for it
seven months before.

The only real problem the Clarkes have with their insurance is
in filing the claim. They have to itemize everything that was

destroyed—down to number of pairs of underpants and pieces of flatware. They should list each item's approximate replacement cost and—if they are able—its estimated depreciated value and where and when it was purchased. After they reach the $54,500 insurance limit, they should keep on itemizing so they can either deduct the excess as a casualty loss on their 1977 tax return* or file suit for their uninsured losses against whoever proves liable for the plane crash.

Reached three years after his story appeared in *Money,* Clarke reported that he had had no difficulty collecting from Travelers but that, yes, they had been underinsured. (And no, they still didn't have a safe-deposit box or a personal inventory of possessions.) The family had taken its time reconstructing its losses, he said, allowing more than six months before finalizing the list. Because of their enormous casualty-loss deduction they had been audited, but encountered no difficulty. Clarke was surprised that Travelers had almost not gone after the owner of the airplane (and, ultimately, four other defendants) to try to recover the nearly $200,000 it wound up shelling out. His neighbor's carrier, Nationwide Mutual of Columbus, Ohio, out nearly $50,000, did not even join in the suit.

The Clarkes' accident itself was unusual, but not the handling of the claim. This is the way insurance is *supposed* to work—and generally does. Admittedly, in this case there was little room for doubt or dispute, and too much publicity for delay. Here's how private detective Irwin Blye describes what he sees as the two basic claims-adjusting approaches:†

> The first technique is that they try like hell to control the complainant. The minute they hear you've had an accident they're at the house or apartment doing you favors. Need money? Here's a couple of hundred. When things get tight they even send men around to poor claimants with suitcases filled with five- and ten-dollar bills. Most of those poor people have never seen so much money in their lives. The guy takes it out of the suitcase a stack at a time. He's doing them a big favor, you see. He's Puerto

---

*Uninsured losses beyond the first $100 are deductible. Thus, for a family in the 50 percent tax bracket, half of any uninsured loss is absorbed by the government in the form of lower income taxes—insurance of a sort for which all taxpayers pay. (Very large casualty-loss deductions naturally lower a family's tax bracket. A family with $50,000 in income doesn't need a $95,000 deduction. But excess losses can be applied to prior and future years' taxes.)

†Nicholas Pileggi, *Blye, Private Eye.*

Rican, just like them. He's Italian. He's black. He's whatever the claimant happens to be and that's why he's looking out for their interests. It wasn't easy for him to get a suitcase full of money out of the company but he did. If they sign the release it's all theirs. He can leave it right in the middle of the dining room table and walk out the door. It will usually be something like $2,000 to $5,000 in cash on suits that would probably earn the claimant $25,000 to $150,000 if they went through the courts.

I don't know too many poor people who can resist. Especially after their insurance company buddy says that there are guys in his company who want to fight the case all the way to the Supreme Court, that even if they win it'll take five, ten years, and by then their lawyers will have taken most of the money. These adjusters can be very convincing and most people fall for their line. They will try to provide the claimant with everything. They are all over you like a blanket. Everything from phone calls to chicken soup. It's called "keeping claimants under control," and the whole reason behind it is to keep the claimant from getting an outside attorney.

That's approach #1.

> The other approach [continues Blye] is the approach taken by most of the mutual insurance companies. These outfits hold out in every single way. No notes about getting well here. They use the theory that by hardnosing each case most claimants will get discouraged and withdraw their suits. It is a conscious corporate policy on the part of many mutuals. They appeal every ruling. They file extraneous motions. They do everything they can to discourage the claim. Mutuals are so tough and hardline that they are often fined by judges for failing to negotiate properly under the state's insurance laws.*

Blye's view is doubtless too harsh, particularly as regards mutual insurers, to apply generally in the 1980s (although it might have fit the 1950s to a T). Even so, the concepts remain valid. The first approach makes sense for open-ended bodily injury claims: settle them as fast as possible. The second applies to property damage: take your time—the fender's not likely to get any more bent, and

---

*Tough? Hardline? Everything is relative. In Mexico City in July 1980, according to the UPI, "thugs working for a bus company kidnapped 20 men, women and children, killed one of them and tortured and poisoned others so they would agree to settle an accident claim."

the guys in the investment department can use that cash in the meantime.

While I could find no manuals with instructions for hardnosing claims, or for "shaving" them—the practice of offering a little less on a perfectly legitimate claim than is owed, knowing it will not be *enough* less to warrant a lawsuit—I did obtain a training manual used by a former training supervisor for a large property/casualty company.

"Timeliness," according to this manual, "is possibly the most important factor in effective adjuster communications. A prompt first call on a claimant can prevent the development of unfortunate attitudes." Not to mention the retention of an attorney. (And yet, see how easy it is to become cynical? Would we prefer that insurance companies *not* provide prompt claims service?) "It is important for the adjuster to maintain communication through regular *control calls*. The frequency of these calls is a matter of judgment. However, when the adjuster keeps in touch, shows interest in the claimant's welfare, and reiterates the company's good intentions, rapport is maintained and an equitable settlement is usually reached."

Under that heading—"control"—the manual has this to say: "The adjuster wants to deal directly with the claimant rather than through an attorney. Under no circumstances should the claimsman advise claimant not to employ counsel. What he should do is create confidence on the part of the claimant so there will be no desire for a lawyer."

Other hints:

• Little "acts of kindness" help to establish rapport.

• Note taking can be off-putting; develop a good memory instead and take notes after an interview.

• "Movement towards the claimant and immediate self-introduction" help to create confidence. "If the claimant calls at his office, the adjuster should not simply sit at his desk, but get up and move toward the claimant with a friendly smile."

• In a claimant's home, try to conduct your interview at the kitchen table. (Unless a life insurance salesman has beaten you to it.)

• "Talking directly across a desk or table should be avoided. Sitting together with claimant on the same sofa is not an ideal situation because eye contact can be achieved only through awkward positioning on the sofa.'' Try sitting ''at a round table or talking across the corner of a rectangular one.''

• Try not to have anyone else present.

• Let the claimant talk. ''No matter how halting his speech may be, no matter how poorly he expresses himself and no matter how inconsistent his statements are, the claimant should be allowed to express his ideas. Do not interrupt, and particularly avoid the use of 'yes, but . . .' form of interruption.'' Nod silently at points the claimant makes with which you completely agree; remain expressionless if he or she says something with which you disagree. ''In short, permit the claimant to talk himself into an equitable settlement.''

• Catharsis (on the part of the claimant) can help to clear the air of pent-up emotion. It does not occur in every interview, but it can occur at any time. *Never interrupt or argue during catharsis.*

To which might be added: Do not laugh at the claimant, no matter how ridiculous he looks; do not get loaded before or during your interview with him; do not push his grandmother out of the way as you rush forward, smiling, to make your self-introduction.

• ''Some words have appeal while others lack it. An example is the word 'sign.' Many members of society have been conditioned against the idea of signing. When asked to do so they are immediately repelled.'' Instead, the adjuster uses euphemisms. He never comes out and says, ''Hi, I'm here to get you to sign a statement.'' He says, ''Hi, I'm here to write up a report on your accident. Could you tell me about it?'' As the claimant tells, the adjuster paraphrases, writing out a statement for the claimant. When it's done, the adjuster asks if the claimant wouldn't mind ''putting his name to it'' to verify he's done his job.

• Be vigilant, but assume that most people are honest. ''If the adjuster actually believes his claimants are all crooks, the attitude will be unconsciously communicated. An immediate barrier to confidence is established. If the adjuster does not trust the claimant, why should the claimant trust the adjuster?''

After reading this particular manual, the claimant might or might not. Here's more on the crucial point of whether or not to retain an attorney:

''It is important that the adjuster show no alarm or even a great deal of concern over [a claimant's threat to retain] counsel. He knows that the claimant does not really want an attorney or else would already have one. The threat is probably an idle one . . . the claimant is probably attempting to judge the adjuster's reaction.

"The adjuster can indicate that he respects attorneys, that he works constantly with them and understands why they are so expensive . . . .Mention can be made of the unpleasantness involved in litigation such as independent medical examinations, interrogatories, depositions and cross-examination . . ."

Assuming the adjuster will work out a settlement directly with the claimant (for once an attorney is retained, it is unethical for the adjuster to deal directly with the claimant), and once catharsis, if any, has cleared the air, the adjuster helps the claimant come up with an itemized list of the specific costs he has incurred. Two words absent from the adjuster's vocabulary for any such list are "pain" and "suffering." He is happy in most cases to make a reasonable settlement for actual, verifiable damages incurred—"three days' lost wages, $187.50," that sort of thing—and even to let the claimant feel he has "beaten" the adjuster out of a dollar or two— if the adjuster can keep from opening *that* Pandora's box.

• Finally: "Once an agreement has been reached . . . the adjuster should leave." Quick. "Further conversation will accomplish nothing. As a matter of fact, the settlement could be lost through post-mortem type of conversation."

Adjusting a claim for a bent fender is not the world's most complicated job. It requires a certain expertise, and there are opportunities for corruption—such as kickbacks from body shops—but by and large it is straightforward work assigned to unexceptional adjusters. Bodily injury claims (there are 1.8 million "bed disabling" motor vehicle accidents each year) are something else again.

As one adjuster put it, "Pain and suffering, anguish—what's that worth? No one knows. Cries in the night—who knows?" And so it lends itself to a lot of corruption. "When I first went into the business, I remember I heard guys in the office talking about 'ten points.' Real low, under their breath. In a normal voice I said, 'What's ten points?' 'Not so loud!' they said—'are you crazy?!'

"Ten points meant that if you were working with an attorney on a case, and the word was he was the kind of attorney who didn't mind sharing some of the wealth, you and he might come to a pretty fast settlement—say, $4,300—and then he'd kick back ten points, or ten percent of the claim.''

Nothing like this goes on in the industry anymore, needless to say; or, for that matter, in business, government or labor generally. Gosh, no! (Well, perhaps in France a little corruption remains.) But however much the business may have been cleaned up, adjusting a bodily injury claim is no less an art than it ever was.

A man fell through the stairs of his landlady's apartment house and was left dangling in mid-air for half an hour before help came. He agreed to settle for $9,000. He thought under the circumstances that was fair. But the insurer refused to settle, so the case was put to a jury. The jury considered $101,000 fair. Well, which was it—$9,000 or $101,000? Which was fair? Jeffrey O'Connell leads into *The Lawsuit Lottery* by citing two nearly identical malpractice suits. In one, just as the jury was about to exonerate the doctors, awarding the plaintiff nothing, attorneys for the two sides—each fearing an adverse verdict—settled for $500,000. In the other case there was the same type of last-minute settlement (for $165,000)—only this time the jury had been set to award the plaintiff $900,000.

Malpractice cases are even more complicated than ordinary bodily injury cases, but in either the claims adjuster has little by way of clear and certain guidelines to go on. So much depends on what a jury might ultimately think if the case went to court. Which is why, at least until late 1968, an Allstate claims manual instructed adjusters to note whether "claimant, insured or witness[es]" clicked their teeth, cracked their knuckles, scratched, had yellow teeth or dirty fingernails, had manicured nails, used perfumes or lotions, used "uncommon words" or frequented race tracks, 5-and-10-cent stores, bars, art galleries, libraries, hotel lobbies, burlesque shows, courtrooms or whorehouses.

Of course, there are precedents. A young professional badly injured will receive more than an older man in the same predicament soon to retire from a low-paying job. In settling claims, insurers and claimants try to guess what a jury would award and then work backwards. Both sides know that a case worth $100,000 when finally settled by a jury is worth a lot less if settled tomorrow. But can they agree on a price?

Because it is so hard to quantify pain and suffering, claims came to be settled based on a multiple of the actual economic damages incurred. Consisting essentially of medical expenses and lost wages, these are known as "special damages" or, simply, "specials." (A better term might be "specifics," as in "specific damages" versus "general damages.") After all, the kind of accident that results in minor medical bills is likely to be one that involves minimal pain and suffering; and vice versa. An imperfect standard, but one both attorneys and adjusters grabbed on to.

But once it became clear that the starting point in any bodily injury negotiation was the sum of the "specials"—multiplied by three or five or whatever—attorneys quickly figured out that if you could increase the specials, you would increase the value of your case. So off you would be sent to doctors and specialists and chiropractors, some of whom enjoyed good relationships with the attorneys who did the referring, to build up your claim.

Settlement of bodily injury claims, many of them auto-related, remains a messy, unsatisfactory process. One reason is that auto insurance, as originally conceived, was designed not to compensate accident victims for their loss but to defend drivers from claims. An intelligent system of no fault insurance would go a long way toward reducing the inequities and inefficiencies, but so far no state has adopted such a system. We *think* we have no-fault insurance in a couple of dozen states, but (Chapter 10) we do not. What follows is the essence of a short training film produced by one of the very largest auto insurers. It is magnificently dated—the company might be surprised to know there is even a print still in existence—but perhaps that's its charm. It is a piece of vintage 1950s Americana.

CONTROLLING EMILY

As the film opens, two men with crew cuts are walking up the path of a neatly kept suburban home. It is nighttime. The two men, in their late thirties, represent Mr. Jackson's insurance company. Driver Jackson, it seems, accidentally hit Mrs. Emily Potter as she was crossing the street from the supermarket. The adjusters have already spoken with Jackson. This is their first visit to the claimant, Mrs. Potter. They purposely did not call to ask if they could come by, preferring instead to drop in unexpectedly. Already this gives them an edge: they knew they were coming, she didn't. The reason there are two men out on this call is that one of them, Roy—the one with the dark suit and the white socks—is a trainee.

They ring the doorbell and Mrs. Potter, prim past all primness, comes to the door.

"Mrs. Potter?"

"Yeeees?"

"My name is George Richardson. I'm with the [giant] Insurance Company."

"Well, now! You've come about the accident!"

"That's right." There is enthusiasm in George Richardson's voice. He's *really* looking forward to this visit with Mrs. Potter, and to making sure she's treated fairly. He's not surprised she's happy to see him.

"Come in!"

"Oh, ah, this is Bloom, a new man riding with me this week."

"A *new* man! Well, isn't that nice! Sit down, for heaven's sake! Make yourselves at home!"

"We were out this way yesterday and a few times this afternoon, but we couldn't find you in." But it did help them establish that she was well enough to go out, and gave them a chance to size up the neighborhood.

"Yesterday I was at my daughter's. Naturally I called her up after it happened. '*Grace!*' I said, 'You'll never guess what happened to me! I got run over!' She came right over in a taxi, bless her heart. I spent the day at her house—er, yesterday, that is."

"And you seem to be feeling all right now."

"Oh, I'm going to live, no doubt about that."

"Well, I'm certainly thankful for your sake that it's nothing serious."

"Not that it couldn't have been! That impossible man!"

"Well, that's what I'd like to hear about—how it happened."

"Well, my dear young man, it couldn't have been simpler. I started to cross the street and Mr. Jackson knocked me down. At Second Avenue and Maple."

"I'm, ah, familiar with that corner"—you bet he is—"let's see if we can get a clear picture of this." He begins to draw a diagram. "Now, here's the intersection; could you show me—"

"Certainly. I was just coming out of the supermarket, right here . . ."

"Supermarket," Richardson echoes, adding it to the diagram.

". . . That's right. And all I wanted to do was cross the street."

"Were there any cars parked in front of the supermarket?" If there had been, they might have blocked Jackson's view, and so lessened or absolved his responsibility for the accident.

"No. And this is where Mr. Jackson knocked me down, right here."

"When did you first see Mr. Jackson?"

"Oh, I guess the first time I saw him was when I was coming out of the supermarket. He was coming around the corner."

"Oh, I see—he was making a right-hand turn." Of course, Richardson has already heard all this from Jackson. "Ah, then what did you do?"

"Well, he seemed to be stopping to let a lady cross, here, and there weren't any other cars coming from that direction, so naturally I thought I had plenty of time to get across while the light was still green."

"Well, did you keep your eye on Mr. Jackson as you started to cross the street?"

"No! Why should I, for pity's sake! Why didn't Mr. Jackson keep his eye on *me? That's* the question."

"Well, ah, you weren't at the crosswalk," Richardson rejoins hesitantly, as if it really pains him to find even the slightest weakness in her story.

"Well isn't that a ridiculous thing to say? The light was green, wasn't it? I had the right of way, didn't I? Like my husband, God rest his soul, used to say, 'Emmy, we're *pedestrians*— we've got the right of way!' Am I right?"

Silence.

"I have no use for drivers who act as if they own the streets, no use at all."

"Ah, what part of Mr. Jackson's car did you come in contact with?"

"The *front* part! The front corner, that is."

"The right front bumper."

"That's right."

"Unhunh. And then what happened?"

"Well, I was carrying a bagful of groceries this high. And the next thing you know I was sitting down and the groceries were all over me. I was so embarrassed I could have cried."

"Ah, Mr. Jackson said that you wouldn't let him take you to see a doctor."

"I should say not! Would you get into the same car with a strange man who just tried to kill you? No thank you!"

"Well, ah, how did you get home?"

"Oh, I walked, of course—it's just around the corner."

"Did you see a doctor?"

"Grace, my daughter, insisted on it. Do you know Dr. Roberts?"

"No, I, ah—"

"A lovely person. Simply lovely. You know, he's the kind of person that makes you feel better just to talk to. You know what kind of person I mean?"

"Ah, Mrs. Potter," answers Richardson after a polite smile, keeping the interview on course, "what were the extent of your injuries?"

"Well, they, ah, weren't very dignified. I, ah, fell in a *sitting* position, you know."

"Oh," says Richardson, pausing, showing that he appreciates the . . . delicacy . . . of the situation. "Um, a few . . . bruises."

"More like one great big solid bruise! I ached all over at work today."

"Oh, I know how that can be! It will probably be a few days before you're feeling *really* all right again. Oh, incidentally, Mrs. Potter, where do you work?"

Mrs. Potter works at the Holly Greeting Card Company. She inspects the cards to make sure they're just perfect. She makes (this is the 1950s) $13 a day.

"And you missed work yesterday because of the accident?"

"Well, I should hope so! One doesn't get run over by a car every day, for heaven's sake. I think I deserved to stay in bed for *one* day."

"You're absolutely right; you did deserve it! And, as far as I can see, you might have a little money coming, besides. Before I leave," he says, pulling out a company check, "I'd like to make this out to you."

"Oh!" Mrs. Potter clasps her hands, "Isn't he sweet!"

"Before I forget though," he says, as if speaking to a school-child, "I'd better make a few notes for my report."

"Go right ahead."

"Ah, what is your full name, Mrs. Potter?"

Time passes. Mrs. Potter is reading, aloud, the "notes" Richardson jotted down:

" 'I had to miss a day at work because of this accident. My doctor bill was $5 for one visit. I plan to see him once more. There were no other medical expenses. I lost a bag of groceries worth about $3.87. My coat will have to be sent to the cleaners. I have reimbursed my daughter for taxi fares. Except for the bruises mentioned above, I did not suffer any other injuries. I have read the above report, of one and one-half pages, and it is true and correct to the best of my knowledge and belief.' You know? You have a very interesting handwriting, Mr. Richardson—very interesting!''

"Well, thank you, Mrs. Potter!''

"Look at the way he crosses his *t*'s,'' she says, trying to let Bloom, the new man, in on some of the excitement. "Obviously you ought to be in some kind of artistic work. Like interior decorating, for instance. Did you ever think of that?''

"Well, it's awfully nice of you to say so. Uh, if you'll just put your name right down here,'' he says in his most matter-of-routine deadpan, pointing with his finger to the conclusion of his night's work.

"I'll have to *sign* something?'' Trepidation has suddenly grabbed Mrs. Potter by the throat.

"Well, now, this *is* your own version of the accident. We've included all the important facts, haven't we?''

"Oh, yes!''

"And all of these facts are *true,* aren't they?''

"Why, certainly!''

"Then if this is a *true* report [statement] you certainly don't have to worry about putting your name to [signing] it, do you?''

"Certainly not.'' What kind of little old lady does he take her for, anyway? "Right here?''

"Umhum . . . And also right here.'' She signs both pages of the report. "And also under 'Diagram Correct.'''

"See how I cross *my t*'s?''

"Why, yeeees,'' says Richardson the way you'd humor a paranoid.

"I'll admit that my job doesn't pay very much. But the work I do is artistic—and, every penny counts, as the saying goes.''

"It certainly does. And I'd like to see to it that you aren't out a single penny.'' Whereupon he itemizes with her all her expenses and lost wages. Mrs. Potter feels a sudden need to confess about the $3.87 she has claimed for the groceries she was carrying. The fact was, she had left most of them lying in the street, but she *had* taken the box of mints. Her voice quickens as the confession pours forth—was this catharsis?— "If you want to deduct for those, I—''

But Richardson, being a right guy and representing a big-hearted company, interrupts: "Let's just consider that a little gift.''

"Oh,'' she coos. "Well, that *is* nice of you.''

Absent a pocket calculator it takes the claimsman a minute or so

to add it all up: $33.37. "I think that about covers every-
thing?"

"Thirty-three thirty-seven," Emily says slowly, the gram of
greed in every grandmother's heart surfacing in hers. "Well,
now, that doesn't seem like very much for a great big old rich
company like yours, now does it?"

Richardson does a double take. My God—has he accidentally
shortchanged this woman? "Have—have we left *out* anything?" he asks with great concern.

"Well, glory be—I'd think it would be worth more than that!
Why, the embarrassment alone!"

"I'll tell you what, Mrs. Potter. I'll add another day for lost
time. That's another thirteen dollars—just in case you feel
like staying home and relaxing."

"Well . . . "

He writes the extra amount carefully in his book. He is giving
her a chance to feel she's beat the company. "Forty-six dollars
and thirty-seven cents. Well! I think that's very fair, don't
you?"

"Hmmm."

"Let's look at it this way, Mrs. Potter. I'm willing to settle this
with you right now, and save myself the time and bother of an
investigation."

"Investigation?"

"Well, Mrs. Potter, there are always two sides to everything, you
know that."

"Yes of course—a right side and a wrong side."

They go around and around on the subject of fairness for a while,
and it is at this juncture that Bloom, the new man, gets to utter his
one line in the film. Richardson is telling Mrs. Potter what a good
job she has done of giving a fair account of the accident from her
point of view—"Don't you think so, Roy?" "Yes, *very* good,"
says Bloom. But Richardson points out that Mr. Jackson has his own
point of view, which he now proceeds to relate. Jackson's point of
view is that it wasn't his fault. Trying to decide between these two
points of view, Richardson says, could be quite time consuming. It
would mean, among other things—and Richardson is sure to throw
this in, because he has already seen how sensitive Mrs. Potter is to
the embarrassing nature of the accident—having the company doctor examine her naked body. He doesn't say it quite that way, but
knows that's what Mrs. P. is thinking.

But all this, he says, "will take time, and money. Personally, I'd rather give the money to you. Like this, well, this extra thirteen dollars, for example. I'd rather give it to you and call it quits. After all, you're not the kind of person who wants to make this into a long-drawn-out federal case [are you?]; all you want is to be reimbursed for what this has cost you. And that's what I want to do. Right now. You'll have your money without waiting, and, well, we'll both be ahead—am I right?"

> "Well . . . like my husband used to say, a bird in the hand is worth two in the bush, take it while you can get it—that was Mr. Potter for you, a quip for every occasion!"
>
> "Well, let's face it, Mrs. Potter. A full day's pay for a few minutes of embarrassment isn't bad, now is it?"
>
> "Well . . . when you put it that way, I guess not."
>
> "Oh, say, I'd better get this form filled out. This is your full and final release of your claim against Mr. Jackson. If you'll just put your name right there . . ."

She does, they thank her, falling all over themselves to get out of the house as quickly as possible. Music up, class dismissed.

And where do our sympathies lie? Do we not feel Emily has been manipulated? But what *was* her accident worth? How much *should* her fellow citizens pay for a little bruise on her backside?

Conveniently, Mrs. Potter's accident was about as sweet and grandmotherly as she herself. *Most* of the accidents this film was designed to train adjusters to settle involved such little uglinesses as snapped bones, gashed faces, terrifying pain—stuff like that. In such cases, settlements everyone would call fair are even harder to arrive at.

For a look at modern insurance adjusters, live and in person, I interviewed two of them. Both are honest and upstanding, out to do their jobs fairly, but in most other respects are not at all alike. One, a young college-educated woman from an upper-middle-class background, was working in San Francisco for a large property/casualty insurer. The other, a twenty-year man, is senior adjuster for a medium-sized Midwestern life insurer.

THE YOUNG CLAIMSPERSON

"I've worked for three years as a field adjuster in bodily injury claims," Lisa said. "I'd estimate a good 90 percent of my files are auto accidents; the other 10 percent, slips and falls.

"We try to deal directly with the person who is injured, but in the Bay area that's real unlikely, because people are very claims-conscious. There are so many attorneys in this area, most people automatically get one. And that's why insurance premiums are so high—one reason, anyway. People bitch about their premiums being so high and at the same time they'll have two lawsuits going for diddly claims.

"Our job is to investigate the claim so that in the event it goes to litigation we have some material we can send to our defense attorneys. And also to know the worthiness of the claim. Let's say I'm dealing directly with the person who's injured. I would gather their medical specials, the verification of their wage loss and that sort of thing. Then on the basis of what I've supposedly been trained to know, I would put a dollar figure on the worth of their claim. And then negotiate."

Some adjusters are retired police or firemen, but Lisa had had no such related experience. Hers was basically on-the-job training. After thirteen months of adjusting claims, she was finally put through the company's formalized two-week training program.

"You go through case studies and what not, but there really are no rules or tables to tell you how to evaluate a claim. It's just something you get a feel for after a while. It's hard to explain how one learns the trade. There used to be—and to some extent I guess there still is—a formula for evaluating a claim: three or four times the medical specials. We use that as a kind of guideline, but it's really flexible. What we want to avoid is litigation. And if there is a lawsuit, we want to settle it before it goes to trial, because trials are so unpredictable. And expensive. You never know what a jury is going to decide. So you really want to try to avoid that. Let's say the claimant is this really sympathetic person the jury is bound to like, and the insured happens to be really obnoxious—well, this might make the person's claim a little more valuable. You might want to spend a little more just to settle it."

One of the biggest cases she ever handled involved an old Chevy station wagon, the owner of which, her company's policyholder, had a summer house near Lake Tahoe—and a very steep driveway. "Our insured and his family had gone up there to work on the driveway—they were going to line it with stones, and they'd filled the back of their station wagon with these little boulders. Our insured's uncle was visiting from Iran. He had been in the U.S. for a couple of months on a visitor's visa, living with the insured. They were all up there working on the driveway, and our insured's brother parked the car at the top of the driveway and set the emergency brake. He got out of the car, heard something snap, and saw that the car was rolling backwards, downhill.'' The uncle, standing right in its path, slipped and fell trying to escape the runaway station wagon, which rolled right over him. He was trapped under the wheels of the car and very seriously injured. A Highway Patrol helicopter flew him to the hospital, where he remained for some time. "He had a collapsed lung, a bruised heart and a very, very serious knee injury,'' she recalls. "He'll be disabled for the rest of his life.''

The case was assigned to a different adjuster in the same office who made just one phone call. "He called the insured and asked, 'Where does your uncle live?' And the insured said, 'He's living with me.' So the adjuster said, 'Fine,' and closed the file, because there's an exclusion in our policy that says resident relatives are not entitled to liability coverage. The adjuster really made a mistake in that he did not investigate it further; he just kind of took the easy way out and closed the file.''

When he was told there was no coverage, the insured got an attorney. The file was reopened and Lisa was assigned to it. "I had to take some very thorough statements, and quickly found out that in actuality the uncle did not live with the insured—that he was only visiting, that he actually lived in Iran—so of course there was coverage.

"The policy limit was $100,000, and it's really hard for us to get $100,000 authority because we have to go through so many channels; there's so much red tape that it's very frustrating. Each adjuster has a certain amount of authority within which to settle claims depending on how long he's been with the company or how experienced he is. Mine was $7,500. My office manager's limit was $15,000.

"I had to go through my manager, who in turn had to go through the regional office—and they had to go to the home office. And then it just kept going back and forth up and down the line, up and down. The home office kept asking for more information.''

Finally the plaintiff's attorney said, "Okay, we're just going to have to sue you for bad faith,'' which in California is no idle threat. Soon the $100,000 authority arrived and the man was paid, seven months after the accident. "Generally claims take much longer than that to settle," Lisa explains, "but his medical bills had mounted so high it was obvious the case had to go for the full $100,000."

The reason her company kept putting off the claim (apart from a general lack of enthusiasm for writing big checks) wasn't doubt the claim was worth that much—it was—but that the home office kept trying to pin negligence on someone else. "They said our insured wasn't negligent, but of course he was. The car was so old you couldn't say that it was a manufacturer's defect. The insured hadn't maintained the car well enough to keep it safe. So in effect he was negligent. But our home office kept asking for engineers' reports, testing the car . . . and it just dragged on. We even had an outfit we use in Oakland tear down the whole transmission to check if there was any manufacturer's defect, but they said they couldn't find anything." Had there been a defect, the company would have paid the claim, but then tried to recover from the manufacturer through what's known as "subrogation."

Are there many women working as adjusters? we asked.

"When I started in 1977, I was the second woman adjuster in the office. Now there are a lot. I think a woman makes a better adjuster than a man because people are more likely to trust women and more likely to settle a claim.

What percentage of your cases go to trial?

"I would say of the files I've seen a good 60 percent go to attorneys; maybe 8 percent go to litigation. I would be surprised if more than half a percent actually went to trial."

Is California a no-fault state?

"No. If it was, I wouldn't have a job."

THE VETERAN CLAIMSMAN

"We don't have much difficulty, particularly with the death claims that come in," says Dick, who arrives at work each morning at seven, leaves at four, lives in a trailer (twenty years adjusting claims doth not a rich man make) and is about as friendly and helpful a fellow as you'll ever meet. "We ran a check and found we were paying 86 percent of all those claims within three working days of proper notification. But here and there you do get some sticky ones. I still like to believe that the bulk of the people are honest, but, unfortunately, there are more and more professionals out to get us.''

He had one case in which a man insured the lives of his four children, three for $2,000, one for $5,000. Later, he let all but the $5,000 policy lapse. Lo and behold, the poor $5,000 child was killed in an auto accident. In Ghana. A claim was filed, but denied. As best the insurer could determine, no such child had ever existed (and no confirmation of the death could be obtained from Ghana). A *different* child, borrowed from a friend or neighbor, had been substituted when the agent came to write up the policy.

Then there was the CPA who died in Tijuana. The company grew suspicious when, for other reasons, the grave was opened and his body wasn't there.

And the case of a young Egyptian couple who had moved here, representing themselves to be attorneys. ''As soon as they got here they started taking out lots of insurance policies. Their first claims were for lost baggage—they lost very little time.'' They had life policies aggregating in excess of $100,000 from three different companies. When the wife went back to Egypt for a visit, she was killed in a car crash. Her death was verified by a whole package of official-looking papers. ''In some countries you can buy a 'death package,' of phony certificates, hospital records and so on. The hospital on the papers may not exist, but if you write them for verification, they'll write back as if it did.'' Out to Los Angeles with his binoculars goes our claimsman, who earns in a year what *The Rockford Files'* James Garner earns in a week, and he begins surveillance of the couple's apartment. Soon a party gets under way. It is surprisingly lively, given the recent sad event. (''It was the deceased's welcome-home party I was watching, but I didn't realize it until later.'') His suspicions grow, and he begins checking TWA flight manifests. Sure enough, ''the deceased'' had flown back into the country using her own name. Confronted with the facts, the woman's husband sullenly agreed to sign a release withdrawing his claim.

No charges of any kind were ever brought against the couple. ''It would have been throwing good money after bad to press charges,'' Dick says resignedly. ''The FBI and the Immigration people are too busy to do anything.''

And sometimes state laws make it difficult for insurers to challenge doubtful claims. ''We run scared in the state of California,''

Dick says. "I think you've been reading about the punitive damages suits out there. Claims that shouldn't be paid we are paying simply because we're scared to death not to."

In his years on the job, Dick has developed a certain professional detachment. I was in his office when he took a call notifying the company that one of its own retired employees had died. Dick remembered the man and did express sympathy—but what could he do? A couple of quick phone calls set the claim in motion and then we were back to our conversation.

"We talk about compassion . . . I remember one claim, years back, involving a policy for just $1,000 we had written on a blind man, knowing he was blind—but we did not know he had had a previous heart attack. So there was definite misrepresentation, and the death had occurred within two years of his taking out the policy, so it was still contestable. My job was to call on the wife, explain why we couldn't pay the $1,000, and deliver to her a check refunding the premiums that had been paid.

"I went out to the home, I knocked on the door, a woman answered, and, lo and behold, *she* is blind.

"I introduce myself, we go inside, and I said, 'Give me the name and phone number of a good personal friend of yours who can sit down with us so that I can show this person what I have and they can tell you that what I'm telling you is the truth.' She said, 'Well that's all right—I trust *you*.' So I sat and explained to her why we could not pay $1,000. She accepted the check for the refund of premiums, no argument, no problems at all, but I've often— You can't administer a claim through your heart, but— Well, I was so close that one day I could have doctored the file. I could have arranged it so we could have paid her the $1,000, even though we didn't owe it to her, and no one would have been the wiser. I went and told our agent, who had sold the policy, and he was extremely upset. Well, in my heart I agreed, but, you know, you don't pay claims out of need or necessity."

Couldn't you have called the home office for authorization?

"I could have, but I know what they'd have said. They'd have said, 'What if you're in the same situation a year from now, but it's *fifty* thousand dollars? Would you pay the fifty?' Well, the answer is no."

TOO MUCH INSURANCE
If Inefficiency Is Built into the Game, Why Not Play Less?

*The system wants to sell the insurance
we don't need.*
—Felix Kloman, President,
Risk Planning Group, Inc.

Two supertankers passing close by one another—on purpose, to shout hello—collided and sank.

A young woman who underwent a tubal ligation begat twins eleven months later.

Accidents do happen. (In Japan, a man riding on an express train was killed by a flying foot. Severed from the leg of a second man in the process of committing suicide by jumping from a train traveling in the opposite direction, it came crashing through the window and into the first man's stomach.) And yet, despite the virtually infinite range of mishaps that can befall even the most timid among us, it's hard not to think that we are, as a society, overinsured. Not in the *depth* of our coverage, to protect us against really serious loss, but in the *breadth* of it. We expect insurance to cover a great many hazards we could in fact afford to weather all by ourselves. From an individual point of view, this means giving two-to-one odds on the flip of a coin more often than necessary. From a national point of view, it means literally tens—possibly hundreds—of millions of work-hours wasted each year providing insurance that's not needed.

A squirrel eats away at a wooden window frame—call the insurance company! A guest falls and bleeds on the wallpaper—call the insurance company! A pebble cracks a car windshield—call the insurance company!

The particular windshield I have in mind—these are all real claims—belongs to a small but prosperous New York ad agency with $300,000 in the bank. Why should it have bought insurance to cover minor losses? Had it retained all risks under $15,000, say, or even under $5,000, it would have saved thousands of dollars in premiums and—more to the point of this chapter—it would have saved everyone the cost and trouble of processing trivial claims. Had it not been insured for small losses, the firm might even have decided not to repair the windshield at all. It might have felt the cost did not justify the repair. Or that the same money could be spent more productively in some other way. When "it's insured," no one has the incentive to make such economic decisions.

Given the choice between living with a scraped fender or paying $275 for a new one, many of us, if it were *our* money, would pull out the spray paint and save $275. But because "it's insured," we automatically have the fender replaced.

Collectively, of course, it *is* our money.

A Midwesterner was involved in a minor motorcycle accident. The repair shop gave him an estimate of $75. "But when the shop learned that the automobile driver's insurance company would pay," reported *Forbes,* "they quickly prepared a new estimate. This time it was for $200; for example, a slightly dented gas tank could have been repaired. Instead, it was replaced. There are thousands of such examples every month in the U.S."

Twenty-four hours after John Lennon's murder in December 1980, Lloyd's paid out $1 million to Warner Communications, his record distributor, which carries a floater policy on the lives of all its artists. The policy reimburses Warner for money advanced to an artist who dies before fulfilling his contract. But Warner's pre-tax profit has been running around $200 million a year. Why do executives of the company feel a need to pay Lloyd's to take this risk?

Ad agencies typically have no insurance to protect against one of their clients' defaulting on $50,000 or $100,000 in unpaid bills—but do buy insurance to cover the theft of a typewriter. Chemical Bank, with $45 billion in assets, has no insurance to cover default by Zaire, or Pan Am, but is fully insured lest someone slip and fall in one of its branches. Likewise, giant Citibank. And AT&T, with assets of $100 billion and annual profits in excess of $5 billion, buys fire insurance to cover losses above $2.5 million (raised only a few years ago from $300,000). Two and a half million dollars is to AT&T what $12.50 is to a man earning $25,000 a year. Why do huge companies buy any insurance at all?*

The claims-settlement battle described at such length in the last three chapters, with its costly fraud and friction, is largely intractable. It may yield to a certain amount of improvement, but in large measure it is inherent in the system. *It's built into the game.* A partial solution, therefore, is simply to play less. To insure only those risks we cannot ourselves afford to bear.

Having said this, and before saying more, it may be well to acknowledge what a splendid thing insurance is. The brochures are correct: insurance has played, and must continue to play, a vital role in the development of our economy.

TOO MUCH OF A GOOD THING

Insurance is, to begin with, and most obviously, the crucial mechanism by which we spread risk. As such, it provides economic security and greatly facilitates commerce and enterprise. It reduces

---

*Partly because they "always have"; partly because managers do not think in terms of the whole enterprise, but rather their own individual profit centers; partly to keep from unnerving shareholders with occasional uninsured losses; and largely for tax reasons. The I.R.S. allows companies to deduct the cost of insurance premiums; but if the same cash is set aside internally as a reserve against losses, it is not deductible. It is taxed as profit. To skirt this, hundreds of corporations have set up their own "captive" insurance subsidiaries, in effect paying insurance premiums to themselves. To combat *that,* the I.R.S. quickly passed a regulation disallowing the status of captives unless they derived a substantial portion of their premium income from insuring outside risks. Suddenly, scores of fledgling insurance companies, many of them with little more than a Bermuda post office box, were plunging into the insurance business for real, insuring other people's risks—and not always doing too well at it. To pick up substantial books of business without actually setting up a marketing and underwriting organization, they concentrated on *re*insurance—accepting on a block basis thousands of risks another company has sold one by one, in return for a share of the premiums. The four largest reinsurers operating in the U.S.—General Re, North American Re, American Re and the Employers Re—wrote two-thirds of the business in 1970. Ten years later, they were down to just *one*-third of the business. Nearly half *Fortune's* 500 had set up captive insurers. All this just to satisfy an Internal Revenue Service ruling!

uncertainty, trepidation and fear; it lubricates the engine of prosperity.

Equally important, it is an orderly means of saving—for all manner of rainy days, yes, but also, with the reserves that accumulate in the meantime, to finance economic undertakings. These range from the building of homes and schools to the financing of corporate America or the construction of the Alaska Pipeline (which might as properly have been called the Prudential Pipeline, considering the Pru's share in its financing). It need hardly be mentioned that capital accumulation is fundamental to a strong and prosperous economy, of whatever type; or that this is an area in which America throughout the past decade has been all too weak.

In addition to spreading risk and building capital, the purchase of insurance helps managers quantify risk, the better to make certain decisions; and the industry as a whole has been instrumental in pushing society toward better risk control. It was the insurance industry, for example, that in 1894 founded Underwriters Laboratories to grant or withhold its "UL" seal of approval with respect to electrical devices and connectors, lest they lead to shock or fire— and insurance claims. And it was the insurance industry, around the same time, that pioneered safer practices for the storage and shipping of cotton, then this country's leading export. From time to time, it seemed, bales of cotton were spontaneously combusting. Investigation determined that embers, as from a cotton baler's pipe, were being caught within the huge, tight bales, smoldering for days or even weeks, like time bombs in a ship's hold, before catching full flame. It was further determined that the way to douse such embers was not with sea water but, ironically, kerosene. Unlike water, kerosene would penetrate the bale to smother the smolder.

Today, certain insurers have developed and actively disseminate expertise in loss prevention. Liberty Mutual, of Boston, the largest mutual underwriter of workers' compensation insurance, is the prime example. Liberty has 760 loss-prevention representatives, health consultants and industrial hygienists working in cooperation with its 45,000 corporate policyholders to reduce losses. It will test a factory's air quality, recommend fire precautions, study lower back pain, issue reports ("Noise Generation in Pneumatic Blow-off Guns," the American Industrial Hygiene Association *Journal*), and more. The company recently tested a "brown and serve" oven bag one of its policyholders planned to market to see if there were any possible circumstance under which it might catch fire. There was, and the bag was withdrawn from production. Or take the "Boston Arm," a prosthetic device Liberty developed for above-the-elbow amputees. The market for such devices (thankfully) is too small to make such a project commercially viable; but to an insurer facing a lifetime of disability payments, it is worth the money. Forty such electronic, motorized arms were in use in 1979, with a hundred of an improved model scheduled for production.

Even so, the industry is not the factor in loss prevention it once was. Today there are so many regulations and government agencies promoting safety—the Occupational Safety and Health Administration, O.S.H.A., prime among them ("Our Savior Has Arrived," as some loss-prevention specialists refer to it)—that the efforts of the insurance companies, if not redundant, are no longer as significant.

In fact, by removing uncertainty and shifting risk, insurance actually removes some of the incentive to keep losses from occurring. In the slums of Newark or Detroit insurance encourages losses. Further, it reduces the incentive to keep the costs of losses, once incurred, low. An important cause of wildly mushrooming health-care costs is that for most Americans health care is virtually "free," paid for by one or another insurance plan. Why scrimp on something free?

Yet I repeat: by and large, like charity, insurance is a very fine thing. The concern is to be sure one's dollars are being spent, insofar as possible, on the benefits they are intended to provide. As is painfully evident from the table on page 72, approximate though it is, there is considerable room for improvement.

TOO MANY CLAIMS

Employment of claims representatives is expected to grow faster than the average for all occupations through the 1980's as the number of insurance claims continues to rise.
—U.S. Department of Labor
1980–81 *Occupational Outlook Handbook*

In 1940, the gross average weekly income for production workers was $25.20. The $50 deductible made sense. Today the average production worker grosses about ten times as much—yet many policies still carry a $50 or $100 deductible.

While deductibles lower than $500 for autos and $1,000 for homes should be available for those willing to pay the price, they should be the exception rather than the rule. Many policyholders would be well served by even higher deductibles.

Lifting the threshhold on claims this way would sweep away *millions* of the most trivial, least efficient insurance claims transactions. How many of Aetna's 42.7 million claims in 1980 were for losses the claimants could actually have borne themselves? Half? Two out of three? (During the Depression, desperate policyholders were fastidious about claiming any money they were entitled to. The INA has a record of one claim in the amount of 50 cents to patch a pair of overalls burned when the policyholder sat on a lighted cigarette.) In return for bearing many of these risks themselves, Aetna policyholders' premiums could have been substantially lower.

The Insurance Services Office, which collects industry-wide loss data to help insurers set rates, tallied 723,723 auto insurance claims paid by its affiliates in 1978 under "full coverage" policies. *Nearly four out of five involved $200 or less.* Of payments to people who had chosen $100-deductible policies, *close to half each year were for less than $400.*

When it came to homeowners policies, 60 percent of the payments to people with $100-deductible coverage were for less than $400. (Eighty-five percent were for less than $1,000, and all but 2 percent were for less than $5,000.) Thus 60 percent of the claims processed could have been eliminated if homeowner insurance payments had started after the first $500 of loss instead of the first $100; 85 percent of all claims could have been eliminated if insureds had borne the first $1,100 of loss

Eliminating 85 percent of the claims would have eliminated just 30 percent of the actual *dollars* insurers paid out to policyholders, as it is the relatively few large losses that account for most of the claim dollars paid—and for which insurance is both indispensable and efficient.

This is not to make light of the pain caused by a $500 or $1,000 loss. But such losses—for which I have a modest proposal—are not what a homeowner needs insurance for. Homeowners need insurance against the house burning down—$20,000 and $50,000 and $150,000 losses, not $700 ones. Losses of a few hundred dollars are (sadly) well within the range of *ordinary* expenses of automobile or home ownership. Homes need new roofs, new paint; transmissions drop out of the bottoms of cars. Even TV sets must occasionally be replaced. Yet we manage to face these risks without paying someone else—handsomely—to take them.

If people chose higher deductibles, and hence made fewer claims, their rates would come down. Only for the unluckiest policyholders would such a shift wind up costing any money. For most of us, lower premiums each year would, on average, more than compensate for higher unpaid losses. It would be a matter of giving two-to-one odds on that flipping coin much less often. What's more, *we* would be the ones earning interest on those premium dollars rather than the insurer. Those who *were* hapless enough to suffer more than their share of small uninsured losses would be able, under current tax law, to lay off part of the loss on the government. Unreimbursed property losses above $100 are tax-deductible. For the 50 percent taxpayer—a rate many Americans approach on the last few dollars that they earn—this means that a $700 loss costs just $400 after taxes. Why pay extra to protect against losses you can afford to bear yourself when Uncle Sam (and his relatives in state and city tax departments) will kick in half the coverage, or close to it, for free?

It's already been established that for every $1 honest policyholders pay in auto and homeowners premiums, less than 50 cents, on average, will be paid back out in claims. But because casualty losses are tax-deductible, 20 or 30 cents of that 50 could come back to you *anyway,* via lower taxes, without your putting up the dollar at all!

As for the policyholder who is constantly running up losses—

YET A THIRD TABLE
Just as Rough in Its Estimates as the First Two*

For Every Premium Dollar Honest 50-Percent-Tax-Bracket Policyholders Pay in Premiums	This Is How Much, Collectively, They Get Back (Beyond What They Would Have Gotten Anyway)
A SAVINGS BANK	$1.03
AUTO INSURANCE	$0.25
HOMEOWNERS INSURANCE	$0.25

*See pages 72 and 95.

$600 here, $1,200 there—in theory, he would be wise to take the lowest deductible available. In practice, his policy might be canceled after the second or third claim.

A chief district judge in North Carolina was burglarized. A new lock had to be installed to replace the one that had been smashed open. When the locksmith sent his bill, he sent two: the real one, for $45, which he wanted paid; and, as a courtesy to His Honor, another for $145 "in case your insurance is $100 deductible." To a *judge!* But why would anyone with a $20,000 or $40,000 income require a deductible as low as $50 or $100 in the first place? Had the judge entered a documented claim for $145, as the locksmith suggested, it almost certainly would have been paid. Chalk up another few dollars of fraud and friction. Had he, however, owned policies with $1,000 deductibles, there would have been no possibility of a claim. (What kind of lock costs $1,045?)

The I.R.S. understands this principle, and so moves steadily toward increasing its own "standard deduction" in order to reduce the number of taxpayers who itemize. Itemized returns are more time-consuming to prepare and to examine, and far more susceptible to cheating. Better than 70 percent of American taxpayers now choose to take the standard deduction, up from 51 percent in 1970.

The insurance industry is far less eager to trim its workload. Handling routine claims is its *business,* and not an unprofitable one. (You don't hear H&R Block shouting for a simplified tax code, either.) In fact, while the really tiny risks may indeed be a nuisance to insurers, it is basically the smallish ones—the $200 to $2,000 bets, for example—that are its bread and butter. These risks are eminently predictable, with all the characteristics of a smooth production-line flow of premiums, paperwork and profit. Given the choice between insuring one RCA satellite launching or all RCA's employees for dental coverage, all but the most aggressive insurers (of which there are about two) will grab for the teeth.

So, many insurers do not give you the *option* of really large deductibles. They may discourage the $50 deductible, but not encourage or even offer $1,000 or $2,500 deductibles. This is hardly surprising. The larger the deductible you choose, the less insurance you are buying. Insurers want to sell insurance.

For the family with little or no savings and a meager income, $500 or $1,000 losses are not acceptable risks. If avoiding them means giving State Farm two-to-one odds on the flip of a coin, so be it. But for the great American middle class, such losses, while painful, are hardly catastrophic. Opting for deductibles this size, when available at fair rates, makes great sense. The premiums saved thereby might, in some cases, at least, be used to increase coverage at the *other* end of the spectrum—to raise the policy limits. That is where people really need protection—to cover losses they could *not* afford to bear themselves. That is where many are *under*insured. And that is the kind of insurance that is relatively efficient to provide. There are far fewer claims; the claims are large in relation to the clerical effort required; the chance of successful fraud or padded payment is much lower.

A MODEST PROPOSAL

To help people save up for small emergencies—the $500 loss not covered by insurance—savings institutions and commercial banks should be allowed to offer "Self-Insurance Accounts." Really, they would be very much like any other savings account. Only, rather than returning just 40 or 50 or 60 cents of each dollar deposited, as insurance policies, on average, do, such accounts would return the full dollar—plus interest. The twist would be that to qualify for such an account, and a high rate of interest, depositors would agree not to withdraw funds before, say, five years' time, *except to pay the uninsured portion of casualty losses*. If your car were hit and required $1,000 of repairs, only $500 of which was covered by insurance because of the $500 deductible you had chosen, you could without penalty withdraw $500 from your Self-Insurance Account. In the event of early withdrawal *other* than to pay for an uninsured loss, interest would be recalculated to a lower rate. This is the same system banks already use for "early withdrawal" from long-term savings certificates.

No doubt some depositors would lie about the reason for their withdrawals, presenting phony documentation of a loss in order to withdraw funds without penalty, but this would present no significant problem for the banks. The banks would not need to investigate or corroborate or "settle" depositors' claims, as insurers do, for they would only be giving back the depositors' own money.

The banks could even offer the option of billing depositors a specified monthly or quarterly amount, to assist them in building their Self-Insurance Accounts. Or they could make automatic monthly transfers from checking and/or regular savings accounts.

For qualified depositors, the banks could also guarantee a predetermined emergency line of credit—$500 or $1,000 or more—in case the depositor suffered an uninsured loss *before* having saved up enough to pay for it.

Such mini-insurance accounts, for small losses, would provide the man on the street with a much more economical way to protect against relatively minor losses. He would get to withdraw $1.05 or $1.10 from *this* insurance plan; he would adjust his own claim; he would not have to pay for the fraudulent claims of others; *and* he could take all but the first $100 of his loss as a tax deduction.

Of course, nothing prevents you from building a $1,000 or $2,000 emergency fund for this purpose right now. The advantage of the plan above is that it would provide discipline and incentive to help you do so. And the banks have the marketing clout to sell the idea. Not everyone is going to think of it on his own.

TOO MUCH TEMPTATION

A Harvard graduate working with one of the nation's most prestigious law firms was told he had to have a wisdom tooth pulled. "No problem," his dentist assured him. "It's not impacted—I can do it in the office for $85." Checking with his personnel department, the young attorney learned his insurance only covered dental procedures that involved an overnight hospital stay. To save $85 he had the extraction performed in the hospital at a cost of $540. He was simply responding to the system as it was constructed.

On a somewhat grander scale: From 1965 to 1975, the number of Americans receiving Social Security disability payments doubled. In the same period, the cost of the disability program quintupled, from $1.6 billion a year to $8.4 billion. By 1980, the program's annual cost had grown to about $12 billion. "Increasingly high benefit formulas of the program have had the undesirable effect of adding a disincentive" to go back to work, Congressman Dan Rostenkowski told a rehabilitation study group in 1980. "As the cash benefits paid as a percentage of predisability earnings rose by 50 percent during the years 1967 to 1976, the recovery rate declined by the same percentage.'' There was less incentive to go back to work, so fewer people did.

At the same time as the insurance industry could be far more efficient if people were offered higher deductibles at attractive rates, so could it be made more efficient by redesigning some of the policies. It makes no sense that in April of 1980 a poor black woman would "pay" $2,000 to have a bunion removed under general anesthesia in a Staten Island, New York, hospital—compliments of Medicaid—when another woman with very much the same sort of bunion but no Medicaid would have hers removed safely and quickly for $200. It makes no sense, but it happened. Consumer affairs reporter John Stossel, having uncovered this anomaly, asked Medicaid's consultant on podiatry to explain. The system was set up that way, he said, in order to protect the poor from being taken advantage of by unscrupulous practitioners. The poor woman would *not* have been reimbursed had she gone the simpler $200 route.

Bunions and wisdom teeth notwithstanding, fire insurance is the most striking example of incentives run amok.

> *In the South Bronx, things were bad enough.*
> *But once the FAIR Plan started and anybody*
> *could get insurance, everything started burning.*
> —A New York City fire marshal

More than a quarter million fires in 1980 were deliberately set. One every two minutes. Arson, the fastest-growing crime in the country, destroys $3 billion in property each year and takes more than 1,000 lives. Something like a fourth of America's homeowners premiums are eaten up paying for arson.

Revenge is the prime motive. Profit runs a close second.* More

---

*Rounding out the list: juvenile vandalism based on anger, juvenile vandalism based on peer pressure (to gain status), coercion or intimidation (as in persuading a tenant or competitor to move), crime concealment, real estate parcel creation (used against the hold-out property owner who holds out just a little too long), property improvement, tax fraud and—in a small category all its own—pyromania.

John S. Barracato, author of *Arson!* and longtime investigator of that crime, now with Aetna Life & Casualty, profiles the pyromaniac: Almost always male (or, when female, lesbian), driven to set fires by a sexual urge. He commonly has a history of bed-wetting, of cruelty to animals (throwing cats beneath subways trains, dogs off rooftops), and cannot urinate in front of others (at least not in the midst of an arson interrogation). He does not use an accelerant, because "he is motivated by an uncontrollable urge, not premeditation. A pyromaniac doesn't walk the streets with a container of gasoline waiting for the urge to strike. Instead, he uses whatever is on hand in the building he decides to burn." Nor does he fit "the Hollywood image than a third of all arson is committed for profit, in most cases to defraud insurance companies. Think of it! Fifty or a hundred thousand fires that would not be set each year if only fire insurance were handled differently. Because as fire insurance policies are currently structured, the most profitable thing many landlords and small businessmen can do is light a match. (Or ignore unsafe conditions that will, given a little time, amount to the same thing.)

People respond to incentives. Tell them, "If your house burns down, we will pay you twice what it's worth," and they will burn their houses down. Tell a failing businessman he can recoup his investment by "selling" his company to an insurance company, and he will respond by hiring a torch. This is exactly what many landlords and businessmen are in effect told, and so their neighborhoods burn.

The problem is that if you don't offer insurance in those neighborhoods—if you redline them—you assure their continued deterioration.

A solution would be to write policies that pay "replacement cost" *only* if the property is in fact repaired or replaced. Otherwise, payment would be no more than *fair market value*—making it no more profitable to burn a building than simply to sell it.

Suddenly the profit motive is eliminated. The incentive is no longer there, even though the insurance coverage remains. And the insurance costs less because there are fewer fires.

Bronx district attorney Mario Merola has long advocated such a scheme. "I've been trying to sell that idea for five years," he told a reporter, "but have met a stone wall. I think it becomes quite

---

of him standing in front of a burning building, watching the flames with a look of ecstasy on his face." His thrill comes from the *setting* of the fire and, "when he has accomplished that, he simply walks away." Thus he is not to be confused with the *vanity firesetter*, whose motivation is not sexual but rather a desire to appear heroic. The vanity firesetter strikes occupied buildings, "is the first to call in the alarm and alert residents of the burning building. He attempts to rescue people and, if he can, he helps the firefighters with their equipment and duties. Fortunately, the vanity firesetter is usually immediately recognizable at the scene of the fire because his heroic efforts are so obvious."

Barracato has learned to reconstruct a fire from its remains (the area of origin is generally the most severely damaged; lightbulbs distend in the direction from which the fire came), and even to assess the likely perpetrator if the fire was deliberately set. Young people generally set fires before midnight, older ones, from midnight to 5 A.M. Female arsonists generally seek revenge or attention, rarely use accelerants. "If a married woman sets fire to her bed, it generally means she is bored with her marriage. . . . But if she piles all her husband's clothes on the bed first . . . it means she suspects or has caught him having an extramarital affair." Barracato has seen these patterns repeated hundreds of times, he says.

obvious that you can take the profit motive out of arson. In other words, if a bodega owner or a supermarket owner or a doughnut shop man knows ahead of time that he is not going to collect the insurance proceeds, he is going to have second thoughts about arson. What I am suggesting is that any businessman looking to burn his place for the insurance money will be deterred if he knows that the insurance company will help him rebuild rather than paying him the money. I think if we publicized the fact that owners must rebuild their property—and insurance companies already have the legal right to rebuild in lieu of making a cash settlement—we would see a 25 to 50 percent reduction in arson almost overnight.''

Catching and jailing arsonists helps; but the best solution, where possible, is to eliminate the incentive to strike the match in the first place.

Logical though this may be, it's taken some prodding, and will take more, to get insurers fully behind such a reform. "After all," noted *Forbes* in the fall of 1979, "an insurance company can simply jack up rates to cover increased payouts. And the higher the premiums, the more assets the companies have to invest."

The Senate Permanent Subcommittee on Investigations issued a report in 1979 contending that insurers often failed to investigate and challenge questionable fire claims, and were often lax in valuing properties for insurance in the first place. Result: a low-risk, high-reward business that organized crime, not just desperate bodega owners, was pursuing with zest.

The committee found that property was often insured for more than its worth, both because of insurers' failure to verify values and because agents' commissions rose in proportion to the size of the policies they sold; that fire adjusters were inadequately trained in arson detection ("A fire talks to you, if you just know how to listen," says Aetna's Barracato); and that some companies—four of the fifteen large ones the committee polled—negotiated claims with suspected arsonists rather than pay to investigate.

Certainly insurance companies do not favor arson. In recent years some have been pushing hard for stiff anti-arson programs. Nor is their job easy. They are required by state laws to pay claims promptly, often before they've had a chance to establish proof of fraud. And if they do allege fraud and can't prove it, they may later be sued for slander. But few have worked for this most logical remedy—removing the profit motive.

TOO MUCH PAPER, TOO MANY INDIANS

The workers battle endlessly with the paper,
keeping it down, beating it back, finding new nooks and
crannies in which to hide it;
but the paper rises and proliferates,
like the magic mill that lies at the bottom of the sea,
forever grinding salt.
—William Hoffman, *The Stockholder*

In the broad sense, insurance inefficiency results from many things; but one of them is just that—plain inefficiency. It is astonishing how slow the insurance industry has been to computerize its operations, a process that is now well under way but by no means complete.

A study spearheaded by Florida's association of independent insurance agents and supported by many of the industry giants, reported in 1973 that "Agencies and companies are not operating anywhere near capacity." Indeed, the report continued, *"the average agency is only 25% to 35% efficient."* These figures were arrived at by actual timed observation of 101 different insurance agencies. Aetna performed the study first; then the Hartford Group duplicated it to confirm the results.

The point was made that "it is not realistic to expect all employees to be 100% efficient." (One hundred percent efficiency was defined as "the pace at which an average well-trained employee can perform throughout the day without undue fatigue.") On the other hand, the study did not take into consideration the kind of computerization that might be possible. With *existing* methods the employees were inefficient.

Aetna has been measuring the productivity of its clerical workers since 1920. When, recently, clerks in the Hartford headquarters were offered $30 weekly bonuses for hitting certain output standards, they began processing policies 50 percent faster than before!

According to *Business Week* (November 1979):

Insurance companies . . . still have done little to reduce the ever-growing mounds of paperwork generated by communications between them and the independent agents who sell the policies. . . . Only a few hundred of the nation's more than 70,000 independent agents have installed even limited data processing hookups

with their insurance companies. . . . Policies often change hands
a half-dozen times as they travel back and forth between agents
and underwriters. And errors are introduced each step of the
way. . . . Aetna estimates 17% of all transactions are rejected
because of errors. But errors are dramatically reduced when companies begin communicating with their agents via the computer.
Information needs only to be keyboarded once, because it is then
stored in the computer memory.

So you don't have to worry about $47 becoming $74 by accident, or
endorsements (those little slips of paper stapled to the policy) becoming detached and falling behind a desk. You don't have to rely
on the mail, either. Documents can be transmitted over phone lines
in seconds.

The same month *Business Week* was surveying the sorry state of
the industry's inefficiency, Elmer N. Dickinson, Jr., executive vice
president of the AIG, was predicting that loss ratios in the 1980s
would climb to 80 percent and beyond. "Personal lines must be
written in such a way that there's a big return to the customer," he
said.

To achieve the dramatic improvements in efficiency that will
make higher payouts possible, all manner of computerized systems
will be, are being, installed.

Example: Rather than estimate auto repair work as it currently is
done —illegibly, by hand, with much looking up of manufacturers'
parts numbers and prices—there is a system called Audatex that
can handle any of 700 different auto models. The adjuster or repair-
man need merely mark the coded spaces corresponding with the
part or parts that need replacing or repair; a computer looks up,
prints out and totals all the numbers and prices.

Will such a system actually work for GEICO and others that are
beginning to introduce it? Will Yankee ingenuity come through for
us once again? There is reason to think so. Audatex has been working in Germany, where it was invented, for nine years. Eighty
percent of all auto repair estimates in Germany and Switzerland are
made this way.

Example: When Weyerhaeuser's personnel department installed
a claims administration system marketed by System Development
Corporation of Santa Monica, an eight-week backlog of unpaid
medical benefits was reduced to a two-day turnaround. With fewer
people.

Says SDC's Jim Foran: "Someone handling accounts manually would probably be processing no more than about twenty-five claims a day. On our system, they can do in excess of eighty a day."

Insurance operations are entering the era of the microchip, and yet, to date anyway, the industry payroll climbs steadily higher. In 1979 the American Council of Life Insurance estimated a total industry-wide employment of 1,839,000. In 1980, 1,895,000. It's conceivable that when the 1981 figure is calculated, 1980 will turn out to have been the peak. But if so, it will be the first time in living memory that the insurance army—tripled in size since 1945—has not grown. Nor does that figure of 1.9 million include lawyers, paralegals, judges and juries not directly employed by insurance companies but engaged in the settlement of their claims; nor "risk management" and "employee benefit" staffs of corporations who work full time to buy insurance and administer group insurance plans; nor employees of government-administered insurance plans.

Employment in Insurance, 1970–1980
(Annual Averages)

	Property/Casualty Companies	Other Companies	Agents, Brokers & Service Personnel	All-Industry
1970	365,800	663,900	430,300	1,460,000
1975	385,400	688,900	554,700	1,640,000
1976	399,400	701,900	573,700	1,675,000
1977	429,000	717,000	544,000	1,690,000
1978	460,600	733,200	582,200	1,776,000
1979	476,700	736,600	625,700	1,839,000
1980	490,500	749,900	654,100	1,895,000

Sources: Company data, Bureau of Labor Statistics, U.S. Department of Labor; agents, brokers and service personnel and all-industry figures, Bureau of Labor Statistics data adjusted to account for American Council of Life Insurance estimates of additional independent agents and staff personnel.
    Courtesy, Insurance Information Institute.

TOO MANY AGENTS

Virtually every state has an "anti-rebate" law, enacted in the distant past at the behest of the insurance industry to prevent agents (life or property/casualty) from giving you back any portion of their commissions. These laws are thus not unlike the Fair Trade laws, repealed in 1975, which used to allow manufacturers to dictate the final selling price of their product.

On whole life insurance, the agency commission may be as much as 120 percent of the first year's premium, 10 percent of successive years' premiums. On property and liability insurance the range is more like 15 to 30 percent, year after year. What if these "fair trade" laws were repealed, just as fixed commissions on Wall Street were abolished (also in 1975)? The "manufacturer"—the insurance company—would price its service to the independent agents who sell it. The agents could then determine their *own* markups. Some might charge even more than they already do, hoping to serve customers not much concerned with price; others might go the low-price, high-volume route, like McDonald's. Consumers would have a choice.*

Insurance sold direct to the public, through the mail or by means of salaried personnel, would not be affected. But insurance sold through commissioned agents—particularly the nation's 70,000-odd *independent* insurance agencies—would be.

The typical independent agent, who may also be called a broker, deals with several insurers. When you come in looking for insurance, he has a number of companies with which to place your business. How does that independent agent decide what insurance you should have? One consideration, to be sure, is what will be best for you. Another consideration, however, will be what's best for *him*. What insurer offers him the biggest commission? Very often, the insurer that offers the biggest percentage commission will also be the insurer that, in order to *pay* that commission and still have enough left over to meet its expenses and make a profit, charges the highest price.

This is by no means to say that your independent insurance agent will always put his interests ahead of yours. Still, a study published by J. David Cummins and Steven N. Weisbart in 1977 found that

---

*Repeal of anti-rebate laws would not lead to horse-trading of the type that goes on in auto showrooms or Moroccan bazaars. States also have "anti-discrimination" laws that would forbid an agent from giving one customer a better price than he gave another. In other words, an agent that had been receiving a 30 percent annual commission could cut his markup to 20 percent—but for everyone, not just me.

nearly half the time (47.9 percent), an agent's decision on where to place a new customer's business was based on which insurer paid the highest commission.

If you were an independent businessman, struggling to pay the rent and the help—and hoping someday to own a Cessna 152— wouldn't it influence you?

In the early days of insurance, commission rates kept leapfrogging each other as insurers competed not for customers but for agents who could deliver those customers. Competition was not based on providing this commodity—insurance—cheaply and efficiently, but on stealing away agents, and their customers, with high commissions, even though doing so meant charging higher prices.

The fact that in recent years the direct writers, who deal directly with their customers and not through independent agents, have carved out a steadily growing hunk of the market suggests that many insurance customers—surprise!—do care about price. The direct writers, not having to pay so much of your premium dollar in commissions, typically are able to offer the same coverage at a lower price.

Independent agents are not pleased to see their customers going direct to State Farm or GEICO or Allstate. In 1980, they decided to advertise. You've probably seen the campaign. In the typical ad, a 700-year-old redwood tree has just fallen through the roof of *your home*. You (and your wife, who has just come in with a bag of groceries to find a horizontal arboretum in her living room) are understandably frazzled. You reach for the phone and call your insurance company. "Let me talk to that nice agent who sold me my policy," you say, foolishly thinking that all agents are alike. "What do you *mean* the agent who sold me my policy doesn't deal with claims?" you scream into the phone, frazzlement having turned to a jumble of outrage and panic. "My *policy number?*" you whine. You look at your wife. Your wife, groceries still held tightly, looks over at the drawer in which such papers are kept and that would now require a buzz saw and crew of lumberjacks to reach.

The soothing voice-over suggests that you should have dealt with an *independent agent*—good old Ralph down the street with whose son your boy plays Little League and who would surely be able to get your claim paid promptly and in full. "We treat you like a person, not like a number," soothes the voice-over.

The implication, not stated, is: *Sure* it generally costs more to buy insurance through an independent agent. But it's worth it.

And for some it may be, although many direct writers have fine reputations for paying claims, while agency companies can sometimes be less than exemplary, despite Ralph's proddings.

The point of all this is *not* that independent agents are not worth the extra dollars they generally cost, although many customers have come to that conclusion. The point is that repeal of the anti-rebating laws would make them more competitive, and eliminate the conflict of interest referred to above.

By providing their product to independent agents at "net cost," insurers would allow agents to add whatever markup they chose. Agents could match customers with the policy that best met their needs, and then add their markup. Your interests would be better served, and insurers would find themselves competing not on how much they could pay their independent agents, but on how much value they could provide.

(Such a change would not be without its bugs. The most obvious involves billing. Until recently, the agency itself would tot up and mail out the bills, some of which were even handwritten, and then pass on their payment, and accounting, to the companies. But now that most of the industry, at long last, bills direct, efficiently, by computer, if each agent charged a different price for his own services, the computer program would obviously have to be modified.)

Repealing the anti-rebate laws would not *require* anyone to do anything differently, just as repealing the Fair Trade laws did not require retailers to sell Sonys below "manufacturer's suggested price." It would just *allow* them to. Competition, with luck, would do the rest.

So what was the reaction when Wisconsin insurance commissioner Susan Mitchell proposed elimination of the law? Life insurance agents went nuts. A highly emotional group, they generated several hundred letters of angry protest. They visited state legislators (seven of them *were* state legislators). Property/casualty agents, although opposed, were more restrained. In private, some of them admitted it wouldn't be a bad idea. Commissioner Mitchell, meanwhile, was philosophical. "It will never pass this time," she said in mid-1981. "The pressure against it is much too strong. But if we keep introducing it, and other states begin to do the same thing, in time we might get it."

NEXT THEY'LL WANT A PIECE OF YOUR SOCIAL SECURITY CHECK

Prior to the enactment of workers' compensation laws, beginning in 1911, an injured worker had to prove negligence on the part of his employer in order to recoup his medical expenses and lost wages, let alone collect damages. The employer, on the other hand—presumably better equipped to wage and wait out a protracted legal struggle—had only to prove that the employee's injury was his own fault or the fault of a fellow worker, or, even, that the worker had taken the job knowing that it could result in his injury. It was a miserable system.

Under the new laws, workers gave up their right to sue employers for damages in return for a guarantee of swift and certain benefit payments, regardless of fault. Benefit levels, which have naturally risen many times since 1911, vary from state to state. They include lump sum payments for specific injuries (see "An Eye for an Ear," page 310) as well as monthly disability benefits that may extend for a lifetime. By far the most generous benefits go to civilian employees of the federal government. They have their own special law. In 1981, 88 percent of America's wage and salary earners were covered by workers' compensation. Coverage was mandatory, with very limited exceptions, everywhere but South Carolina, New Jersey and Texas. Claims—millions of them—ran from things like paper cuts and ankles sprained in company softball games to ruptured discs, mangled arms and worse. There were 13,000 on-the-job fatalities in 1980.

Most states allow the private insurance industry to provide workers' compensation insurance. A dozen states have workers' compensation funds of their own that compete with the private carriers. And six states, as well as Canada, have exclusive funds, prohibiting private carriers from writing any of the business at all (but allowing qualifying employers to self-insure).

Now, don't give up, because this gets interesting.

In those six states—Ohio, West Virginia, Washington, Nevada, North Dakota and Wyoming—the insurance industry periodically fights for a chance to compete. The last time this happened in the state of Washington, then governor Dixy Lee Ray retorted, "There should be no profit in pain." Which is one way of looking at it. But the real question is which system provides the most benefits at the least cost. For example, is it really worthwhile to pay 6 cents of each premium dollar in commissions for selling coverage that everyone is required by law to buy? You can be sure the insurance agents think so.

When New York was considering an exclusively state-run system like Ohio's (a proposal the industry managed to scotch), Warren J. Smith, secretary-treasurer of the Ohio AFL-CIO, was invited by the legislature to testify. Here is some of what he had to say:

> In Ohio at the present time [April 1979] our own exclusive system is under attack by the Independent Insurance Agents Association of Ohio. The attack by agents is not new, but is a phenomenon that appears unsuccessfully about every ten years. This effort has once again caused the joining of Ohio labor and business into a coalition to defeat the agents' initiative. This is a historic coalition that has formed every time the insurance industry has attempted to wedge its way into Ohio's workers' compensation system.
>
> Labor wants benefits to be as high as possible; the employers want the cost of workers' compensation coverage as low as possible. These are conflicting goals, and the ability of either party to achieve its goal is impaired if a third party seeking to maximize its own profits enters the equation.
>
> The Ohio Manufacturers Association, which opposes the insurance agents' present effort, reports that under the private insurance plan it would cost the employer $1.45 for every $1 in benefits paid to an injured worker. Under the present system, the cost is only 84 cents. The reason the cost per $1 paid is less than $1 is that the Ohio employers receive the benefit of investment income.

Ohio's agents argued that the state bureaucracy was slow in making payments and that with competition costs would be lower. Yet the AFL-CIO contended that private carriers were much more likely than state funds to contest or delay claims. Smith cited an unreleased study by the U.S. Department of Labor showing that private carriers contested 11.9 percent of all workers' compensation claims compared with 6.2 percent challenged by state insurance funds.

Of course, questionable workers' compensation claims *should* be contested. But Smith believed private insurers were using their bargaining advantage (having all the time and money in the world) to negotiate settlements for less than claims were truly worth. This helped keep costs down, by paying workers less than they were entitled to by law; but the savings, by and large, went not to employers or to other workers but to insurance companies.

As for cost, a study by the Minnesota legislature ranked Ohio's workers' compensation system in the top six among all states for benefits, but eleventh from the bottom in cost.

The Independent Insurance Agents of Ohio were not impressed. They argued that Ohio's little guy was getting a raw deal. *That's* why they were fighting to change the system—not the commissions they would earn. Heck, no. It was the principle that counted. (Still, with an annual premium volume of $500 million or so, there would have been in excess of $25 million in new commissions for Ohio's independent agencies to go after each year—an extra $12,500 apiece.) It was in pursuit of this principle that the agents attempted to obtain the 250,000 signatures needed to place their constitutional amendment on the ballot. So great was their zeal for this principle, in fact, that they would tell passersby just about anything to get them to sign the petition. "Sign this to lower your income tax," people were told, for example. Confronted with tape recordings of such solicitations, the agents quietly agreed to back down rather than be sued for fraud.

But Ohio is viewed as a bellwether in the workers' compensation field. If a few other states switch to exclusive funds (and drives are on in several to do just that), it's thought the momentum could become formidable. So after Ohio's independent agents backed down, the American Alliance of Insurers stepped in. They brought with them a high-class Washington public relations firm and more than $5 million to sway public opinion. It was too late for the 1979 election, but after more than a year's work, with three months to go until the November 1981 election, they were leading in the polls. Their appeal was to competition and free enterprise, God and country. Never mind that the state's large labor unions and employers were both opposed.

As it turned out, the $5 million (*our* $5 million, added on to *our* insurance premiums) was wasted. The industry's initiative was defeated by a four to one margin.

10

TOO MANY LAWYERS
The Case for No-Fault Insurance

A lawyer is a person who profits by creating confusion.
—James Dale Davidson, *The Squeeze*

A Department of Transportation study released in 1971 found that permanently disabled traffic-accident victims suffered, on average, $76,000 in economic losses, but received only $12,000 from the auto liability insurance system. Sadly, after allowing for inflation, little has changed. Our automobile insurance system stinks. We get from our premium dollars barely half the benefits we should—and *could,* if only the system were structured differently. In this chapter (about no-fault insurance) and the next (about an insurance plan called "Pay As You Drive") I will explain how. But first a few words about lawyers.

Lawyers, as a group, have never been much more popular than insurance companies, and yet in America's litigious soil they have flourished, twining a tangled, strangling and near impenetrable mesh. Some of my best friends are lawyers—and they agree. Thirty thousand new lawyers enter the mainstream each year (like beavers, preparing to clog it up). There are more lawyers in the U.S. than in the rest of the world combined. Half a million! West Germany makes do with just one-fifth as many lawyers per capita. France manages with one-tenth as many. Japan has one-twentieth as many lawyers per capita (but seven times as many engineers). There are twice as many lawyers in *California* as in all of Great Britain.

It is in the direct interest of at least one lawyer in almost any lawsuit to stall.

170

"I was born to be a protractor," CBS News quoted a senior partner in IBM's thirteen-year antitrust defense as once having said. "I could take the simplest antitrust case and protract it for the defense almost to infinity. And as you know, my firm's meter's running all the time." And we're paying for it.

Often, when both attorneys are paid by the hour, it is in the interests of both to drag things out—which just serves to intensify the animosity between their clients. Stanley Faust and his wife were getting divorced in San Jose, California. They drew up a five-page division of property, amicably, and went to a lawyer to make it legal. *There were no remaining points of dispute.* Three years and more than $25,000 in legal fees later, in 1980, reported CBS, the divorce—which had become decidedly less amicable—was still in the courts.

For an accident victim, the quicker the case can be settled, the faster will be the psychological and physical recovery. "It has always been axiomatic in medical circles," writes Professor Jeffrey O'Connell, "that promptness is essential to good medical treatment of trauma. The victim must be made to put the accident behind him." Yet the insurance system is designed not for the victims (workers' compensation being the important exception) but for the lawyers. Far from putting the accident behind them, victims are instructed to keep detailed diaries of their pain and disability—an hourly account of what hurts and what they are prevented from doing. Sometimes they will even forgo rehabilitation, consciously or unconsciously trying to "prove" that their claim for pain and suffering is worthy. It would hardly do, after all, to get up before a jury all smiles and in the peak of health. And yet the trial may come only years after the accident. O'Connell quotes a colleague who calls this "the schizophrenic choice between 'recovery' in the medical sense and 'recovery' in the legal sense." And he concludes: "Given the purposes of the tort liability system, lawyers cannot be blamed for thus advising their clients. But many in the medical profession are understandably shocked by a system that, contrary to all medical wisdom, encourages accident victims to preserve, hug, and indeed nurture and memorize every twinge and hurt from an accident."

Nothing supports lawyers like insurance. In 1979, new lawsuits were being filed against the Hartford Insurance Group—just the

Hartford—at the rate of *one every five minutes* of each working day. Reliable figures are hard to come by, but it has been estimated that nearly half the civil jury trials in this country may be lawsuits over auto liability. No wonder lawyers, who control the legal system, have fought so hard, and with great success, against "no-fault" insurance. No fault, no lawsuits. No lawsuits, no lunch.

As stated, some 30,000 new lawyers graduate each year. What are they going to do? Well, they are lawyers—they are not going to sit idle. They'll file lawsuits! It's no mystery why California is the country's most litigious state—it has the best climate. Desirable living conditions attract a disproportionate share of young law graduates, who in turn generate litigation.

To expand the demand for their swelling ranks, lawyers have been expanding the horizons of liability. It is by now old hat, at least in some states, that the bartender or party giver who serves one drink too many may be held liable for the accident his patron or guest subsequently causes. A man in New York's City Hall slipped and fell on someone's half-eaten tunafish sandwich. He sued the city for $1 million. Are we no longer responsible for looking where we're going? How long will it be before Hellmann's mayonnaise is named co-defendant in such a suit?

Once, people *were* responsible for watching where they were going. Today it is well established that if you slip on someone else's ice, or twist your ankle in a pothole, or go sprawling among the guavas and avocados at the supermarket, you have a potentially lucrative cause of action. It is equally well established that between a third and a half of whatever you are awarded under your right not to watch where you're going goes directly to your attorney for his time and expenses. But if society has decided to aid those who slip and fall, why not aid as well people who slip and fall on their own premises or on the premises of the not so well off? ("Couldn't you have dragged yourself down to May's?" shouts Matthau. "From them you can collect!") And why must such a large chunk of the aid we provide routinely go to lawyers instead of victims?

A 68-year-old blind woman living in New York's Greenwich Village stumbled and fell, breaking the wrist she used in "tapping" her way along the street. She incurred nearly $5,000 in medical fees. Far worse, where up until that time she had been highly independent, she now had lost her confidence. She could no longer "see" with her wrist, and in any event was afraid to go out alone. There was no question that her fall had resulted from a gaping flaw in the sidewalk which the city had been negligent in not repairing. A six-person jury heard the case. What would a fair award have been? To pay all her medical expenses and provide, in addition, a monthly stipend for life (with a provision for inflation) so that she could hire someone part-time to accompany her around the neighborhood? That would have cost the city $5,000 or $7,500 a year for (according to the actuaries) about thirteen years.

A friend of mine was on the jury. My friend, filled with compassion for the plaintiff—as who would not be?—had in his ten years living in New York paid *maybe* $3,000 in city taxes. Total. He and his fellow jurors awarded the blind woman (and her lawyer, of course) $225,000. Which meant that the city would borrow yet another $225,000, paying around 10 percent interest, or $22,500 a year. Forever! (Unless you think one day New York will be able to pay off its debts.) Long after the poor woman has died, taxpayers will be chipping in $22,500 a year to pay for this woman's broken wrist and resultant hardship. Would it not be wonderful if we could afford to deal so generously with all society's victims? Instead, under the present system, a few are overcompensated while most get little or nothing at all.

Wrote the *Economist* in 1977, "A legal system in which the parents of a young man who jumps off the Golden Gate Bridge find it worthwhile to sue the bridge authority for $1 million, charging that the suicide could have been 'predicted and foreseen,' or in which manufacturers are made responsible for injuries inflicted by machines built 30 years ago, is clearly out of control."

Insurance perhaps works worst when it is forced by the courts to provide benefits much of society clearly wants but which the legislature has failed to prescribe. When the legislature fails to provide an efficient means of achieving a social objective, the objective does not go away. It just sets the courts looking for a second best way to achieve it.

"As a result," says industry consultant Richard E. Stewart, "we have a hodge-podge of second best solutions devised by the courts. Often they are inefficient and unpredictable."

Simply put, society does not want innocent parties to be hurt—

or, if hurt, to go uncompensated. Having no national system of catastrophic health insurance, we have, through the courts, managed to patch together pieces of a not very satisfactory one.

A 10-year-old boy playing hooky at Manhattan Beach, California, was hit by a motorcycle and hurt terribly. A court ruled that the boy was entitled to sue the school for allowing him to play hooky. "The case is still awaiting trial," reported CBS's Fred Graham four years later, in 1980, "but meanwhile insurance costs for the whole school district have gone up 1300 percent." Meanwhile, too, the insurance system had not paid this victim a dime. Is this the logical and efficient way for society to help? Through lawsuits against school districts that will take years and tens of thousands of dollars to resolve? If we want to care for the catastrophically injured among us—a worthy aim—then that's what we should do, directly and efficiently, through national catastrophic health insurance.

Failing such a health plan, it is remarkable the lengths to which we look to find *someone* to pay for our misfortune.

A man driving with a suspended license, no insurance, and a brake line he knew to be in immediate need of repair, was speeding home from a party when he illegally passed another vehicle. When a police car began giving chase, the driver sped up. (He would later testify that his accelerator pedal stuck.) Careening along at 80 miles an hour, without brakes, he approached a set of flashing red lights and saw an oncoming train. With police lights flashing behind him and railroad-crossing lights flashing in front, he closed his eyes. The train sent his car hurtling through the air. A man was in a phone booth nearby. The car went flying into the phone booth, shattering the man's legs, which would later be amputated. The driver suffered a cut on his forehead. Far from losing *his* legs, he used them to run from the scene of the accident. He turned himself in about an hour later. He was uninsured and owned no appreciable assets.

So from whom could the tragically injured man recover? Not that any amount of money would truly suffice.

The *telephone company,* along with the driver, was ordered to pay $216,761 in damages. A dangerous place, the jury felt, to locate a pay phone. Reaching into the bottomless coffers of the phone company—and thereby spreading the cost among millions of customers and shareholders—the jury was, in effect, voting national health insurance for this innocent victim.

• • •

As Walter Matthau is exiting temporarily, Mr. Cimoli asks him: "How much do you think my pelvis is worth?"

"By itself," says Matthau imperiously, "nothing. So it's a good thing you came to me. Before we're through with them, we'll have them begging for mercy."

"Who's them?" asks Cimoli.

"*That* I haven't figured out yet," says Matthau. "But don't go away. I'll think of an angle."

There are reforms that could reduce the legal overhead of the insurance system. No-fault auto insurance is by far the most important, but two others are worth mentioning first.

LOSER PAYS COSTS

"In practically every other country in the world," writes James Dale Davidson, "a person bringing a false or frivolous legal action must indemnify the party he sues for all legal costs if he fails in the action." Had this been the case in the U.S., the by-now famous tourists who sued the National Park Service after being struck by lightning—holding that the Service was negligent for failing to post warning signs—might have thought twice before cluttering the courts with their suit. Likewise the student who sued the University of Michigan for $853,000 for the mental anguish he suffered upon receipt of a D in German. And the prisoner who sued the county sheriff and his guards for not preventing his escape, and with it, the time that was added to his sentence.

What has a plaintiff or his attorney-on-contingency currently to lose by suing? The attorney has his time and expenses, which can be considerable. But he also knows that an insurer may settle even the most tenuous claim simply to avoid the cost of litigation. *American Lawyer's* Steven Brill cites the example of his own doctor, who had been sued seven times in the past five years. "He has won every suit," Brill reports, "but . . . in several instances, he's had to fight off the insurance company's request that he settle."

The reason unsuccessful plaintiffs do not have to pay defense costs in America is our wish to "keep the courtroom door open" to the poor and those of modest means. (When it comes to litigation, practically anyone is of modest means.) But—again using Britain as a guide—the loser-pays-costs rule need not be strictly applied. Wealthy British defendants rarely attempt to recover defense costs from the less well-heeled. It would be enough to *allow* judges and/ or juries here to award such costs to the defendant, in full or in part, as they saw fit. The important thing is that the *risk* be there. "Suing someone *should* be riskier," argues Brill.

ARBITRATION

A second reform would be far greater use of arbitration to resolve insurance claims. For example, both parties to a disputed insurance claim might be required, as a standard provision of the insurance policy, to submit to prompt arbitration. Either party could reject the arbitrated settlement, preferring to go to court; but the party that did so would be required to pay a 25 percent penalty. If it was the claimant who refused the arbitrated settlement, whatever he eventually won in court would be reduced by 25 percent. If it was the insurer who rejected the settlement, it would have to pay 25 percent beyond whatever was decided in court. This would be an incentive to prompt, efficient settlements. And, for those cases that went no further than arbitration, attorneys could afford to charge much lower contingency fees and still come out very well.

It would be different if, by drawing civil lawsuits out over many years, as now occurs, and involving a great many lawyers, stenographers, judges, jurors, and experts-for-hire (each side having its own trusty stable), the "truly just" verdict and award could be arrived at. But there is little reason to think that panels of trained and experienced arbitrators could not, in most instances, and with far less expenditure of time and effort, do about as well. These are not criminal trials, after all, where every precaution must be taken to ascertain innocence or guilt; these are disputes over money.

The arbitration scheme described above would be "compulsory, non-binding" arbitration. You'd have to submit to it, promptly, but not necessarily abide by the result. It was not in use anywhere in 1981. Many states had authorized *voluntary* non-binding arbitration and set up panels to assist in resolving medical malpractice claims. Thirteen states, including California, Illinois, Michigan, Ohio and Virginia, had authorized voluntary, *binding* arbitration; you don't have to submit to it, but, if both parties do, they must abide by the result. But the use of arbitration is as nothing compared to what it might be.

NO-FAULT AUTO INSURANCE

The reform that fairly screams to be made is the institution of true no-fault automobile insurance. No-fault would be of great benefit to everyone but the lawyers.

Traditional auto liability insurance has been characterized as "the worst system imaginable: A system that not only fails to spread most of [the] loss but is cruel, corrupt, self-righteous, dilatory, expensive and wasteful." It *over*compensates petty and groundless claims, because they are too expensive to fight, and grossly *under*-compensates the seriously injured, and then only after much delay. Each time a $100 case is settled for $400, to get rid of it, insurers are in effect paying a "toll" to lawyers for letting them pass without a lawsuit. Even when no attorney is involved, it is protection money, paid under threat that the claimant *could* retain an attorney. Settling petty or groundless claims for several times their economic value (medical expenses and lost wages) leaves too little of the insurance dollar for the people who really need it.

With no-fault, the idea is to get an accident victim reimbursed promptly and as fully as possible for medical expenses and lost wages. In return for sure, swift compensation, the policyholder gives up his right to sue for pain and suffering.

True no-fault auto insurance eliminates the potential bonanza for a man struck down by a chauffeur-driven Rolls-Royce, but eliminates, too, the current norm: woefully inadequate payments, much disputed and long delayed. It assumes that accidents are, by and large, just that—accidents, not intentional assaults—and that society's effort should be primarily directed not at finding fault but at aiding the victim. It is rehabilitation specialists, not lawyers, we should have chasing after ambulances. Indeed, in many auto injury cases more professional hours are logged by lawyers than doctors! "The courts are overwhelmed, swamped, inundated, choked," Daniel Patrick Moynihan has written. "In a futile quest to carry out a mundane mission—deciding who hit whom on the highway when every day there will be thousands and thousands of such events . . .—we are sacrificing the most precious of our institutions: the independent judiciary, which dispenses justice and maintains the presumption and perception of a just social order that is fundamental to a democratic political system.''

Many years earlier, a young law student had argued the impracticability of trying to assign, let alone prove, fault in auto-accident cases. "In the days of poor roads and low speeds," wrote Richard Nixon in 1936, "the fact of an accident could be reconstructed in a courtroom with some degree of accuracy, and the problem of determining fault did not present unusual difficulties. But with high-powered cars and concrete highways, the probability that an accident—often the consequence of a fractional mistake in management—can and will be described accurately in court has become increasingly remote, especially where court congestion has delayed the time of trial.''

And note this: Even under no-fault, drivers have enormous incentive not to cause accidents. They risk personal injury, death, criminal penalty or, at the very least, property damage, license suspension and hiked insurance rates.

True no-fault auto insurance allows a much larger proportion of each premium dollar to reach the accident victim. Fair, fast and efficient, it was recommended to the nation by a team from Columbia University as long ago as 1932. But the fight for no-fault only got under way in earnest in the late 1960s. To the casual observer, the fight would seem to have been won. Many states today have one or another form of no-fault insurance. In fact, however, *no state had a true no-fault auto insurance system in 1981.* In all but a few "no-fault" states, the threshold of damages beyond which the fault system took over was so low—$500 or less in many cases—that it merely encouraged victims and their lawyers to incur unnecessary medical expenses in order to "build up the claim," exceed the threshold and thus qualify to sue for pain and suffering.

A report issued in 1970 by the New York State Insurance Department assailed the efficiency of the traditional auto liability insurance system.

"What becomes of the personal injury liability insurance dollar?" the report asked, answering:

> First of all, insurance companies and agents use up 33 cents.
> Then lawyers and claims investigators take the next 23 cents.

NO-FAULT IN NAME ONLY: WHEN YOU MAY SUE FOR DAMAGES

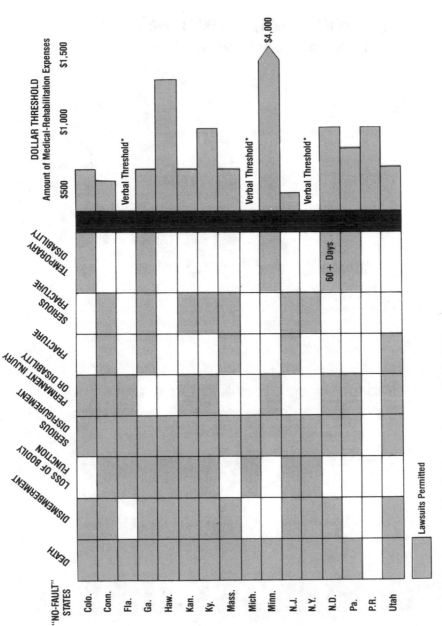

*Threshold is based on a description of the injury rather than any specific dollar amount.

If plaintiff's medical/rehabilitation expenses exceed the dollar amounts shown at right, the accident is deemed to have been serious enough to allow a lawsuit to determine fault and to assess non-economic damages—pain and suffering.

SOURCE: Summary of Selected State Laws and Regulations Relating to Automobile Insurance. American Insurance Association, 1981.

WHAT CURRENT "NO-FAULT" PAYS
Maximum Benefits for Medical Expenses

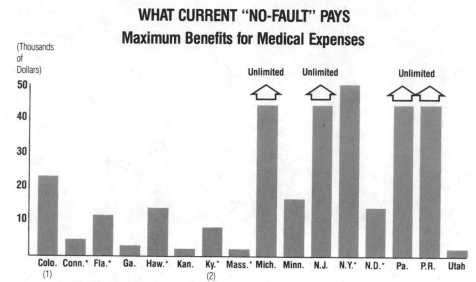

(1) $25,000 rehabilitation benefits also available.
(2) $2,000 rehabilitation benefits also available.
 *Total includes all benefits available (loss of income, etc.). Receipt of this amount of medical benefits possible only if no other benefits received.

Maximum Aggregate Benefits for Loss of Income

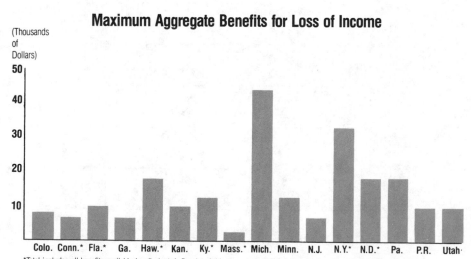

 *Total includes all benefits available (medical, etc.). Receipt of this amount of work loss benefits possible only if no other benefits received.

SOURCE: American Insurance Association.

Together these items make up the operating expenses, or frictional costs, of the fault insurance system—56 cents out of every premium dollar.

What happens to the 44 cents that get through to the accident victim?

First, 8 cents of the 44 go to pay for economic losses that have already been reimbursed from another source. Subtracting these redundant benefits as having low priority leaves 36 cents of the premium dollar to pay net losses of victims.

But of those 36 cents, 21.5 cents go for something other than economic loss. The 21.5 cents are lumped together as "general damages" or "pain and suffering" which, in the typical case today, are simply by-products of the bargaining process of insurance adjustment. Once we look beyond the name which the operators of the fault insurance system have given this non-economic portion of liability payments and understand what it really is in the usual case, it assumes a low priority by any social or humane standard.

That leaves just 14.5 cents out of the premium dollar as compensation for the net economic loss of the accident victim—$100 million out of $686 million which New Yorkers spend each year for automobile bodily injury liability insurance.

Under the fault system, again to quote Daniel Patrick Moynihan, "the victim has every reason to exaggerate his losses. It is some other person's insurance company that must pay. The company has every reason to resist. It is somebody else's customer who is making the claim. Delay, fraud, contentiousness are maximized, and in the process the system becomes grossly inefficient and expensive."

And the lawyers fight tooth and nail to preserve it.

Assuming no drastic changes in safety statistics, more than half of all drivers will be involved in one or more automobile accidents within the next three years. Three-fourths of those who drive will have an accident within the next five years. All but one in a hundred will have at least one within the next twenty years.

Fortunately, most of these accidents will be trivial in nature. But once an accident is set in motion, "luck" has a lot more to do with its severity than "fault." A drunk driving without headlights runs a red light and smashes into the passenger side of another vehicle in which no passenger happens to be riding. Later that day, a usually fastidious motorist, spotting his spouse passing in the arms of an-

THE AUTO LIABILITY PREMIUM DOLLAR

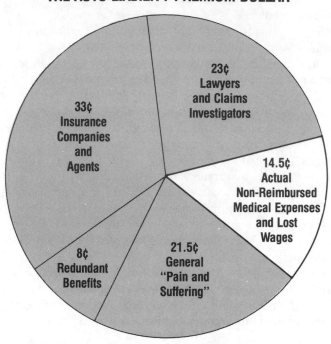

other driver, momentarily loses his concentration, runs the same red light—and plows through an entire class of fourth-graders. Twenty-seven of them. Under the fault system, the first man—the drunk—would likely encounter no extraordinary hardship. His insurance company would pay for the damage he did and perhaps raise his rates or cancel his policy. The *second* man would see his life virtually ruined. His insurance would never be enough to pay all the claims, so it would protect neither him *nor the children he had injured*. It's all very well to be able to sue a driver under the fault system for $2 million. But if he's only got $20,000 of insurance and insignificant personal assets, $20,000 is all you are going to get. (Less legal fees.)

So many people are involved in auto accidents each year one can only conclude that "even nice people" may, to their great regret, occasionally be at fault in the way they drive. It would be hard not to forgive all but the most reckless among them—for whom criminal penalties are available. That being the case, and with luck rather than fault such a large determinant of how bad an accident actually turns out to be, the question becomes: How important is it—even when you can do it—to assign fault in auto accidents? Should society commit tens of thousands of its best minds to the task? Or are accidents not simply a hazard of whizzing around in 160 million registered motor vehicles?

Lawyers object that to compensate innocent victims only for their medical costs and lost wages, and not also for their pain and suffering, is unfair. Which is true. But life is unfair, and it is only a relative few serious accident victims who have the good fortune to have been injured by someone rich, or richly insured. *The drivers with the least insurance cause the most accidents.* And even if the offending party *is* well insured, there is the small matter of *proving* he was at fault. Years may pass. And then in all but a few cases it is questionable whether the injured party, after giving up a third or a half of his award in legal fees and expenses, retains more than would have been paid, promptly, under no-fault. (Remember, attorneys take a portion not just of the pain-and-suffering award, but of the award for medical expenses and lost wages, as well. In arriving at awards, juries are instructed to take no account of legal fees.)

Nor need no-fault necessarily exclude compensation for pain and suffering, even though thus far all such plans do. At increased cost, a schedule of "pain and suffering" awards, on top of economic damages, could easily be added to a state's no-fault law if the citizenry so desired. (Or it could be offered as an option, or sold separately.) Rather than tie such a schedule to a multiple of medical expenses—which just gives victims an incentive to increase their medical expenses—there might be prescribed levels of pain-and-suffering compensation: Level I, for a minor accident involving no broken bones or extensive medical treatment—no extra payment at all. Level II, for a relatively minor injury—$500 or $1,000. All the way up to Level V, say—$50,000 for a really tragic disability (with that money to be paid *on top* of actual economic damages, remember). The insurance adjuster would classify the accident by level; a state insurance department appeals board could be established with authority to review policyholder challenges to those classifications. But the bulk of the award would be for economic damages, promptly paid, undiluted by legal fees. That being the case, the pain-and-suffering award would be relatively less important to both parties. At worst, one or the other might believe the appeals board had misclassified the injury by one level.

Insurers have been divided on no-fault. Their lawyers tend to oppose it, naturally, as it would put many of them out of work. Some companies fear, too, that no-fault, because it is so simple, would eventually lead to the same sort of group coverage as group life and health. Employers would provide it as a fringe benefit. That would be good for the firms that already specialize in group business, and good for the public at large, but a major blow to the insurers and 70,000 insurance agencies that exist to sell each policy separately. (Of which more in the next chapter.) Not to mention the fact that, by shortening the time between accident and payment, an insurer also shortens the length of time it has to invest our premiums. Or that, by making auto insurance more efficient, no-fault could make it a smaller business, with fewer premium dollars to invest.

Those who oppose no-fault—primarily America's personal injury lawyers—take public opinion surveys to show that the public doesn't want it. "Do you believe," they ask, "that the person who causes an accident, or his insurance company, should pay for the injuries he does to others?" Naturally, everyone answers yes. This is then taken to show overwhelming grass-roots support for the traditional fault system of auto insurance.

Or they will cite the soaring costs of insurance in states that have adopted no-fault. But this is equally misleading. In the first place, auto insurance rates have been going up everywhere; but most of this is the cost of theft, collision, and the other coverages to which no-fault (except in Michigan) does not apply. Second, because most "no-fault" states have such a low threshold of damages beyond which the fault system takes over, drivers in those states are in effect paying for *both* systems.

Where fair comparisons have been done, by the U.S. Department of Transportation and others, they show—what else *could* they show?—that under no-fault payment is faster, fairer and more efficient. A higher proportion of the premium dollar is paid in benefits; and, of benefits, a higher proportion is paid for medical costs and wage loss, where it's most needed.*

---

*The following exchange of letters, while more than fifteen years old, is illustrative of the fault system at its worst:

From an Oregon claims adjuster to the claims manager in the Illinois home office: "Liability is most unfavorable. Our insured, as we previously advised, admits drinking. As a matter of fact, our insured indicates that he does not know just what happened as he came up the hill. . . . We feel that we could put [the injured party] off for possibly six months through legal maneu-

Our failure to adopt true no-fault auto insurance is a nuts-and-bolts example of the country at its most obese, arteries hardened and clogged by special interests, its heart having to pump $1 in liability premiums to get 14.5 cents where it is most needed—the economic losses of the accident victim. But what special interest group is better able to strangle the system than the lawyers? They write the laws.

"If you've wondered about such reforms as arbitration or small-claims courts or no-fault laws," Fred Graham concluded his hour-long CBS report ("See You in Court," July 1980), "what we found is that very little reform is really going on, apparently because the lawyers control the system and they lack the will to reform it."

---

vers, but finally a trial would take place. We feel the longer this can be put off without suit being brought, the more hungry they will get and the less they will demand."

Reply from the home-office claims manager months later (there may have been intervening correspondence, but the case was still dragging on): "Obviously, we will have no alternative but to [pay] the policy limits. . . . However, before you make the offer, kindly advise whether or not we would be liable for the plaintiff's attorneys' costs in the event suit is filed. If we are not, I would suggest you let the matter go to suit, and we can always settle on the courthouse steps."

11

TOO MANY UNDERWRITERS, TOO MANY AGENTS
A Plan to Cut Auto Insurance Costs in Half

Think of insurance as a straight line with a point someplace in the middle. Up to that point, the insurer is working to get your business and collect your premiums. Beyond that point, it is working to settle your claims. For that's really about all automobile insurers do: they take in premiums and pay out claims. True no-fault insurance would greatly streamline the second function, the settlement of claims. But even more of their effort, and your dollars, are spent in the first: getting your business and collecting your premiums. To do this, hundreds of thousands of people are employed. They sell insurance, assign premium rates, examine applications, send out policies, send out bills, send out past-due notices, send out cancellation notices. It is all unnecessary.

We pay some $40 billion annually in auto insurance premiums. Insurers earn an extra few billion dollars investing those premiums. Of the total, say $44 billion a year, $20 or $25 billion makes it back through the system to you and me. This chapter will describe a system under which we would get back very nearly the whole $40 billion. For their trouble, insurers would keep the extra few billion dollars in interest.

But first (having surely said enough about lawyers) a few words about underwriters.

Beverly Bingham, of Amusement Business Underwriters (Birmingham, Michigan), once arranged for a policy on the life of a macaw trained to disrobe a strip-tease artist. She knows whether Italians or Australians are more likely to sue if they slip and fall at a rock concert (Australians) and whether it is riskier to insure rides at amusement parks or rides at traveling carnivals. (Carnival rides are considered safer because they are dismantled and reassembled— and thus checked out—so frequently. Also, where a park is likely to have a single owner who can tolerate the breakdown of one or two rides, each ride in a carnival is typically owned by a single individual or family for whom it is the sole means of support. It thus receives better care.)

Commercial insurers depend on two things: the enormous capital surplus that makes it possible for them to take risks in the first place; a handful of seasoned underwriters who know which risks to take.

Imagine the expertise and judgment required in deciding whether to insure a newspaper for libel and, if so, how much to charge. Or in deciding the rate for an $80-million offshore oil rig—particularly one of untried design. It would be a shame to charge a $2 million annual premium only to see the damn thing capsize in a bad squall. But if it didn't, you could be $2 million richer just for having affixed your initials to a scrap of paper.

Because most of us do not have oil rigs to insure, the bulk of this chapter, as I say, deals with auto insurance—how we are rated as risks and how the entire system might be radically improved. But by way of illustration, consider the importance of underwriting to one small commercial line of insurance known as "surety."

The surety business in the United States takes in $800 million or so in premiums each year, of which about 40 percent gets paid back out in claims. Want to put up scaffolding? You may have to put up a surety bond, as well. This kind of coverage assures some third party, often a government, that the policyholder will perform as agreed.

A few years ago, to take just one of a million routine examples, Avon Products had to obtain a $115,528.28 bond to guarantee the state of New York that the prizes in a contest it was running would in fact be awarded. Anyone running a contest in New York must post such a bond. The standard premium rate for games-of-chance bonds is $7.50 per $1,000. But Avon, because it could part with $115,528.28 without batting a false eyelash, qualified for a 50 percent "net worth discount" and so paid its insurer just $433 to put up the bond ($3.75 x 115). Had Avon somehow failed in its obligation to the state, the insurer would have made good its guarantee— and then sued Avon to recover its loss. Instead, Avon gave out its prizes as promised; and the insurer, having taken virtually no risk whatsoever, pocketed $433.

There are bonds for auctioneers guaranteeing "faithful accounting for auctioned goods"; bonds for automobile clubs guaranteeing that "services contracted for will be furnished"; for bowling alleys ("freely written for reputable applicants"); blasting and explosives contractors ("Dangerous . . .")—and so on through the alphabet. "Collectors of Birdnests & Eggs, Fish, & Frogs for Scientific Purposes," advises an insurer's surety manual—each page a grain of the sandstone from which our great legal-economic edifice is carved— may be "freely written for reputable applicants." Escort agencies, on the other hand, present a "high moral hazard. Applicant should be established and reputable." Florists may be freely written; fish removers (those who contract to "remove undesirable fish from state waters") should be experienced, lest they "remove desirable fish."

"The basic rule in surety," one executive confided, "is, if there's any risk, don't write the business."

This is easier said than done, however, in the "contract" end of the business, where the insurer guarantees timely completion of a construction company's work. Construction bonds are required for all federal projects over $25,000; by most local governments; and by many of the lenders that finance private construction. They are required because not infrequently a contractor will bid too low, run into difficulties and go broke. When that happens, the insurer must put up enough cash to allow the contractor to finish the job, or hire some other contractor to do it. The insurer's loss is limited to the face value of the bond, less whatever it may be able to recover from the bankrupt construction company.

Most insurers that write construction bonds have a tough time. They may be going along well for a few years, then—bang—they get hit with a big loss. Overall, the return in the surety business has been low. One company, however, Chubb, makes money every year charging rates *lower* than the competition. They clean up in this business because they have built the expertise and relationships to know which risks to write. They bond the contractors that *don't* go broke.

(No one is perfect. On the wall of an office at Chubb hangs a photocopy of a check for $11,269,155.47. Above it is a photograph of an enormous road-grading machine, headlined, "This Train Is Bound for Glory . . . This Train." A venerable Cleveland construction company, with eighty years in the business (but it had never built anything in *New York* before; it had never built a *road* before), won a highway-construction contract and favored Chubb with the surety business. The construction outfit was very proud of the job, only it hadn't counted on so much rain! So much mud! The caption of the photograph, written while the sun was still shining, ran: "Hunkin-Conkey's Autograde Train Highballs Down New York's Southern Tier Expressway." Straight into bankruptcy. Out came Chubb's checkbook.)

Personal-lines underwriters deal not with multimillion-dollar construction projects but things like whether to insure your life (next chapter) or your Buick Cutlass (this one). They are like a bank's retail loan officers, trying to distinguish the good risks from the bad.

From the standpoint of any given company, risk selection is crucial. An insurer who accepted poor risks at standard rates would soon find itself enormously popular and entirely broke.

From the standpoint of any given individual, underwriting is also of great concern, for it determines whether he can obtain coverage and the rate he will have to pay.

Just how crucial personal-lines underwriting is from a *social* standpoint is another matter; for again there is that trade-off between equity and efficiency. Take group life insurance. As arranged by many employers for their employees, it is at once highly efficient and ridiculously "unfair." Under most plans everyone pays the same rate! Regardless of age! Quite clearly, the younger workers are subsidizing the older ones. Yet sales and administrative costs are pared to the bone, allowing 90 or even 100 cents of each premium dollar to be paid out in benefits. When life insurance is sold one on one, in small amounts, over the kitchen table, much less of the premium dollar makes it through the insurance machine and out the other end.

Are young workers being duped into participating in these plans? Often they have no choice.* But there are strong justifications for such plans.

First, what's *wrong* with young, healthy members of the group subsidizing the old and less healthy? Consider how the older members of the group have subsidized the young! Eighteen years of food and shelter, for starters.

Second, the young will surely grow old, so they, too, will have their turn at being subsidized. Why erect a bureaucracy to even things out, when time alone will do so?

Third, the efficiency of a group plan is so great that even the youngest members are likely to be getting a reasonably good rate as compared with what they would pay for small amounts of life insurance purchased individually.

So this insurance, like group health insurance, is written without appreciable sales costs and *without* individual rating or underwriting. If anyone is greatly upset by the inequity, he has not been shouting about it.

Where shouts are heard is in the area of automobile insurance. Here policies are sold one at a time, and in an effort to make things fair, rates for the same coverage vary tremendously from driver to driver. A California applicant to State Farm will be assigned one of 70,560 rates, depending on which of eighty-four territories he lives in, which of fourteen categories his vehicle falls into, and which of sixty driver categories (determined mostly by age and mileage driven) he fits (84x14x60 = 70,560).

Here are the principal factors insurers use to determine our automobile insurance rates:

Age. Drivers under 25 represented 22 percent of the driving population in 1979, but 38 percent of all drivers involved in accidents. The record would be even more damning if it were based on fault rather than mere "involvement." But while strict equity demands

---

*As contrasted, say, with credit life insurance, issued without regard to age, where participation is voluntary. The credit insurance banks offer, to pay off the balance of your loan if you die, is a terrible deal for young healthy borrowers, a virtual gift to the elderly and infirm.

Indeed, one way for the otherwise uninsurable to obtain life insurance is to take out a bank loan, accept the credit-life option, and invest the proceeds. On D-day, the loan is paid off by the insurance; the investments are your heirs' to keep. Such a scheme, however, is not likely to help your case later the same day.

that young drivers (or urban drivers or reckless ones) pay their disproportionate share of losses, it does not follow that they should also bear a disproportionate share of an insurer's expenses. It costs no more to sign up a young urban driver than an older rural one. Yet, typically, sales and overhead costs have been loaded into premiums on a percentage basis. Thus the urban male with a $1,500 premium may be paying $450 toward selling costs and overhead, while the older man with a $150 premium pays only $45. This is unfair.

Marital status. Single persons have more accidents than those who are married. However, this rating criterion is applied only in distinguishing among youthful drivers. The married 22-year-old will get a lower premium rate than his unmarried twin.

Territory. Accidents and thefts vary markedly from place to place. Yet even within the context of traditional auto insurance rating (which I will argue should be abandoned altogether), there is a point to be made: "Inner-city residents have to pay more for their auto insurance due to the fact that they live in more congested areas. Actually," writes Professor Michael Etgar, *"the congestion is generated by suburban cars coming into the city."* (Italics mine.) In San Francisco, for example, "almost every other person who works in the central city arrives there from one of the surrounding bedroom communities."*

So commuters should perhaps pay the higher urban rate. But it's more than that. In many cities, the surrounding population is relatively so large that the impact of even occasional visits by noncommuters adds substantially to congestion. The visitors may also be less familiar with city streets and driving conditions, a further hazard. They add to the conditions that make urban driving hazardous, with no practical way to charge them for doing so. In this respect, urban drivers subsidize their fellows.

The issue of subsidization in our advanced economy, with its taxes, transfer payments, subsidies and cross-subsidies, is almost impossibly complex. Which is why it is sometimes sensible simply to do what's best for the population as a whole rather than go to great expense attempting to apportion costs and benefits among individuals.

---

*"Unfair Price Discrimination in P-L Insurance and the Reliance on Loss Ratios," *Journal of Risk and Insurance*, December 1975.

Loss history. As any actuary will tell the irate policyholder who has received a "non-renewal" notice: statistically, policyholders who have made claims in the past are the most likely to make claims in the future. A California Department of Motor Vehicles study of 113,525 drivers published in 1976 found that those who had been involved in an accident in the prior two years were almost twice as likely to be involved in one the third year as those who had been accident-free. *Two*-accident drivers had nearly *three* times as many accidents in the third year as the no-accident group. Insurers very logically tend not to renew the policies of customers who make large or frequent claims.

Driving record. Similar studies have shown traffic violators to be loss-prone. A study of 2.5 million drivers published in 1972 by the Highway Safety Research Center at the University of North Carolina showed that drivers who had had two traffic violations over a two-year period were 2.6 times as likely to have an accident in the next two years as drivers who had had no violations. The more violations, the greater the expectation of future accidents.

Sex. Did you grow up thinking "lady drivers are the *worst*"? Perhaps because they are less likely to drive aggressively, females of all ages tend to have fewer auto accidents per mile than males, and significantly fewer serious ones. Males are more likely than females to drive at night, and to drive under the influence of alcohol. Add to this the fact that males on average drive many more miles a year than females, and there is reason to expect the average male to be involved in about twice as many accidents as females, and the more expensive ones, at that. As a result, some companies will give preferred rates in instances where the only household member is an adult woman.

Vehicle use. Distance driven and business use are considered in assigning rating classifications.

Vehicle type. It used to be that rates were tied simply to the value of the insured vehicle. Increasingly, insurers are relating insurance rates to actual loss experience of different makes and models. Almost no one seems to want to steal a Plymouth.

Relating insurance rates to vehicle type is particularly appealing these days because it helps avoid the increasingly touchy problem of rating *people*.

Once the insurance agent, just following the book, has assigned you to the proper driver classification based on the factors above, it is the underwriter's turn to decide whether the company wants your business at all. In the old days, insurers would actually send someone around to look you over and chat with your neighbors before deciding whether or not to take on your business. This has become prohibitively expensive, but in describing "traditional underwriting practices," Robert B. Holtom lists a whole raft of criteria underwriters used to use. One was (and to a limited extent still is) property condition: "A vehicle which was in poor condition," Holtom writes, "perhaps with unrepaired damage, was usually unacceptable to most underwriters. Physical damage coverages could not be written because of the difficulty of determining whether new or old damage needed repair after a loss. But liability coverages were also refused in many cases, on the grounds that the poor maintenance showed that the owner was not interested in presenting a good appearance, which could give an unfavorable impression to a jury in case of a suit. Furthermore, the owner who was not interested in the appearance of the vehicle was probably not interested in its mechanical maintenance, which could lead to accidents because of faulty brakes or steering."*

Likewise, too *much* attention to appearance. Vehicles with decals, racing wheels, or names—other than "Prudence" or "St. John the Divine" (and perhaps even those)—also give an underwriter pause.

Underwriters have always preferred the norm, which, by definition, conforms to actuarial expectations. Why take unnecessary chances? "Homosexuals, as a group," writes Holtom, "were considered to be deviates whose life style and sexual preference could lead to insurance problems. They were considered to be less stable and more susceptible to unnatural influences. Furthermore, the impact on a typical jury could be disastrous if the sexual preference were to be revealed during a lawsuit in which the person was a defendant."

Salesmen who drive a lot (dictating follow-up notes as they go); students; young servicemen; professional athletes; farmworkers— some occupations have traditionally held little appeal for auto underwriters. The Hartford Group was in 1978 cautioning against airline stewardesses and construction workers, among others. Con-

---

*Robert B. Holtom, *Restraints on Underwriting*.

tinental Insurance, while leery of advertising employees, antique dealers, caterers, hairdressers, restaurateurs and others, stressed in its underwriting manual that "To say some occupational groups have a higher-than-average frequency of loss does not, in any sense, imply anything derogatory to anyone's character or integrity." Other bad risks, in Continental's estimation, are "the swinger, the high flier, the ostentatious, the excessive entertainer, the celebrity, the slow payer who lives beyond his means, the excessive drinker or gambler (including amateur), the emotionally unstable and quick tempered, the exhibitionist, the jet set member, the divorce repeater and the just plain ornery.

"There is also the type who has never lived anywhere but in a rural area. He commutes to an industrial plant, does odd jobs, lives on relief or lets his wife make the living. You can usually spot his place. Sometimes in the summer he can be seen sitting on his front porch without his shirt. He is not a good risk."

Even "clergy were considered to be a problem by many underwriters," writes Holtom. "Often their minds are more on the concerns of their calling than on driving conditions. There was even a feeling by some underwriters that some clergy operated on the premise that God would take care of them, so they need not be bothered with traffic signals or other human restraints. Whatever the reasons, the few studies which were made of actual loss experience by occupation indicated that clergy had among the highest loss ratios. . . . Underwriters tended to reject the clergy."

Homeowners are more stable than renters, longtime employees more stable than job hoppers. Regarded askance are: heavy drinkers; drug users; those "known to" collection agencies, welfare agencies, bail bondsmen and v.d. clinics; those exhibiting belligerence; mental incompetents; the physically handicapped; those prone to seizures or blackouts; the deaf; and those who speak or read English poorly. "A driver who cannot read . . . signs, or who needs time to understand them," writes Holtom, "can be in serious trouble. Accidents could result. Another problem with such people is their difficulty in understanding messages sent by the insurer." (One need hardly be foreign-born to have difficulty understanding messages sent by an insurer.)

Much of the underwriter's sleuthing—at least in the days when much sleuthing was done—was really an attempt, however obnoxious, to assess a driver's personality. For, as a study on "accident proneness'' noted in 1971, ''an individual's personality exerts such a powerful and overriding effect on his accident potential that it can make a bad risk out of someone with all the necessary attributes of skill and physical fitness, and a good risk out of someone whose qualifications for driving are anything but ideal.'' An Iowa-based insurer, Grinnell Mutual, studied the accident records of 30,000 insureds to whom it had given a battery of personality tests. Sure enough, those who tested ''safest'' *were* safest; those who seemed most prone to aggressive or reckless behavior suffered nearly twice as many accidents overall as those who scored best, and ten times as many fatal accidents.

Underwriters have even looked to an applicant's housekeeping and the length of the children's hair in trying to assess the family character, and thus its driving habits. Safeco was for many years advising its agents to steer clear of common laborers and minorities, not to mention drivers who ''liked to be called by a nickname, such as 'Shorty' or 'Scotty,' '' as possibly lacking maturity or the proper conservatism.

Holtom and others do not *advocate* all these selection criteria, despite the fact that even the most repugnant of them generally have some statistical validity. Increasingly, state legislators and regulators are banning use of such factors as occupation, race, sex, physical handicap, sexual preference and place of birth as underwriting criteria. That being the case—and considering the expense of trying to analyze each applicant individually, apart from simply assigning him to the right rate classification based on his application and a check of his motor vehicle record—some auto insurers have been toying with the notion of getting rid of their underwriters altogether. ''We talk about that here often,'' says the senior underwriter at an auto insurer with $2 billion in annual premiums. ''But we still feel we can spot some of the extra risks, and that it's worth the expense of the underwriting department in order to turn them down.''

So that some other insurer has to take them.

But why do we need auto insurance rating and underwriting *at all*?

From a single company's point of view, there is no substitute for charging rates commensurate with risks. But consider the matter from a broader perspective. What good does all that paperwork do for society as a whole?

There's no question young drivers have far more accidents than older ones—but is it our aim to keep them off the roads? Or to allow only *rich* young people (who can afford the premiums) to drive? Do we think charging them through the nose for auto insurance will somehow encourage young people to drive more safely?

The answers to these questions, most would agree, are no. Drivers below a certain age, or unable to pass competency tests, or guilty of recklessness—these should be, and are, denied licenses to drive. But young drivers? Urban drivers?

We want everyone competent to drive to be able to do so. Further, in most states we require them all to buy (woefully inadequate) insurance coverage. But then we make it so expensive that a large proportion of the worst risks drive without it. There are today *millions* of uninsured motorists traveling the nation's highways. In states that require proof of insurance to obtain a registration, applicants merely purchase insurance, pay the first month's premium, obtain their registrations, then fail to pay further premiums.

What you gain in equity, you lose in efficiency. It costs 20 cents to send a first-class letter anywhere in this country or Canada. Regardless of weight (up to an ounce); regardless of legibility of the address or inclusion of zip code; regardless of distance or destination. In the interests of efficiency—not having a wildly complicated tariff structure—everyone pays the same. Which inevitably means that some subsidize others. Inequitable, but sensibly efficient.

The proposal that follows may seem at first blush to strike a blow against free enterprise. But auto insurance is already a much-tampered-with commodity. We are required by law to buy it. (Not much "free market" there.) And in most states auto insurance rates are set subject to government regulation. (Not much free market there, either.) There are even "assigned risk" pools into which millions of drivers are thrown (many having never had an accident or filed a claim), to be insured by insurers who would rather not take them (but must, in proportion to the amount of voluntary business they write in the state).

Harkening back to the flight insurance example, isn't insurance that "everyone needs" just the type that lends itself to being provided automatically? Why sell things one at a time if everyone, by law, must buy?

A quick answer might be: Auto insurance must be sold separately so people can choose exactly the coverage they wish. But no!

Choosing auto insurance coverage is *not* like choosing a wardrobe. In auto insurance, everyone wants precisely the same thing: complete coverage. Only, because the current insurance system is so inefficient, all but the wealthiest drivers must settle for less.

Auto insurance could be provided much more efficiently—automatically—at enormous savings.

PAY AS YOU DRIVE:
HOW GOD WOULD RESTRUCTURE AUTOMOBILE INSURANCE

Imagine a true no-fault system called Pay As You Drive. Instead of buying auto liability insurance as we currently do, 25 or 30 cents would be added to the federal (or each state's) gasoline tax. The proceeds—some $25 billion a year—would fund a no-fault insurance pool. Drivers would not be able to sue—or be sued—for pain and suffering. (Manufacturers would still be liable for defects.) *But anyone injured in a vehicular accident would automatically be covered for all his medical expenses and, within certain limits, for lost wages and future disability*. (At modest additional cost, as described in the previous chapter, a schedule of pain-and-suffering benefits *could* be provided. Or, private insurers could sell this extra coverage —or any other—to those who wished to buy it.)

Gone would be billions of dollars in unnecessary sales costs, underwriting costs, policy-issuance costs, billing costs! Gone would be much of the painstaking, litigious claims process! Billions that currently go to *administering* auto insurance could be paid out in benefits. Instead of 14 or even 44 cents of the auto liability premium dollar making its way through the sticky insurance mechanism, nearly the whole dollar would go, as intended, to pay for losses. *Each dollar of auto liability premiums, paid automatically at the gas pump, would provide more than twice as much insurance as it currently does*. Without raising the overall national auto liability insurance bill (which in 1980 totaled $23 billion), *everyone* could be assured full, prompt payment in the event of an accident. A victim's compensation would not depend on his luck in who hits him; nor would it be watered down by legal fees or endlessly delayed in the courts.

What's more, there are simple ways of building equity into *this* system *without* sacrificing efficiency.

• Age. Because young drivers will, with tedious predictability, grow up to be older drivers (unlike reckless drivers, who may not grow up to be safe ones), one wonders what would be lost if young drivers *were* subsidized in their insurance rates. But if the voters wished, it would be a simple matter of adding fees tied to age to the currently nominal cost of a driver's license. Paid into the no-fault kitty, such fees would serve to lower the tax on gasoline that would be required.

• Place of residence. License fees could also be adjusted—efficiently, by computer—for a driver's residence. A rural Illinois driver might pay the standard license fee, while his Chicago counterpart paid an extra $50. Again, such fees would serve to reduce the gasoline tax needed to fund the plan.

Alternatively, the *deductible* feature of this plan could be adjusted for *the place the accident occurs*. An accident in a low-hazard area might be subject to a mere $100 deductible; in a medium hazard zone, $250; and in places like Los Angeles, New York or Boston, $500. Under such a scheme, it would no longer do any good to lie about where a vehicle was garaged or principally used. What's more, urban drivers would no longer subsidize suburban visitors. There would even be some incentive, however slight, to drive less, or more cautiously, in hazardous areas.

• Driving record. It would be a simple matter, too, to impose surcharges in the driver's license fee based on traffic violations. The point systems many states already use in determining license revocations could carry a financial penalty as well.

Of course, traffic violations already carry fines. No-fault doesn't mean no *penalty*. Under no-fault, the truly reckless driver would still have his medical bills paid—just as the state provides medical attention for a wounded bank robber awaiting trial—but he could lose his license or even go to jail.

Under a point system, rather than penalize all young drivers just because they are young, as most states do now, only those who compiled poor driving records would pay extra—which *would* be an incentive to drive safely. Under the current system, the penalty—high insurance premiums—is assessed *in advance*, whether an infraction occurs or not. Indeed, under the current system so many ''poor risks'' are already paying maximum insurance rates that if they *do* cause an accident, their insurance rates can't go any higher.

• Mileage. Under this system, the more one drove, the more he would pay for insurance. What could be more equitable than that? Accidents do not rise in direct proportion to miles driven, but there is a strong correlation. Big cars, often the safest, would be penalized in favor of smaller ones that get better mileage. But as it happens, we have every reason to encourage good mileage. (As for electric cars, public policy could either be to encourage their use by allowing them to skirt the cost of insurance—or else, simply, to add some appropriate insurance charge to their annual registration fee. Efficiently. By computer.)

• There could be other adjustments, as well. "X-rated" muscle cars could have a surcharge in their initial sales price or in their annual registration fee; males or females could be charged extra— or given a discount—in their license fee. These adjustments would be up to the legislators who designed the system.

The key in all of this is *not* how pay-as-you-drive no-fault auto insurance should be fine-tuned to make it equitable or politically palatable—although the industry would doubtless try to scuttle any such plan by engendering endless debate. The key is that, however much or little fine-tuning were done, the system would provide 90 cents in needed economic benefits for each dollar collected rather than just 15 or 25 cents.

But who would administer the claims? (Please—not another federal bureaucracy!) *Claims would be administered by the very same insurers who do so now.*

Each state's licensed drivers could be divided, randomly, by computer, into groups of 2,500 or 5,000. (The same computers that already spew forth drivers' licenses would now simply be programmed to add one more task to their near instantaneous, highly efficient routine.) Insurers could then *bid* for these blocks of business, just as, currently, they will bid for the right to handle a group health insurance plan. The low bidder—the company that offers to insure the block of licensed drivers for the least—would then have the franchise to service the claims of that group. Each computer-generated driver's license would have on it the name and phone number of the company to call in case of an accident. Periodically, each block of business would be put out again for competitive bid, just as employers occasionally switch from one group health carrier to another.

Insurers would settle claims as they do now. Only, because there would be a true no-fault system, it would be much easier and less costly. Legal fees on both sides would be greatly diminished.

It would still be very much in the insurers' interest to foil fraudulent claims and to try to keep the lid on costs, because, as now, whatever they didn't have to pay out in benefits would be theirs to keep. Insurers whose claims-handling practices drew significantly higher than average levels of complaints could be suspended from bidding in that area for a period of time. (In extreme cases, of course, they could, as now, be sued for acting in bad faith.)

To make most sense, an efficient auto insurance system ought to include *all* coverages: collision and theft as well as personal injury and liability. Otherwise, you would still need the elaborate sales, underwriting and billing apparatus currently in place.

To add these coverages to the pay-as-you-drive plan outlined above would cost about 15 or 20 cents per gallon of gas. Everyone would automatically have it (subject to a $250 or $500 deductible), and it would be administered by the insurance companies exactly as above.

Total for the entire package: 40 to 50 cents a gallon. (Less, if licensing and registration fees were levied.) Fifty cents a gallon would amount to $300 a year for someone who drove 12,000 miles a year at 20 miles to the gallon. *And there would be no other auto insurance premiums to pay!* Almost all drivers would find the "policy limits" of their present coverage greatly expanded. No longer would they face the possibility of $350,000 in medical bills and lost wages, but only $50,000 in insurance coverage.

How can pay-as-you-drive no-fault provide so much more in benefits at such low cost? Under the current system, insurers and their agents must deal, one on one, with 125 million separate automobiles. Under the new system, all 125 million would be covered automatically. Insurers would have to deal only with the much smaller number that were involved in accidents. After all, what useful services does an insurer render a policyholder until he has a claim?

In 1980, Americans paid $40 billion in auto insurance premiums and purchased something in excess of 100 billion gallons of gas. If instead of paying premiums directly they had paid 40 cents a gallon at the pump, the same $40-odd billion would have been collected. But $10 billion of that amount would *not* have gone for selling and underwriting costs; it could have been used for benefits. Instead of having $30 billion available to adjust and pay claims, there would have been the full $40 billion, or fully a third more. Even today $10 billion goes a long way.

Setting reasonable deductible levels, too, would eliminate hundreds of thousands of inefficient claims—the ones most often inflated and overpaid—leaving billions more available for the serious ones that currently get short shrift.

And billions that had previously gone to legal fees would go to benefits. The incentives would have shifted: we would be sending rehabilitation specialists out after the ambulances instead of lawyers.

The auto insurers would still be settling claims, as they do now. They would make a good profit on that service, as they do now. But they would not be selling or underwriting or billing or issuing policies. All that would no longer be necessary.

The problem in providing automatic theft and collision insurance would, as usual, be one of equity. Drivers of expensive cars might be subsidized by drivers of inexpensive ones. But, also as usual, it would be easy to compensate in any number of efficient ways. You could tie the deductible feature of theft-and-collision coverage to a *percentage* of the value of the car—say 5 percent—rather than to a fixed amount. Thus a fellow whose '78 Chevy had a bluebook value of $4,000 would be subject to a $200 deductible, while the man in the $30,000 Mercedes would have to pay the first $1,500 of any loss. (There could also be ceilings beyond which the Rolls-Royce set would have to obtain their own insurance.) Or you could apply an "insurance adjustment fee" to the sticker price of all new cars, amounting to, say, 5 percent of the amount by which the sticker price exceeded $6,000. Those fees, as easily and efficiently assessed as the sales or excise tax, would simply be added to the insurance fund. That, in turn, would serve to reduce the size of the gasoline tax needed to fund the system.

Or perhaps no adjustment would be required. Because expensive cars tend to get relatively poor gas mileage, under Pay As You Drive their drivers would *automatically* be paying more per mile than small-car drivers. Also, researchers of the Insurance Services Office have found that four-door and more sturdily built auto models actually suffer less damage in accidents on average, and are easier to repair, than most inexpensive compacts and subcompacts.

The problem comes not with figuring out an efficient, equitable auto insurance system that would give almost everyone very substantially more than he is currently getting. The problem comes in figuring out a realistic way to implement such a system in the face of the powerful entrenched interests—insurance companies and agencies and trial lawyers—who fight so hard and with such selfish dedication to preserve the status quo.

Surely the industry itself cannot be expected to propose such sweeping reforms, nor even to ask unorthodox questions. And who else cares? State legislatures are heavily influenced by the legal and insurance lobbies; many state legislators are themselves lawyers or insurance agents. The federal government might be expected to represent our interests, but the federal government is virtually prohibited from even looking into the insurance business.

Dear Licensed Driver [the letter introducing the new system might begin]:

Congratulations. On January 1st a simple, comprehensive, efficient and relatively inexpensive auto insurance plan will go into effect. As detailed below, it will pay *all* damages you incur, after the first $300.

All drivers will pay to fund this program through a 40-cent-a-gallon gasoline tax,* levied at the gas pump. In addition, so that drivers most likely to have accidents contribute their fair share to the program, some will have to pay an extra fee when they renew their drivers' licenses. A table of surcharges is detailed below. Principally, those living in high-risk areas and those with moving traffic violations will have to pay extra.

But there will be no other auto insurance premiums to pay.

Because this system eliminates sales costs, policies, billing and the expense of handling the smallest claims, most households will find that their annual cost for auto insurance declines substantially at the same time as the limits of their coverage are greatly expanded.

After January 1st, if you are involved in an accident and wish to make a claim, simply call the company listed below. Through

---

*This figure would have to rise with inflation, just as auto insurance premiums already do. And it would rise as the average car on the road came to get more miles to the gallon (but of course then we would be buying fewer gallons).

competitive bidding, it has won the right to serve you and many of your neighbors. The company is pledged to handling all claims promptly and fairly. Should you ever have any difficulty obtaining fair and prompt service, however, please write to us, your state insurance department, for assistance.

Signed,

Details would follow. There would be an explanation that, under no-fault, lawsuits would be neither necessary nor permitted, just as they are not under workers' comp. (Insurers could be sued, however, if they failed to settle claims with good faith; manufacturers, highway authorities and the like could be sued if they were believed to be guilty of gross negligence.) There would be a note, too, explaining that benefits would only apply to damages not reimbursed by *other* health plans to which the injured party might belong.

But by and large, the message would be simple and straightforward. No forms to fill out; no six-part coverages to puzzle through. No *need* for an experienced insurance agent to help policyholders choose among an array of baffling coverages and alternatives. And, as the whole subject would have been hotly debated for years prior to passage, if passage ever were possible, most people would probably already understand its particulars, its pros and cons, long before receiving the letter.

Perhaps the most frequently posed objection to this or any similar no-fault plan would be: "If I am seriously injured in an accident that is someone else's fault, why shouldn't I be entitled to extra damages for my pain and suffering?" The answer (other than that the plan *could* incorporate a schedule of such benefits): Under the present system it is generally only those who are *not* badly injured who receive, by way of pain-and-suffering payments, more than their medical costs and lost wages. Those who are badly hurt, unless they've had the good fortune to be hurt by someone rich—and sometimes even then—generally receive substantially *less* from auto insurance, after paying their attorneys, than even their actual out-of-pocket damages.

A survey of 60,000 accident victims and 29 insurers published in 1979 by the All-Industry Research Advisory Committee, an insurance-industry organ, found that, under the current system, "persons with economic losses [medical and lost wages] up to $2,500 received payments of more than $2 for every $1 of economic loss [before paying their lawyers]" while those with losses above $10,000 received *less* than a dollar back for each dollar of loss —*before* paying their attorneys and *after* taking into account health insurance payments other than auto insurance coverage. The study also found that under fault systems, only about 46 percent of the claimants had begun receiving insurance payments within 90 days of notifying the insurance company of their injuries. Under no-fault systems, the comparable figure was 81 percent.

(Interestingly, the study also found that under a "fault" insurance system, claimants with economic losses under $500 received more from the system if they were represented by an attorney, even after paying the estimated attorney fees. But *"claimants with economic losses greater than $2,000 received a larger net return if they were not represented by an attorney."* Also, "Attorney-represented claims took considerably longer to settle than nonrepresented claims. For BI [bodily injury] claims, those with attorneys took an average of 500 days from first report of injury to final payment, compared with an average of 100 days for nonrepresented claims.")

Pay As You Drive is not a new idea. It has been proposed in a few places, such as the California legislature in 1975 (it got nowhere) and, in an even more modest form, in Florida in 1976. (There the premium was to be paid as an add-on to the licensing fee, not a gas tax, and would have been higher for drivers who caused accidents than for those who did not.) It, too, got nowhere. "Immediate opposition from the insurance lobby" was cited by the bill's sponsors as one of the reasons.

A system of pay-as-you-drive no-fault liability insurance was introduced in New Zealand in 1974. It works.

WELL, THEN, HOW ABOUT GROUP AUTO?

If it is foolish to hope for a fair and efficient auto insurance system—if our insurance industry and elected representatives, with a little help from the trial bar, will protect us from it—then one step in the right direction that's *not* a pipe dream is group auto insurance.

Already some insurers have begun offering pseudo group plans, under which an employer in effect negotiates a group rate, thereby saving its employees some of the sales commission and overhead charges they would otherwise pay. But the insurers behind these plans must then still rate each applicant and issue individual policies.

As of mid-1980, the only insurer offering genuine group auto insurance—under which all employees were automatically covered, with their dependents, for both bodily injury and property damages—was Aetna. Already in the group life and health fields, Aetna Life & Casualty in 1974 set up a subsidiary, Aetna Casualty & Surety Company of America (as distinct from Aetna Casualty & Surety, set up in 1883, or Aetna Casualty & Surety of Illinois, set up in 1971), to offer group casualty coverages—auto first, but someday group homeowners insurance and group legal insurance.

With just 2,000 people insured under this experimental coverage recently, the difficulties Aetna was encountering were three. First, there was opposition from the agents and brokers who make their living selling auto insurance one policy at a time. Second, many states, including California, under pressure from these tens of thousands of local businessmen, no small number of whom serve on state legislatures, refused to allow Aetna to offer group auto coverage. If Aetna offered low rates to participants of group plans, the states argued, it would be discriminating unfairly against *non*-group participants. Aetna is in the process of fighting each such state one by one. Third, to the extent employers contributed to the cost of this coverage, it would be taxed as income to the employees. This is not the case with other fringe benefits, such as an employer's contribution to an employee's health plan. Aetna was hoping this could be changed, also.

Group plans will probably proliferate. Unions may be instrumental in pushing for this eminently sensible fringe benefit. One incidental advantage may turn out to be a reduction in fraud. Whether out of loyalty or fear, employees may be more hesitant to submit padded or fraudulent claims to their personnel departments than to some distant, faceless and relatively powerless insurance company. But useful as group auto insurance would be in trimming fat from the national auto insurance system, it *is* unfortunate that so many licensed drivers would be left out of these plans. With national no-fault pay-as-you-drive auto insurance, we could all be members of the group.

•　•　•

Attention must now be paid to the impact all this would have on the 70,000 property/casualty insurance agencies that dot the landscape.

The Independent Insurance Agents of America, as they are known, are already under attack and have been for some time. They have been losing business to the direct writers, like Allstate, State Farm and GEICO, who sign up auto and homeowners policies by mail or through their own network of agents. The reason for this is simple. The direct writers are more efficient; they can charge less; people like low prices.

National no-fault pay-as-you-drive auto insurance would wipe out many independent agents. What would they do instead? And who would provide the *non*-automotive coverages, like homeowners insurance, that they sell?

The second question is easy. There are any number of ways that homeowners insurance could be sold much more efficiently than it is now. In addition to the direct writers who sell a great deal of it already, one logical sales agent for homeowners insurance would be real estate agents. We have them aplenty, Lord knows, and it would be a simple matter for them to provide property insurers with information, photographs and appraisals. They could, logically and efficiently, offer homeowners insurance to their clients. Many already do.

An equally good candidate would be the banks, either acting as sales agents for insurers (as they already do when they sell credit insurance) or, if the law were changed, providing the insurance themselves. The bank that provides a mortgage *already* has to appraise the property—and the lender. Why fill out two sets of applications? Why make two appraisals? Why duplicate billing?

"Truth in Lending" safeguards would have to be extended to be sure that a borrower could sort out the cost of his loan from the cost of his insurance, thus to be able to compare rates with competitive banks. And the borrower would have to be clearly guaranteed the right *not* to accept the insurance coverage (provided it were obtained elsewhere) once the mortgage commitment was made, so that a bank couldn't force the sale of one by threatening to withhold the other. But such safeguards would not be hard to enact. And if banks could offer a better rate by virtue of the economies of combining the mortgage and the insurance—all the better.

And then there are those independent agents who would manage to remain after most of their colleagues had closed up shop. These would be the agents who are strong in commercial lines, providing insurance to small businesses and, perhaps, to the carriage trade of the individual market—the Rolls-Royce owner who finds pay-as-you-drive theft coverage insufficient for his needs.

Undeniably, a much more efficient auto insurance system would put a lot of people out of work. Mechanized farm equipment did the same thing. But keeping men and women employed at jobs that don't need doing can hardly be the way, long-term, to keep them, and the rest of us, prosperous.

12

THEY BET YOUR LIFE
What Kind of Risk Are You?

*Individuals having an abdominal girth greater than their chest
expanded measurement are the least desirable type of
overweights. An extra mortality debit in addition to that
assessed for their overweight is applied. See BUILD.*
—**Life Insurance Underwriting Manual**

Are you insurable?

How long are you likely to live?

Among the first to study longevity was Edmund Halley, the British astronomer. In 1693, Halley published "An estimate of the Degrees of the Mortality of Mankind drawn from Curious Tables of the Births and Funerals at the City of Breslaw." By analyzing the deaths that occurred in Breslau (now Wroclaw, Poland) between 1687 and 1691, Halley concluded (with perhaps just a bit more precision than was justified):

A Breslavian Aged	Might Expect to Live Another	To Age
0	33.50 years	33.50
5	41.55 years	46.55
10	39.99 years	49.99
15	36.86 years	51.86
20	33.61 years	53.61
25	30.38 years	55.38
30	27.35 years	57.35

(continued)

A Breslavian Aged	Might Expect to Live Another	To Age
35	24.51 years	59.51
40	21.78 years	61.78
45	19.22 years	64.22
50	16.81 years	66.81
55	14.51 years	69.51
60	12.09 years	72.09
65	9.73 years	74.73
70	7.53 years	77.53
75	5.99 years	80.99
80	5.74 years	85.74

Today people live longer. American life expectancies in 1980 were about as follows:

An American Aged	Is Expected to Live to
0	73.3
5	74.5
10	74.6
15	74.7
20	75.0
25	75.4
30	75.7
35	76.0
40	76.4
45	76.9
50	77.6
55	78.5
60	79.8
65	81.3
70	83.2
75	85.4
80	88.2

Notice that an 80-year-old today—notwithstanding the benefits of modern medicine, hygiene and central heating—may be expected to live only two or three years longer than would have been the case in the seventeenth century. Man's natural life span, 75 to 90 years or so, has not increased. It is the number of us who manage to attain it that has increased.

There are several ways of arranging longevity statistics. Here is another:

Of 1,000 Americans Born Today

It Is Expected That About This Many	Will Still Be Alive at Age
1,000	0
984	5
982	10
980	15
975	20
968	25
962	30
955	35
946	40
932	45
911	50
877	55
829	60
759	65
670	70
555	75
409	80
260	85
116	90
35	95
7	100

But life insurance—being in fact death insurance—can best be understood by considering not how long people are likely to live (longevity), but how likely they are to die (mortality).

Of 1,000 Americans Aged	About This Many Are Expected to Die This Year
0	14.2
5	.4
10	.2
15	.8
20	1.3
25	1.3
30	1.3
35	1.7

(continued)

Of 1,000 Americans Aged	About This Many Are Expected to Die This Year
40	2.5
45	4.0
50	6.3
55	9.5
60	15.1
65	21.3
70	31.5
75	50
80	75
85	125
90	185

Armed with data like this—knowing the odds—one could start one's *own* life insurance society.

Say you belonged to a club of 1,000 45-year-olds and wanted to provide each with $100,000 of life insurance protection. How much would you charge? You could simply pass a hat around every time somebody died, with each of your 1,000 members chipping in $100. That would raise $100,000.* But what if you wanted to do the billing annually, in advance? Expecting about four deaths during the year (see above), you might charge $400 per member. Or, to be on the safe side, you might charge $800 or $1,000, promising to refund whatever might be left over at the end of the year. (You could call this refund a "dividend," as the life insurance companies do, but it would actually just be the return of an overpayment.)

If you and your members were arranging this scheme purely for each other's mutual benefit, refunding any excess premiums, yours would be a mutual insurance company. Or—mutual benefit be damned—you could form your *own* company to offer life insurance to your fellow members, keeping for yourself whatever might remain after expenses and death claims. Yours would be a stock company.

In 1981, Presidential Life (a stock company) was offering $100,000 of life insurance to 45-year-olds at an annual premium of just $320 for men, $234 for women. Impossible? The "catch," if you can

---

*I know—with the deceased out of action there would be only 999 members. But this club has a *waiting list*, and no sooner does a member drop out than another rushes in to fill his place.

call it that, is that, like virtually all life insurance offers, this one wasn't open to just anybody. Rather, the worst applicants were screened out. In an *average* group of 1,000 45-year-old Americans the annual death toll is expected to be about four. But that includes diabetics, alcoholics, manic depressives and Air Force test pilots. Weed out the worst risks, and the expected mortality drops sharply. The process of screening risks is called underwriting.

Just as claims adjusters are paid to keep an insurer's losses low by looking out for bad claims, so are life underwriters paid to keep them low by weeding out bad risks. They are not unlike the credit managers in an industrial concern who will occasionally infuriate salesmen by rejecting an order from a poor credit risk.

"If I bring in a $4 million sale," says a life insurance salesman who occasionally does, "the underwriter is immediately suspicious. There may be a perfectly legitimate reason for so much insurance, but the underwriter is thinking, What's the scam? What are they hiding from me?" The underwriter is especially suspicious, this salesman says, if, heaven forfend, there should be a $180,000 check for the first year's premium stapled to the application.

The underwriter may perhaps be forgiven his suspicious nature. He is up against a feature of all life insurance contracts called "incontestability." No matter how outrageously misleading or false a policyholder's insurance application may have been, after two years it becomes incontestable. Forgot to mention that your favorite sport is Russian roulette? That your urine is fluorescent? If the omission or fraud is material and you die within two years, your beneficiary will receive only a refund of the premiums paid plus interest. But thereafter the policy is payable in full.*

The earliest British life insurance societies accepted members with no selectivity of any kind. All but the very young and very old

---

*"This clause is of vast importance and benefit," ruled a court in 1906, "both to the insured and the insurer. It enables the latter to increase his business by giving an assurance to persons doubtful of the utility of insurance, that neither they nor their families, after the lapse of a given time, shall be harassed with lawsuits when the evidence of the original transaction shall have become dim, or difficult of retention, or when, perhaps, the lips of him who best knew the facts are sealed by death. That this consideration is a powerful inducement, especially to the poor and obscure, to take out insurance, cannot be doubted; and after the lapse of this reasonable time, it must, of necessity, be of great consolation to the insured to feel that the insurance money, to secure which he has, perhaps, so often endured privation, will be paid over to his family undiminished by court costs or lawyers' fees. . . . The incontestable clause is upheld in law, not for the purpose of upholding fraud, but for the purpose of shutting off harassing defenses based upon alleged fraud . . ." *Kansas Mutual Life* v. *Whitehead*.

were admitted, so long as they paid their entry fee and dues. This naturally tended to attract a preponderance of the unhealthy and infirm.

Some people were insured without their even knowing it, as others bet on their mortality. *George looking a bit pallid this morning? Perhaps I'll take out a small policy on his life.* "A practice . . . prevailed of insuring the lives of well-known personages as soon as a paragraph appeared in the newspapers announcing them to be dangerously ill. The insurance rose in proportion as intelligence could be procured from the servants, or from any of the faculty attending, that the patient was in great danger. This inhuman sport affected the minds of men depressed by long sickness; for when such persons, casting an eye over a newspaper for amusement, saw their lives had been insured in the Alley at 90 per cent, they despaired of all hopes; thus their dissolution was hastened."*

Lacking a sound actuarial basis and effective underwriting techniques (fat people were considered the best risks until the early 1900s), the mortality rate of fledgling life insurers themselves was high throughout the eighteenth and nineteenth centuries.

In 1725, the London Assurance Company struck an early blow for prudence when it instructed its representatives to meet prospective insureds personally. The company's agents were concerned primarily with fire and marine insurance, but from time to time received applications for life insurance, as well. They did not actively sell it. The home office was now directing them to verify applicants' identities; to verify the "insurable interest" (that is, to be sure the proposed beneficiary had a legitimate need for the insurance); and, finally, to ascertain whether or not the applicant had had smallpox. Those who had were granted a lower rate in recognition of their resultant immunity. That was the extent of the life insurance underwriting process. (It is easy to forget the shadow smallpox once cast across Europe and the British Isles. "Every tenth person and one-tenth of all mankind was killed, crippled or disfigured," wrote one who had been spared. "No man dared to count his children as his own until after they had had the disease.")

Greater selectivity and medical sophistication gradually evolved. The two "landmarks" in this evolution were the introduction of routine urine testing, in the late nineteenth century, and the intro-

---

***The Mystery and Inequity of Stock Jobbing,* by Thomas Mortimer, 1781.

duction of sphygmomanometry, early in the twentieth. Sphygmo-
manometers measure blood pressure.

By now, mortality statistics have been honed quite fine. This is
not to say that a plague could not throw them askew. Halley's own
comet, should its tiny icy nucleus collide directly with Brooklyn or
Detroit when it returns in 1985, could cause a jag in the otherwise
smooth computer curves. But under ordinary circumstances we do
know with a fair degree of statistical confidence how long people of
various ages, sexes and states of health, on average, will live. And
this is where the "law of averages" (or "law of large numbers"),
so crucial to the insurance game, comes into play.

On average, a coin flipper will flip heads half the time. *Unquestionably.* But it would hardly astound anyone to hear that, in the
course of ten coin tosses, heads came up six times. Or seven times.
Or even eight. Any tenth-grade math student can easily calculate
the odds of these not-so-unlikely events occurring. (That those of
us beyond the tenth grade are helpless in the face of this calculation
makes it no less valid.)

Someone who bet $100,000 on each of ten coin tosses would
thus face the slim but daunting chance of losing eight or nine times
out of ten. As the number of tosses increases, however, the chance
that the outcome will vary significantly from the norm declines
rapidly. For example, what do you think are the chances of tossing
800 heads out of 1000?

The chances of tossing eight heads out of ten are about 1 in 19.
(While you were reading this, I was out scouring the neighborhood
for a tenth-grader.) But the chances of tossing 800 heads out of
1,000 are *nil*. Even tossing just 600 heads out of 1,000 will occur
no more than once or twice every 10 billion times you try it.

It would be risky indeed to go into the life insurance business
with just ten lives under contract. (Or into the casino business for
just ten minutes.) Insurers like the Prudential spread their bets over
millions. (Twenty-six million, in the case of the Prudential.)

One of the principles of life insurance underwriting—in part out
of respect for the law of averages—has thus always been to include
as many lives as possible in the "standard" pool. Marketing consid-
erations aside (it being a lot easier to sell insurance if you don't have
to turn down applicants or concoct a special rate for each one), the
idea is to have as large a pool as possible to conform to statistical
expectations. *Ninety out of a hundred Americans who apply for life*

insurance today are able to obtain it at standard rates. Of the ten remaining, seven are considered "substandard" risks, charged correspondingly higher rates; three are considered such poor risks that their business is declined altogether.

The odds of qualifying are even better for people in their twenties and thirties, exceedingly few of whom are in such poor health as to be uninsurable at standard rates. And, of course, once an insurance contract *is* issued, it remains in force no matter how bad your health subsequently becomes.

APPLICANTS FOR LIFE INSURANCE

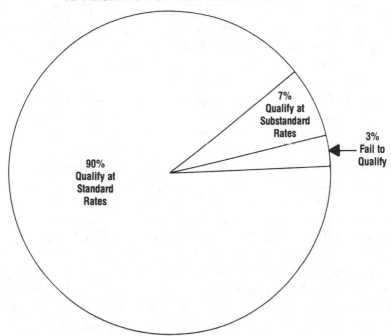

CAUTION: THE INSURANCE INDUSTRY IS BEGINNING TO THINK SMOKING MAY BE HAZARDOUS TO YOUR HEALTH

What may seem a relatively small difference in terms of longevity—for example, that women live five or six years longer than men—becomes an enormous difference when viewed in terms of mortality.

In the long run, it is true, we are all dead; our mortality is 100 percent. But from the point of view of an insurer, it is those relative few who die prematurely—in their twenties, thirties, forties, fifties and sixties—who are of particular concern. *Among* those relative few, men outnumber women two to one. Only half as many women as men fail to live out a full natural life span.

It is only reasonable, therefore, to charge women less for life insurance than men. Most life insurers have been doing so for a very long time. (For medical and disability insurance the reverse is true. Women in comparable occupations incur a higher level of medical and disability claims than men, and so are charged more.) Rather than construct separate rate books for men and women, most insurers simply "subtract" three to five years from a woman's age in figuring the rate she pays. A 47-year-old woman might pay the rate for a 43-year-old man. At most ages, this does not fully reflect the degree to which women are better risks than men. Their rates should be lower still. Even so, an insurer wouldn't dream of accepting applicants without regard to sex.

The insurance industry is frequently credited with having helped society to see and reduce risks. But it was not until late 1979 that an insurer finally compiled and released data that compared the mortality experience of insured smokers and non-smokers. Looking at the mortality of 105,000 of its policyholders, State Mutual Life (Worcester, Massachusetts) found death rates at all ages to be more than twice as high among smokers as among non-smokers. In the case of respiratory cancer, the rate was fifteen times higher. Smoking shortened the life expectancy of a 32-year-old male by 7.3 years. It proved to have an even greater impact on mortality than sex. (Indeed, one of the *reasons* women live longer than men is that fewer smoke, although the gap is narrowing.) Yet *this* is an underwriting criterion that until very recently received little attention. Only in 1980 did the practice of offering (modest) discounts to non-smokers become at all widespread.

Prompted by the famous Surgeon General's Report, first published in 1964, State Mutual began offering discounts to the nearly two-thirds of the adult American population that does not smoke. But it was one of the few insurers to do so. Had an enterprising actuary at one of the scores of large life insurers undertaken a similar study in the 1920s, or surely the 1950s, he or she might have preceded the Surgeon General by many years. No other industry had so much to gain by confirming the connection between death and tobacco—and none was so neatly situated to quantify it. Such a head start in public awareness of the dangers of smoking would unquestionably have saved thousands upon thousands of lives. An effective way of dramatizing the health menace would have been the life insurance price differential only now beginning to be applied.

In theory, the non-smoker discount (or smoker surcharge) should be very large—not just the "substantial" savings "up to 14 percent" that Prudential announced proudly in the fall of 1980.

"In fact," says an executive of Britain's Prudential Assurance Company, "the practical difficulty is quite simply stated: we know that we ought to apply a steeply increasing scale of surcharges to proposers who smoke 20, 30, 40 or 50 cigarettes per day, but in practice we have not much redress against a proposer who conceals excessive cigarette smoking; nor is there much we can do about someone who says he has given up smoking and then, three months after he has effected a policy, relapses into his former habits."* Can insurers rely on applicants to describe their smoking habits accurately? How should they differentiate between heavy and light smokers? Between never-smokeds and quit-last-years?

Apart from such practical problems, many insurers hesitate to differentiate between smokers and non-smokers because they want the standard risk classification to be as broad as possible. "This principle of insurance would be completely undermined if preferred risks were taken out of the standard class," Brackenridge writes. "Furthermore, if nonsmokers receive preferential treatment, what right is there to withhold such treatment from applicants who are somewhat underweight, have ideal blood pressures, do not drink, and do not drive automobiles?" What right, indeed? As life insurance becomes increasingly price competitive throughout the remainder of this decade, as there is reason to expect it will, insurers are likely increasingly to differentiate among the 90 percent of all lives now simply rated "standard." On large policies, where more than a few dollars are involved, they will attempt to attract the best risks by offering them the best rates.

RATING YOUR LIFE EXPECTANCY

The numerical rating system most underwriters use—explicitly, with a tally sheet, or implicitly, based on years of experience and

---

*As quoted in Dr. R.D.C. Brackenridge's authoritative *Medical Selection of Life Risks*.

"feel"—starts out by assigning each applicant a base of 100 points. This is the score of an average life insured at standard rates. From this base are subtracted credits for particularly favorable attributes; and to it are added debits for unfavorable attributes. The final "score" thus compares the candidate with people who have already qualified for insurance at standard rates. Anyone who scores in the range of 80 to 125 or so—whose risk of dying at any given age is 80 percent to 125 percent of standard—qualifies for standard rates. Higher scores, representing higher mortality rates, bring with them proportionately higher premiums.

An applicant who scores 200—who is thought, that is, to be twice as likely as the standard risk to die prematurely—will likely be rated "Class D" or "Table 4" (see below) and pay twice the normal premium. (For whole life, because of the savings element, the calculation is different, but the principle is the same.)

SUBSTANDARD CLASSIFICATIONS

Class*	Table*	Numerical Score	Mortality	Effect on a $1,000 Standard Term Premium
Standard	Standard	80-125	100%	$1,000
A	1	125-130	125%	1,250
AA	1½	135-140	137½%	1,375
B	2	145-155	150%	1,500
BB	2½	160-165	162½%	1,625
C	3	170-185	175%	1,750
D	4	190-210	200%	2,000
E	5	215-235	225%	2,250
F	6	240-260	250%	2,500
G	7	265-285	275%	2,750
H	8	290-325	300%	3,000
J	10	330-380	350%	3,500
L	12	385-450	400%	4,000
P	16	455-550	500%	5,000

*Some insurers use alphabetical ratings, others numerical. It amounts to the same thing. The idea of "class underwriting" is to group like classes of risk together, and then allow them to share that risk.

Even the least intuitive mind is likely to sense a relationship between one's mortality classification and his or her life expectancy. Experience has shown the relationship to be roughly as follows:

THE UNFORTUNATE EFFECT OF MORTALITY ON LONGEVITY

A Man This Age	Is Expected to Live This Many More Years If His Expected Mortality Is					
	Standard	150%	200%	300%	500%	1000%
25	48	44	41	37	32	25
35	39	35	32	28	24	18
45	30	26	23	19	16	11
55	23	20	17	14	11	8
65	16	13	11	9	7	4

Example: The average 45-year-old male who qualifies for insurance at standard rates may be expected to live another 30 years or so, but only nineteen years more if his mortality is rated three times standard.

Life expectancies for women follow the same pattern; simply add three to five years across the board.

Numerical rating is neither rigid nor entirely scientific. Each underwriter interprets applications his own way; each company applies its own degree of conservatism. It is not at all uncommon for an applicant to be rated standard by one insurer, substandard by another. In part it is a question of business strategy. An insurer can do very thorough and strict underwriting, paying for medical exams and turning away or discouraging a lot of business in the process; or it can charge rates high enough to accommodate a somewhat less rigorously screened pool of applicants.

Too, a 49-year-old applicant for $2 million of coverage is scrutinized rather more closely than a 29-year-old applying for $50,000. Medical exams are frequently dispensed with for candidates under 40 applying for coverage of $50,000 or less. In such cases, underwriters rely on the information the candidate himself provides and, often, a brief corroboration from his physician.

Insurers may also query the Medical Information Bureau, in Boston, a non-profit information bank subscribed to by more than 700 life insurers. Originally founded in 1890 as the "Rejection Exchange," the bureau currently maintains records on 11 million of us—in code, to maintain privacy. Typically, an insurer will send to the bureau information on an applicant who has failed to qualify as a standard risk. That by no means keeps him from obtaining insurance elsewhere—bureau bylaws forbid blackballing an applicant without further examination—but keeping records for seven years, as the bureau does, makes it less likely he will get it by lying about his medical history. Underwriters can call up an applicant's file from the M.I.B. as an airline clerk might call up your reservation, in a matter of minutes. (In the fine print of most insurance applications is the statement whereunder you grant permission for all this.)

Without in any way attempting to describe all the possible debits an applicant might merit (there are relatively few credits), the underwriting guidelines that follow may provide some sense of the art.

Age and sex. These essential criteria do not figure into the rating process, because premiums are already geared to take them into account. The question in deciding whether you qualify for standard rates isn't how old you are but how well you compare with others your own age.

Family history. Alexander Graham Bell (no less), whose own parents lived to 86 and 88, and who himself reached 75, demonstrated that longevity most definitely runs in the family. He compared children whose parents both died under 60 with children whose parents both reached 80. The former group lived, on average, a mere 32.8 years, while the latter reached an average age of 52.7— almost twenty years more! American longevity has of course improved dramatically in the hundred-odd years since Bell's subjects expired; nor is it at all clear how much of the longevity inheritance is hereditary ("good stock") and how much economic (good stocks). The wealthy tend to live longer; and, in turn, to pass along the benefits of the best medical care, hygiene and nutrition. (Affluence, rather than genetics, is the primary reason whites live significantly longer than non-whites.)

Whatever accounts for it, inherited longevity is of interest to underwriters. Applicants whose parents both died under 60 may have 15 or more mortality points added to their scores (especially if they exhibit similar medical characteristics themselves); offspring of long-lived parents and grandparents may have their scores *reduced* by up to 15 points.

Marital status. People in stable relationships—married couples primarily, but others as well—live longer than those—single, widowed or divorced—who live alone. Professor James Lynch, scientific director of the Psychophysiological Laboratories at the University of Maryland Medical School and author of *The Broken Heart: The Medical Consequences of Loneliness,* estimates that among divorced white males under 70 who live alone the incidence of fatal heart disease and lung cancer about doubles. The fatal statistics on cirrhosis of the liver and hypertension are even more grim (not to mention suicide). Insurance applicants will not automatically be debited for living alone, but it is a factor an underwriter may consider.

Build. Until the early part of this century, thinness was associated with tuberculosis; heft with plenty of food and a good disposition. When studies relating build to mortality were finally published, just the opposite proved true. The best life insurance risks tend to be lighter than average; excess weight poses a serious hazard. (Except in the case of suicide. Overweights show a markedly *lower* suicide rate. "Thus the expression 'laugh and grow fat' may after all contain a grain of truth," writes Brackenridge.)

An applicant's weight in relation to height is often the first clue an underwriter considers. Following this page is a table, applicable to both men and women, that underwriters use to assign credits and debits. The number in italics indicates the number of mortality points to be subtracted or added to an applicant's score. Note that *severe* underweights have points added to their mortality rating, but that those moderately under average have points deducted.

A person six feet four inches tall who weighed 320 pounds would have 110 points added to his (or her) score, which, if there were no other debits or credits, would then total 210. Meaning that in any given year the chance of death would be a little more than twice as great as for someone in the standard pool. Life insurance would be available, but it would not be cheap.

A mitigating factor to which underwriters look in rating overweights is body type. To a layman, people are "skinny," "fat" or "muscular." To an underwriter, we are "ectomorphs," "endomorphs" or "mesomorphs." The 320-pound applicant above would be looked on more kindly if his or her expanded chest measurement substantially exceeded his or her waist—but with dismay if the opposite were true.

(This table, abbreviated slightly, leans toward the conservative. Particularly for female applicants, underwriters may be less strict in assigning rating points.)

Blood pressure. Pull out your sphygmomanometer and then find your debit in the tables that follow. With luck, you *won't* find yourself. Your blood pressure will be too low to be of concern to a life insurance underwriter. But if you are 45 and your blood pressure is

RATING YOUR BUILD (*mortality ratings shown in italics*)

Weight in pounds

Height																					
4 ft. 10"	82	88	95	101	107	113	120	126	132	139	145	151	158	164	170	176	189	202	214	227	239
	20	*20*	*0*	*-10*	*-10*	*-5*	*-5*	*-5*	*0*	*0*	*10*	*15*	*20*	*25*	*35*	*50*	*75*	*95*	*130*	*170*	*205*
5 ft. 0"	86	92	99	106	112	119	125	132	139	145	152	158	165	172	178	185	198	211	224	238	251
	20	*15*	*0*	*-10*	*-10*	*-5*	*-5*	*-5*	*0*	*5*	*10*	*15*	*20*	*25*	*35*	*50*	*75*	*100*	*135*	*175*	*215*
2"	90	97	104	110	117	124	131	138	145	152	159	166	173	179	186	193	207	221	235	248	262
	20	*15*	*0*	*-10*	*-10*	*-5*	*-5*	*0*	*0*	*5*	*10*	*15*	*20*	*25*	*35*	*50*	*75*	*100*	*135*	*175*	*220*
4"	95	102	110	117	124	131	138	146	153	161	168	175	183	190	197	204	219	234	248	263	277
	20	*15*	*0*	*-10*	*-10*	*-5*	*-5*	*0*	*0*	*5*	*10*	*15*	*20*	*25*	*35*	*50*	*75*	*105*	*135*	*180*	*220*
5"	98	105	113	120	128	135	143	150	158	165	173	180	188	195	203	210	225	240	255	270	285
	20	*15*	*0*	*-10*	*-10*	*-5*	*-5*	*0*	*0*	*5*	*10*	*15*	*20*	*25*	*35*	*50*	*80*	*105*	*140*	*180*	*230*
6"	100	108	116	123	131	139	146	154	162	169	177	185	193	200	208	216	231	246	262	277	293
	20	*15*	*0*	*-10*	*-10*	*-5*	*-5*	*0*	*0*	*5*	*10*	*15*	*20*	*30*	*40*	*50*	*80*	*105*	*140*	*180*	*235*
7"	103	111	119	126	134	142	150	158	166	174	182	190	198	205	213	221	237	253	269	284	300
	20	*15*	*0*	*-10*	*-10*	*-5*	*-5*	*0*	*5*	*10*	*15*	*20*	*25*	*30*	*40*	*50*	*80*	*105*	*140*	*180*	*240*
8"	105	113	122	130	138	146	154	162	170	178	186	194	203	211	219	228	243	259	275	292	308
	20	*15*	*0*	*-10*	*-10*	*-5*	*-5*	*0*	*5*	*10*	*15*	*20*	*25*	*30*	*40*	*50*	*80*	*110*	*140*	*180*	*240*
9"	108	116	125	133	141	149	158	166	174	183	191	199	208	216	224	232	249	266	282	299	315
	20	*15*	*0*	*-10*	*-10*	*-5*	*-5*	*0*	*5*	*10*	*15*	*20*	*25*	*30*	*40*	*50*	*80*	*110*	*140*	*180*	*240*
10"	111	119	128	136	145	153	162	170	179	187	196	204	213	221	230	238	255	272	289	306	323
	20	*15*	*0*	*-10*	*-10*	*-5*	*-5*	*0*	*5*	*10*	*15*	*20*	*25*	*30*	*40*	*50*	*80*	*110*	*140*	*180*	*240*
11"	114	123	131	140	149	158	166	175	184	193	201	210	219	228	236	245	263	280	298	315	333
	20	*15*	*0*	*-10*	*-10*	*-5*	*-5*	*0*	*5*	*10*	*15*	*20*	*25*	*30*	*40*	*50*	*80*	*110*	*140*	*180*	*240*
6 ft. 0"	117	126	135	144	153	162	171	180	189	198	207	216	225	234	243	252	270	288	306	324	342
	20	*15*	*0*	*-10*	*-10*	*-5*	*-5*	*0*	*5*	*10*	*15*	*20*	*25*	*30*	*40*	*50*	*75*	*110*	*140*	*180*	*240*
1"	120	129	138	147	156	166	175	184	193	202	212	221	230	239	248	258	276	294	313	331	350
	20	*15*	*0*	*-10*	*-10*	*-5*	*-5*	*0*	*5*	*10*	*15*	*20*	*25*	*30*	*40*	*50*	*75*	*110*	*140*	*180*	*240*
2"	123	132	142	151	161	170	180	189	198	208	217	227	236	246	255	265	284	302	321	340	359
	20	*15*	*0*	*-10*	*-10*	*-5*	*-5*	*0*	*5*	*10*	*15*	*20*	*25*	*30*	*40*	*50*	*75*	*110*	*140*	*180*	*240*
4"	130	140	150	160	170	180	190	200	210	220	230	240	250	260	270	280	300	320	340	360	380
	20	*15*	*0*	*-10*	*-10*	*-5*	*-5*	*0*	*5*	*10*	*15*	*20*	*25*	*30*	*40*	*50*	*75*	*110*	*140*	*180*	*250*

RATING YOUR BLOOD PRESSURE

Ages 40 to 49

Systolic Pressure

	132	136	140	144	148	152	156	160	164	168	172	176	180	184	188	192	
84	0	0	0	0	10	15	25	35	45	60	75	95	105	120	140	160	84
86	0	0	0	10	15	20	30	40	55	70	85	105	115	130	150	170	86
88	0	0	10	15	20	25	40	50	65	80	95	110	125	145	165	185	88
90	0	10	15	20	25	35	50	60	75	90	105	125	140	160	180	200	90
92	10	20	30	40	45	55	65	75	85	100	120	140	155	175	195	215	92
94	20	30	40	50	55	65	75	85	100	115	135	155	170	190	210	235	94
96	35	50	60	70	70	80	90	100	115	130	150	170	185	205	225	250	96
98	45	60	80	90	90	95	105	115	130	145	165	185	200	220	240	265	98
100	60	75	85	90	100	110	120	130	150	165	185	205	220	240	260	285	100
102	80	90	100	110	120	130	140	150	175	190	205	225	240	260	285	305	102
104	90	110	125	135	150	160	170	180	200	215	230	245	260	285	310	335	104
108	150	160	170	190	200	220	230	240	250	260	275	295	315	335	355	385	108
112	—	—	220	240	260	275	295	305	310	320	335	355	375	395	415	445	112
	132	136	140	144	148	152	156	160	164	168	172	176	180	184	188	192	

Diastolic Pressure (left axis label)

Ages 1 to Under 40: The table for those under 40 is very similar to that above. Just add 5 to 10 points to the low ratings, 15 to 20 points to the higher ones.

Ages 50 to 59: The table for these ages follows the same pattern. Simply find your rating, if any, from the tables above and below and take a rough average of the two.

Ages 60 and Over

Systolic Pressure

	132	136	140	144	148	152	156	160	164	168	172	176	180	184	188	192	
84	0	0	0	0	0	5	10	10	20	30	40	50	60	80	100	125	84
86	0	0	0	0	5	10	15	15	25	35	45	60	70	90	110	135	86
88	0	0	0	0	10	15	20	25	35	45	55	70	85	100	120	145	88
90	0	0	0	10	15	20	25	30	40	50	65	80	95	110	130	155	90
92	10	10	10	15	20	25	30	35	45	60	75	90	105	120	140	165	92
94	10	15	15	25	25	30	40	45	55	70	85	105	115	130	150	180	94
96	15	15	15	25	25	40	50	55	70	80	95	115	125	140	160	190	96
98	20	25	25	30	35	55	65	70	85	95	110	130	140	155	175	205	98
100	30	30	35	40	50	70	80	85	100	110	125	145	155	170	190	220	100
102	40	45	45	55	65	90	100	105	120	130	145	170	180	200	220	250	102
104	50	60	60	70	80	115	125	130	140	155	170	195	210	230	250	280	104
108	85	95	115	120	130	170	180	190	200	215	225	250	270	290	310	340	108
112	130	150	165	175	185	220	240	260	270	285	300	320	340	360	380	410	112
	132	136	140	144	148	152	156	160	164	168	172	176	180	184	188	192	

Diastolic Pressure (left axis label)

"140 over 95" you are likely to be rated up an extra 50 points or so.

Medical history. Underwriting manuals cover everything from cancer and cerebral palsy, which preclude an applicant's obtaining insurance at the standard rate, to acne and blepharitis (inflammation of the eyelids), which do not. Even fluorescent urine gets a mention. ("May be due to drugs or various dyes used in the manufacture of sweets and candies.")

Hemorrhoids—no problem. Hemophilia—add 100 to 400 points depending on the amount of clotting factor lacking in the blood.

One guide devotes 46 oversized pages, its longest section, to helping underwriters interpret medical data on just the heart. Guidelines for amnesia are more easily summarized: If present at the time of application, postpone writing the policy (and do not rely too heavily on the applicant's recollection of his medical history). If recovery has occurred within the past year, and a cause for the memory loss was identified, such as a concussion, write the business but add 100 points. After two to three years, add 50 to 100. From the fourth year on, 0 to 50.

It is the same sort of scheme with apoplexy (stroke). If the stroke occurred after age 60, if it left serious aftereffects, or if it was not the first, underwriters are advised to decline the risk altogether. But other stroke victims will be able to obtain insurance, with the number of rating points they are assigned diminishing with the number of years that have passed uneventfully since the occurrence.

These are guidelines only, of course. The medical director of a Canadian insurer is particularly liberal in rating applicants who've undergone open heart surgery. Why? Because he himself had a triple coronary bypass and feels fine. Similarly, the medical director of an insurer in Kansas was always liberal in his underwriting of diabetics; he had himself lived with diabetes for 30 or 40 years.

The best life underwriters are accomplished medical and psychological sleuths, flexible enough to break rules when warranted and possessed of considerable insight into what makes people tick (and for how long). Sometimes they draw clues from disorders that are in themselves insignificant:

• Supernumerary nipples—extra ones—are routinely found, according to Brackenridge, in about 1 percent of the population. They pose no hazard in themselves; yet a study of 191 diabetics found no fewer than 57 supernumerary nipples.

• Hay fever sufferers tend to be above average in intelligence, according to Brackenridge, mercurial, and, very often, only-children. Supposedly, they "suffer infections badly," contracting respiratory illness with more than average ease.

• The nearsighted "seem to be more than usually prone to anxiety," while "susceptibility to fear" seems to correlate with the blood coagulation that can become phlebitis. Now you know.

Brackenridge thinks that perhaps the most important observation of all to be made during an insurance physical, and one which is not usually requested, "is an evaluation of personality, temperament and constitution. These have an undoubted influence on future health and longevity." He admits that most moderate personality defects are likely not to be evident during a brief physical. However: "A notable exception is the anankastic or obsessional personality. The individual with this defect is amongst the most exasperating of characters to examine for life insurance; he is always at pains to disclose every minor illness he has had together with their precise dates, for which he often consults his diary. Before signing his statement he insists on reading word-by-word the doctor's account of his history, pointing out unimportant inaccuracies here and there, and when requested to prepare for the physical examination wastes more precious minutes while he slowly undresses, meticulously folds his shirt and vest and neatly places them across a chair before announcing himself ready. [Such individuals] are particularly liable to develop agitated or involutional depression in later life which, if untreated, holds a high risk of suicide." If not for the patient, then surely for the examining physician.

Alcohol. Light drinkers have actually been found to outlive non-drinkers, but alcoholics are three times as likely to die in a given year as the population at large. A good portion of the extra mortality shows up on the highways, which doubles the risk to the company in cases where the insured has chosen the accidental death and disability rider ("double indemnity"). In fact, accidents being the leading cause of death for those under 45, many underwriters will attempt to weed out from their standard pool drivers with a history of recklessness.

One insurer assigns rating points for drinkers this way:

	Social drinking	Mild Excess (bubbly)	Marked Excess (loud, boisterous)	Severe Excess (drunk)
1. 6 times/yr.	0	0	0	25-50
2. Monthly	0	0	50	100+
3. Weekly	0	25-50	100+	150+
4. 3 times/wk.	0	75-100	150+	200 or decline
5. Daily	25+	150+	decline	decline

Other drugs. The same underwriting manual that docks mild inebriates 50 points makes no mention whatever of tobacco. But marijuana is a concern. And current use of hallucinogens or narcotics would generally rule out an applicant for insurance if known.

Kinky Sex. "The individual acting in defiance of laws and customs accepted by society departs from social mores," writes Gaylord L. Payne.* "Often these aberrations involve psychiatric difficulties associated with an unstable personality. Among individuals with social aberrations the incidence of violent death and suicide is high. The underwriter does not seek to judge the morality of these departures in social mores; he seeks only to measure in a reasonable manner the effects on mortality" (lest the stay-at-home Idaho high school principal and his wife subsidize the insatiable West Hollywood masochist). Homosexuals may be rated standard, substandard or declined altogether, depending on the case. Transsexuals are assigned 50 to 150 rating points in "the best cases"; others, ordinarily are declined.

Occupation. Because occupational and avocational risks do not increase with age, they are not dealt with in terms of rating points. Instead, flat surcharges—so many dollars per $1,000 of coverage— are applied. Piloting planes that tow gliders or that report on rush-hour traffic is about as risky for a 25-year-old as for a 50-year-old, so either one is charged, at least by one insurer, an extra $3.50 per $1,000 of insurance. On a $100,000 policy, that comes to $350 a year on top of the regular premium.

Commercial airline pilots—even sky marshals—are billed at standard rates. But air-show participants (including wing walkers) have to lay out an extra $10 per $1,000 annually. Pilots of "experimental hypersonic planes" pay $25 per $1,000. On a $100,000 policy—$2,500 extra per year. The irony is that Francis Gary Pow-

Life and Health Insurance Handbook.

ers survived being shot down in a supersonic high-altitude U-2 reconnaissance plane, but died when his traffic-control helicopter ran out of gas over Los Angeles.

Non-professional pilots are charged no extra if they have sufficient experience and fly no more than 150 hours a year. Beyond that, surcharges may be added. Some insurers will issue pilots otherwise-standard policies that specifically exclude death in the cockpit. A hundred years ago much the same thing was done with dueling, which voided many contracts.

Marine aquarium divers are not charged extra, it being difficult for a professional diver to drown in a fishtank. But cave divers are charged a *"minimum"* of $5 extra per $1,000, while divers who work below 750 feet pay an extra $25 per $1,000 and cannot get waiver of premium or accidental death and dismemberment coverage at any price. Officers and enlisted men in the Naval Submarine Service are rated standard.

Farmers, college teachers and Anglican ministers are considered such good risks that some underwriters will credit them a few points.

Just how often an underwriter is called upon to quote some of these rates is unclear, but there they are, neatly printed: Workers aboard orbiting space stations, $15 per $1,000. Passengers on "extraterrestrial flights beyond earth orbit," $20 per $1,000 "if no landing-and-exit on foreign body" (not some Frenchman, you understand), $25 per $1,000 otherwise.

Ratings change from time to time, and from company to company, so astronauts, and others, are advised to shop around. One suspects the missile-silo workers who in the late 1970s could obtain their life insurance at standard rates have had to pay more since, in 1980, a Titan missile blew up in its silo.

In the nineteenth century, whalers were charged an extra premium. Today's fishermen are rated standard. So are: high-rise window cleaners, amateur boxers, bank guards, cliff divers (except international competitors and professionals), exterminators, municipal police, nuclear energy industry employees, prison guards and sawmill hands. Carnival and circus roustabouts—standard. But trapeze artists and human cannonballs—$3.50 per $1,000. Wild animal trainers (you laugh, but this stuff is important!)—$5.

Chemical warfare workers are rated standard, except for "participants in exposure tests," who pay an extra $2.50 or $3.50 per

$1,000 and periodically have their heads examined.

Also, of course, *overweight* chemical warfare workers, et al, may be rated up like anyone else for their high blood pressure whether or not they pay occupational surcharges.

At $2.50 per $1,000: bomb disposal crew members, cloud seeders and forest-fire water bombers, woodsmen (outside the Pacific Northwest) and snake milkers.

At $5: pilots who fly into hurricanes, who fly search-and-rescue missions, who thin animal herds. Also, woodsmen in the Pacific Northwest.

At $7.50: pilots of single-engine planes in Arctic regions, pilots who transport explosives, professional boxers, stuntmen.

Have I left anyone out? According to the American Council of Life Insurance, only about one applicant in 10,000 is denied insurance because of a hazardous occupation; only about one in 250 is required to pay a surcharge.

Criminal record. Arsonists, extortionists and multiple murderers—as well as loan sharks, prostitutes and madams, according to one guide—should all be turned down for life insurance. First-degree murderers, however, if released from prison or on parole (and single offenders), may be written after a three-year delay at an extra $10 per $1,000 for the first five years of the policy and at standard rates thereafter.

Avocations, sports. It's said insurance is a mirror of society, and, indeed, for just about every human activity there is a set of attendant risks—and an underwriting guideline. One has to think, however, that when insurance underwriters gaze into the mirror they do not, by and large, see themselves.

They rate as standard iceboaters, white-water rafters, jet skiers, judo and karate competitors, hockey players, spelunkers, skin and scuba divers to 50 feet or less, ground-skimming hang gliders affiliated with a club, para-sailors, surfers, skiers, scooter skiers, wind surfers, motorboard surfers, sand surfers—do people actually *do* these things? Even demolition derbyists and those who race their cars across frozen lakes may be surprised to find, should they fill out their insurance applications with sufficient candor to include these insane pastimes, that they are rated standard. Because vehicle speeds in these sports are not great, they are not considered particularly hazardous. Auto-crash enthusiasts, by contrast—this is all printed in the manual—are rated up $2.50 per $1,000 of coverage.

Their sport is defined as "competitive events where the driver purposely attempts to roll the car, 'dive bomb' off a ramp into a parked car (the object being to land directly on top of that car and stay there), or perform similar type stunts involving relatively high speeds and deliberate collisions." Skydivers, too, pay an extra $2.50 to $5 per $1,000. Motorcycle acrobats and jet-propelled dragsters—$15.

Which brings us, I should think, to:

Attempted suicide. Underwriters do not view suicides, even failed ones, with enthusiasm. In the case of a single attempt they will postpone issuing a policy for at least a year, adding 50 to 100 rating points in the second through fifth years, if they accept the risk at all. *Two* attempts are taken even more seriously. A wait of five years is suggested before issuing insurance, with 200 to 300 rating points added if and when a policy is issued. Suicidal *gestures,* however— those in which the victim has arranged the attempt in such a way as to be certain of discovery and rescue—are not to be confused with the real thing, nor viewed so harshly. *Multiple* gestures, on the other hand, are to be rated as if they were two genuine suicide attempts, above.

Foreign residence. In the last century, American life insurers charged an extra premium to those living or traveling in the Deep South, where there was a higher incidence of disease. Mortality among the California gold rushers was determined by New York Life to be about four times normal. Surcharges were added for anyone traveling west of present-day Kansas. With the advent of rail transportation in the 1860s, however, travel restrictions began to disappear.

Today, apart from war and revolution risks, which an underwriter must consider separately, certain areas of the world are thought to present extra risks to American residents or frequent visitors. For "the more habitable and settled areas" of such places as Algeria, Antigua, Argentina, Australia, Western Europe, Mexico and the like, no surcharge is suggested. Likewise Tasmania. But Tanzania is another story. If you are IBM's man in Dar-es-Salaam, or in Togo, Zambia or much of the rest of Africa, you may be charged an extra $3.50 per $1,000—more if you are out beating the bushes for business. Of course, the glaring, gaping flaw in all this, from an insurer's point of view, is that once you have a life insurance policy in force—taken out while IBM had you stationed in Springfield,

Illinois—you cannot be charged extra when you land in Djibouti. Among those countries and provinces whose capital cities rate a $5 per $1,000 surcharge (in peaceful times): Papua New Guinea, Uganda, Vietnam, Manchuria, Rwanda, Mali and Malawi.

And what of the 40-year-old male (100) with a family history of heart trouble (+50) who stands five feet two inches tall but weighs 229 pounds (+175), who lives alone (+50), in Manchuria (+$5 per $1,000), drinks to mild excess with regularity (+100) and has a complicated childhood history of attempted rapes and suicides (+250)?

"I CAN INSURE ANYONE"

Warren B. Eller, of Farmington, Michigan, specializes in placing substandard risks. He once obtained $40,000 of whole life coverage for an 80-year-old woman so sick that she had to cancel her physical five times—which the doctor duly noted on his report. The premium came to $7,000 a year, but, says Eller, who advertises nationally for agents to bring him their hard-to-place risks, it was a way of reducing her potential estate taxes. (The premiums she paid reduced her taxable estate; the proceeds of the insurance, when she died, would pass free of tax to her beneficiary.)

In another case, a 39-year-old executive wanted $250,000 of coverage. Seven years earlier, in 1972, he had lost feeling in his left side—possibly the result of a stroke, although all his tests were normal. Feeling returned, but the next year he had a similar seizure. This time he recovered quickly, Eller says, but again no cause could be found. And then it happened in 1978. In the eyes of most underwriters, such a series of unexplained episodes made the fellow uninsurable. To Eller (whose own life is rated standard and insured for $1.5 million at a level annual premium of $38,000), their uneventful recurrence just proved that the problem, whatever it was, was like water rolling off this odd duck's back.

He met with a German reinsurer on a stopover at Kennedy Airport and described the case. "For all we know," he told the German, "it could be psychosomatic. The guy's under a lot of pressure at work." The German bought the risk at a "Table B" rate (see page 218). The premium came to $5,530 a year. (Standard for this whole life policy, from this insurer, would have been $4,715.50.) The executive was so pleased he almost had another seizure; and Eller, for his trouble, got more or less what he always gets (and splits with the agent who referred him the business)—90 percent of the first year's premium ($4,977) plus 10 percent in each of the nine succeeding years (another $4,977).

To clients who might not be able to get insurance any other way, Eller's commission is but a small detail. Eller tells of the 46-year-old angina sufferer whose "heart was shot" and whose condition precluded follow-ups to the coronary bypass that had been performed in 1978. He had managed, during a treadmill stress test at a recent physical, to reach 90 percent of the maximum expected for a healthy man his age—only to collapse on the treadmill. Cardiopulmonary resuscitation had to be administered to revive him.

Everyone had rejected this case, but Eller chose to look on the bright side. He was encouraged by the fact that this man's father, with a similar heart condition, had survived to 63. And by the fact that he was enrolled in a supervised coronary program, swimming three times a week, walking two miles a day. Says Eller: "He had the will to live!" All that was needed was an insurer willing to bet $200,000 on the fellow's willpower.

Eller found an insurer that rated the man "Table N plus $40 per $1,000 for the first five years." The premium for $200,000 of whole life came to $19,510 for each of the first five years, $11,510 each year thereafter. At those rates, the insurer stood to make out very well. Eller points out that his own commission on this case was limited to the Table N rate—$11,510 a year—and did not apply to the $40 per $1,000 surcharge. The argument is made—indeed, the Federal Trade Commission once tried to make it—that an insurance salesman should be paid commission on the standard portion of the insurance premium only, and not on the additional "rated" portion, which requires little or no extra salesmanship. Why should he profit from the client's ill health? A few companies do limit commissions to the standard portion of a substandard premium. A few others leave the decision to the agent, allowing him to take the extra commission or pass it along to the client. Eller takes the commission.

He has become wealthy specializing in a field relatively few understand, exploiting the reluctance of most insurers to take unusual or aggressive risks. There is really no reason anyone still breathing should be *totally* uninsurable. At some price, any life is a good bet. One relatively new development is a life insurance product called "guaranteed issue graded death." Just about anyone can qualify, albeit at stiff rates, but if death occurs within three years, the beneficiary receives only repayment of premiums plus interest. Thereafter, the full face amount of the policy is paid. Roughly put, Eller says, the logic of such a policy is that "if they can make it three years, they can live forever."

13

GERBER LIFE: LIKE TAKING CANDY FROM A BABY

What Term Insurance Should Cost

We found that the insurance delivery system does not
naturally provide life insurance purchasers
with the information they need to be effective consumers.
The adverse consequences for consumers are grave.
The regulatory initiatives undertaken recently
by the states have been too long delayed
and are inadequate to the task.
—**Representative John E. Moss, December 28, 1978**

There is little that is subjective in determining what life insurance should cost. Life insurance is a commodity, not a bottle of perfume—a fairly simple transaction, like buying a savings certificate or taking out a mortgage. Who would be satisfied with 7 percent interest from a six-month savings certificate when banks right down the street were paying 15 percent? Who would take out a 30-year mortgage at 18 percent when other banks were offering similar mortgages at 11 percent? Not many. But with life insurance, the equivalent happens all the time. Because people cannot compare prices, the industry is not particularly competitive. As a result, it tends to be overpriced and inefficient.

The Gerber people, with nearly 70 percent of the U.S. baby food

233

market, branched out into life insurance in 1968. The plan for young families that they were promoting a dozen years later wouldn't "grate, grind, chop, slice, dice and peel," but it was being pitched on late-night TV almost as aggressively as the gadgets that do.

On its face, it seemed attractive. If you were anywhere from 18 to 45 years old, Gerber would sell you up to $20,000 of life insurance, generally without a medical examination. Premiums, which Gerber repeatedly emphasized were "low cost," naturally depended on the age of the applicant. But once the policy was in force, the premium would not rise for 20 years. Gerber called it "Budget-Priced 20-Year Term Life Insurance."

Respondents to Gerber's ad received a "TV Viewers' Information Center" package, complete with a wide-eyed little baby looking up at them, that laid out the offer in question-and-answer form.

"Why should I have term insurance?" the brochure asked itself.

"Because [it answered] most folks on their way up need maximum protection with a minimum cash outlay."

Gerber Life's "Low Monthly Rates" ranged from $4.04 a month for a man of 18 buying $10,000 worth of insurance up to $26.92 a month ($20,000 of coverage for a 45-year-old). Were these good prices? Awful prices?

The brochure said it was just "16 cents a day for a man age 26 . . . and this low premium is guaranteed not to increase for a full 20 years." Yet far from being a "low premium," 16 cents a day was more than double what a man should have been paying for $10,000 of term insurance at age 26. Even a man of 36 needn't have been paying more than 8 or 9 cents a day. Only by around the last year of this 20-year policy, at age 45 or 46, would 16 cents a day be a good low rate. But as the folks at Gerber must have known when they designed this package, most people, however good their intentions at the time of issue, don't hang on to their policies for 20 years. Most let them lapse much sooner. So most people who accepted Gerber's offer would be paying too much in the early years of their policy—and never getting the benefit of the low rate in the last few years.

There are two ways of determining what life insurance should cost. One is to check out the competition.

Here's how Gerber's rates compared with those of two other companies—Beneficial National (now National Benefit Life) and

Bankers Security Life, both of New York—that sent offers of term insurance to millions of Visa cardholders at about the same time Gerber was advertising *its* policy.

**WHAT A MAN SIGNING UP AT AGE 20 WOULD PAY
EACH YEAR FOR $10,000 OF INSURANCE**

When He Is	Gerber	Beneficial	Bankers
20	$50.88	$19.92	20.20
21	50.88	19.92	20.20
22	50.88	19.92	20.20
23	50.88	19.92	20.20
24	50.88	19.92	20.20
25	50.88	21.04	21.20
26	50.88	21.04	21.20
27	50.88	21.04	21.20
28	50.88	21.04	21.20
29	50.88	21.04	21.20
30	50.88	23.04	23.20
31	50.88	23.04	23.20
32	50.88	23.04	23.20
33	50.88	23.04	23.20
34	50.88	23.04	23.20
35	50.88	29.52	29.80
36	50.88	29.52	29.80
37	50.88	29.52	29.80
38	50.88	29.52	29.80
39	50.88	29.52	29.80

Over the course of 20 years, one would have paid $1017.60 to Gerber, but just $467.60 to Beneficial! What Gerber was charging for $10,000 worth of term insurance over 20 years would have bought you approximately *$25,000* worth from Beneficial. And yet Gerber's material boasted of providing "maximum protection with a minimum cash outlay."

It would be one thing if that extra $550 bought you something. Prestige, convenience, special service. But it doesn't. In the unlikely event you actually did die while one of these policies was in force, Gerber's $10,000 check wouldn't be worth a nickel more to your beneficiary than Beneficial's. Life insurance is a commodity.

One might argue that it is worth paying a little extra to deal with a company you know to be financially impregnable. (Both Gerber and Beneficial are rated B+ by A.M. Best & Co., the "Standard & Poor's" of the insurance industry. Bankers Security is rated A+.) With whole life policies, the financial strength of the insurer *is* important. You want to be sure the savings you build up over the years are safe. But with term insurance, which is "pay-as-you-go" and *not* also a form of savings, you take little risk. If your insurer went broke, you would simply stop making payments and take your business elsewhere. The only real risk is that you could in the meantime have become uninsurable. But as we have seen, only three insurance applicants out of a hundred can't buy insurance; and, in any event, very few life insurers go broke.

Similarly, with auto or homeowner's insurance, you might want to pay extra to deal with a company known for honoring its claims promptly and equitably. But life insurance claims are easy to settle. An insurer might argue that a burglary did not take place, or that you left your keys in the ignition; but it can hardly argue, after a few hours of observing you not breathe, that you are not dead. There can be relatively little variation in the quality of life insurance. The big difference is in the price. *Life insurance is a commodity.*

Gerber's plan could hardly have been designed worse for the "young homeowners" it was pitched at. ("Honey, *here's* something we should send for," exclaimed the young husband in the television ad.) It had you paying much more than necessary when you were young and least able to afford coverage, in order that when you're older, more senior in your career—with the kids much closer to an age when they could fend for themselves—your premiums wouldn't rise. That is what is known among scions of actuarial philosophy as "ass backwards."

Now here is a table that assumes you are 30 years old—and which includes rates not just for Gerber, Beneficial and Bankers, but for Savings Bank Life Insurance as well. SBLI is readily available at savings banks throughout New York, Massachusetts and Connecticut, and is rated A+ by Best.

(It should be noted that under the Beneficial and Bankers "group" plans, offered to bank credit cardholders, rates could rise (or fall) if the mortality experience of the group turned out to be significantly worse (or better) than anticipated. The plans could even be canceled. "In the unlikely event this should happen," wrote Citibank, "Citibank Visa would work to arrange continuance of your insurance under another plan." Finally, because the group premiums were billed automatically, giving up your credit card meant dropping out of the plan.

The SBLI plans had no such restrictions and, like the Beneficial and Bankers plans, were renewable to age 70. Gerber's was renewable only to 65.)

WHAT A MAN SIGNING UP AT AGE 30 WOULD PAY
EACH YEAR FOR $10,000 OF INSURANCE

When He Is	Gerber	Beneficial	Bankers	N.Y. SBLI*	Mass. SBLI*
30	$66.48	$23.04	$23.20	$36	$21
31	66.48	23.04	23.20	36	21
32	66.48	23.04	23.20	36	21
33	66.48	23.04	23.20	36	21
34	66.48	23.04	23.20	36	21
35	66.48	29.52	29.80	41	21
36	66.48	29.52	29.80	41	21
37	66.48	29.52	29.80	41	19
38	66.48	29.52	29.80	41	19
39	66.48	29.52	29.80	41	18
40	66.48	41.56	44.00	47	29
41	66.48	41.56	44.00	47	28
42	66.48	41.56	44.00	47	27
43	66.48	41.56	44.00	47	27
44	66.48	41.56	44.00	47	27
45	66.48	67.40	67.80	57	40
46	66.48	67.40	67.80	57	40
47	66.48	67.40	67.80	57	40
48	66.48	67.40	67.80	57	40
49	66.48	67.40	67.80	57	40

Included in all rates above and on pages 235, 239 and 240 is the waiver-of-premium benefit, which relieves policyholders of the obligation to pay premiums while they are disabled.

*These rates are approximate, as they include an allowance for dividends that could turn out to be higher or lower.

Gerber would charge you $1,329.60; Beneficial, $817.60. But it was much worse than that, because most of the difference comes in the early years, when money is much more valuable. (Given the choice between $50 in cash right now or the promise of $100 in twenty years, which would you select?) In the first ten years of the policy—longer than most people are likely to keep it in force— Gerber charges $665 to Beneficial's $263. Two and a half times as much!

The comparison with Massachusetts Savings Bank Life Insurance is even more remarkable. (The rates in New York and Connecticut, although much lower than Gerber's, still leave a little to be desired.) Do the low rates in Massachusetts presage imminent collapse of their Savings Bank Life Isurance system? Unlikely: Massachusetts SBLI was founded in 1907 by future Supreme Court justice Louis Brandeis and has remained financially sound ever since. Despite the insurance industry's oft-repeated line that "almost nobody *buys* Savings Bank Life Isurance," more than three quarters of a million residents of Massachusetts have had the good sense to do so. They account for $3 billion of life insurance in force.

The question is: What's so special about Massachusetts? Do people live longer there? (No.) *Then why aren't such low rates—or rates close to them—readily available to healthy applicants throughout the U.S.?* Why has the insurance industry been able to keep SBLI out of all but three states; and in those limit the amount of coverage that SBLI can sell? Only New York, Massachusetts and Connecticut allow Savings Bank Life Insurance.* In New York, the banks are limited to policies of $30,000 or less—even though they have repeatedly requested legislative authorization for a higher limit. In Connecticut—where the insurance industry is nothing if not influential—it is just $10,000. Might not residents of Illinois, California and Texas like the low rates SBLI provides? Might not New Yorkers wish to buy more than $30,000 of coverage? What has the insurance lobby been protecting us from all these years?

In Massachusetts, the ceiling on SBLI is $1,000 of coverage multiplied by the number of mutual savings banks offering it. There are currently fifty-three banks in the system, hence a $53,000 ceiling. This doesn't mean that if you want $25,000 of coverage you have to visit twenty-five different banks to get it; but it did mean, up until 1955, that the issuing bank actually had to prepare twenty-five separate policies and mail them to the other banks. And that if you sent in a change-of-beneficiary notice, the clerk would have to make twenty-five copies, without the aid of photocopiers, and mail them out to each bank. It was a stricture imposed by the state legislature at the behest of the life insurance industry to hobble SBLI. In 1955, the $1,000-per-bank limit was raised to $5,000. "So if you bought

---

*You must either live *or* work in New York, Connecticut or Massachusetts to apply for their SBLI. However, New York and Connecticut allow a blood relative to apply for you if he/she lives or works in the state. Of course, once you have SBLI, you do not forfeit it if you move to another area.

$40,000 of insurance," says Francis Pizzella, president of the Massachusetts SBLI Council, "you still got eight policies. Keep in mind there's no legitimate reason for this, and if we could issue one policy it would save a heck of a lot of money. It's just that the people who opposed SBLI would not allow that change." Pizzella introduced legislation on five separate occasions trying to unshackle SBLI. Finally, in 1976, he succeeded in getting the per-bank policy limit raised from $5,000 to $15,000. "So now if you buy the $53,000 limit you need only four policies."

The industry argument goes essentially as follows: Life insurance is a terrific, socially valuable product; the more that is sold, the better for everyone; selling it in any quantity requires an admittedly expensive person-to-person agency force; SBLI just takes sales away from those hard-working agents by skimming off the easiest sales—the ones that need the least persuading—and thus damages the health of the agency system on which our great free enterprise system, in part, depends.

In short: Readily available low-cost life insurance would be a threat to the industry, and whatever threatens the life insurance industry threatens America.

"We have all the consumer interests helping us," continues Pizzella. "But the fact is that the insurance lobby is a very powerful lobby."

The third table, which assumes you are 40 when you sign up, includes term insurance rates for the Aetna and the Equitable, as well.

WHAT A MAN SIGNING UP AT AGE 40 WOULD PAY
EACH YEAR FOR $10,000 OF INSURANCE

When He Is	Gerber	Beneficial	Bankers	N.Y. SBLI*	Mass. SBLI*	Equitable*	Aetna
40	$118.32	$ 43.56	$ 44.00	$ 54	$ 37	$ 91	$ 91
41	118.32	43.56	44.00	54	36	91	91
42	118.32	43.56	44.00	54	35	91	91
43	118.32	43.56	44.00	54	34	91	91
44	118.32	43.56	44.00	54	32	91	91
45	118.32	67.40	67.80	67	40	107	120
46	118.32	67.40	67.80	67	40	107	120
47	118.32	67.40	67.80	67	40	107	120
48	118.32	67.40	67.80	67	40	107	120
49	118.32	67.40	67.80	67	40	107	120

(*continued*)

When He Is	Gerber	Beneficial	Bankers	N.Y. SBLI*	Mass. SBLI*	Equitable*	Aetna
50	118.32	104.84	105.40	88	71	151	175
51	118.32	104.84	105.40	88	68	151	175
52	118.32	104.84	105.40	88	66	151	175
53	118.32	104.84	105.40	88	65	151	175
54	118.32	104.84	105.40	88	62	151	175
55	118.32	163.24	164.00	144	124	192	266
56	118.32	163.24	164.00	144	122	192	266
57	118.32	163.24	164.00	144	120	192	266
58	118.32	163.24	164.00	144	117	192	266
59	118.32	163.24	164.00	144	113	192	266

*These rates are approximate, as they include an allowance for dividends.

Compare Gerber and New York Savings Bank Life Insurance. In order to save a few dollars 15 or 20 years from now, you would have been paying an extra $730 in the first fifteen years.

And all these numbers would have been about twice as large, the price differences about twice as dramatic, if costs were compared for $20,000 of coverage instead of $10,000.

Aetna and Equitable, as you see, offered prices every bit as inflated as Gerber's. The difference was that, far from pushing these plans on TV and calling them "low cost," both companies were downright embarrassed when called upon for rates, explaining that at such low levels of term coverage they really weren't very competitive. A senior executive at Equitable confided that anyone who did not first purchase all the Savings Bank Life Insurance he or she qualified for, before buying additional coverage elsewhere, was throwing money down the drain.

Gerber Life is a mere peanut within the context of the life insurance industry. The reasons for singling it out are, first, that they have been so aggressive in promoting their "low cost" plan; second, that customers are more likely to lower their guard for "the baby people" than for some more traditional insurance salesman; and third, in the frequently faceless world of insurance, Gerber does stand out of the crowd. *But what's important is not Gerber.* What's important is that most consumers, reading Gerber's offer or any other, are ill-equipped to make good buying decisions. As a result, the life insurance industry is not nearly as efficient as it could be.

Unable to discern good value, the market rewards elaborate selling efforts instead.

The second way to know approximately what life insurance "should" cost is to do exactly what the insurance companies do: Check the probability of your dying. For example, the chances of an average American dying in his or her thirtieth year are about 1.3 in 1,000. So if 1,000 30-year-olds signed up for Gerber's plan, each sending in $66.48 for $10,000 of coverage, Gerber would collect $66,480 from the lot of them. When the 1.3 policyholders, conforming neatly to statistical expectation, met their maker, Gerber would have to pay out $13,000 in benefits, leaving it more than $50,000 to cover expenses and profit. In later years, for those who kept their policies, the payout would climb. But for the first 15 of the 20 years, it would be very low indeed. The disclosure notice for the first ten years might read:

It Is Expected That
APPROXIMATELY *25 to 35* CENTS
Of Your Premium Dollar Will Be Used to Pay Claims.
The Remainder, Plus the Interest on Your Money,
We Keep.

This is not to say that, after paying for all those TV ads and brochures, Gerber even makes a profit on its life insurance. I don't know. What matters is not how much or little a given insurer earns in profit, but how much we get for our money.

WHAT YOU SHOULD PAY FOR TERM INSURANCE

Following this page are the odds of your demise. Assuming you are insurable at standard rates, the righthand columns apply. *To ascertain the approximate cost of insuring your life for $1,000 for one year, simply place a dollar sign in front of the number for your age and sex.*

That is the "pure cost" of insurance, before allowing anything for the insurer's expenses or profit. For a 40-year-old male, it comes to $1.91. It simply means that with 1.91 out of 1,000 expected to succumb during the year, the cost of paying each of their beneficiaries $1,000 will total $1,910. (I realize people do not succumb in fractions, but actuarially they do.) Spread over 1,000 policyholders, that's $1.91 apiece. Or, for $*100*,000 coverage, a hundred times as much—$191.

THE ODDS OF YOUR DEMISE
Annual Deaths Per 1,000

AGE	U.S. Population as a Whole 1969–1971		Those Qualifying for Insurance at Standard Rates*	
	MALE	FEMALE	MALE	FEMALE
20	2.12	0.72	1.28	0.48
25	2.17	0.81	1.08	0.53
30	2.10	1.02	0.94	0.63
31	2.18	1.10	0.96	0.66
32	2.28	1.19	0.99	0.69
33	2.39	1.29	1.04	0.72
34	2.52	1.40	1.10	0.77
35	2.68	1.52	1.18	0.82
36	2.88	1.65	1.28	0.90
37	3.12	1.80	1.41	1.00
38	3.39	1.97	1.55	1.12
39	3.69	2.15	1.72	1.27
40	4.01	2.33	1.91	1.44
41	4.35	2.51	2.13	1.62
42	4.73	2.73	2.36	1.81
43	5.18	2.97	2.62	1.99
44	5.68	3.25	2.89	2.18
45	6.23	3.54	3.19	2.37
46	6.81	3.84	3.50	2.57
47	7.44	4.16	3.84	2.77
48	8.12	4.49	4.19	2.99
49	8.87	4.84	4.58	3.23
50	9.69	5.23	5.01	3.50
51	10.59	5.65	5.51	3.79
52	11.61	6.11	6.08	4.11
53	12.75	6.60	6.74	4.48
54	14.00	7.12	7.48	4.86
55	15.34	7.68	8.28	5.26
56	16.76	8.29	9.15	5.65
57	18.27	8.94	10.06	6.01
58	19.87	9.62	11.02	6.35
59	21.28	10.35	12.05	6.70

(*continued*)

	U.S. Population as a Whole 1969–1971		Those Qualifying for Insurance at Standard Rates*	
AGE	MALE	FEMALE	MALE	FEMALE
60	23.39	11.13	13.20	7.11
65	34.63	16.78	21.52	11.45
70	49.91	26.32	34.07	17.79
75	72.64	43.25	56.35	31.99
80	103.67	70.97	87.28	56.56
85	147.30	112.82	135.33	101.10

*Actual insured deaths, particularly among preferred risks, are likely to be fewer. These are the raw data, based on industry-wide mortality experience from 1970–1975. To these data will be added a further safety margin to produce the "Tables K." The Tables K, when approved by the various states, will supplant the "1958 CSO Table" currently used in determining the adequacy of life insurance reserves (based on 1950–1954 mortality experience). Twenty-four years may seem a long time for the insurance industry and its regulators to have waited to update one of its most basic mortality tables—mortality being fairly central to the business—but professionals do not act in haste.

Source: "The Report of the Special Committee to Recommend New Mortality Tables for Valuation," to be published in late 1981 in *Transactions* of the Society of Actuaries.

Actually, the pure cost may be even lower. Mortality has improved significantly since the early 1970s, the period on which the figures in the table are based, and will likely continue to do so. Also, if you are a non-smoker, or otherwise a better-than-average insured risk, the pure cost of insuring your life will be substantially less. But if you can find insurance as cheap as this, with the insurer in effect returning practically 100 cents of each $1 it collects, and living off the interest it earns on that dollar, you will be doing very well indeed.

The idea is not to pinch every last penny out of your insurance costs (although, if this is your objective, be my guest), but to be sure not to pay significantly more for insurance than necessary. The table on the next page includes three $100,000-and-up policies. The non-smoker rates introduced in 1981 by Fidelity Union Life of Dallas—ironically, a company long noted for its *poor* values—were among the lowest available (even lower on larger policies). Two other A+ rated firms with low rates: Old Line Life of Milwaukee; First Colony Life of Lynchburg, Virginia. These are non-dividend-paying policies.

The New England Life and Prudential policies do pay dividends. (Accordingly, the rates shown on the next page would be higher for someone signing up after age 30: he would not have accumulated as

ANNUAL PREMIUM PER $1,000 COVERAGE

Age	"Pure Cost" Male[1]	Mass. SBLI*[2]	Ger- ber[3]	Fidelity Union Life[4]	New Eng. Life*[5]	Pru- den- tial*[6]
30	$0.94	$2.04	$6.04	$1.75	$2.47	$2.29
31	$0.96	$2.04	$6.04	$1.77	$2.52	$1.78
32	$0.99	$2.04	$6.04	$1.79	$2.57	$1.78
33	$1.04	$2.04	$6.04	$1.82	$2.64	$1.80
34	$1.10	$2.02	$6.04	$1.84	$2.71	$1.80
35	$1.18	$2.13	$6.04	$1.88	$2.82	$1.83
36	$1.28	$2.02	$6.04	$1.97	$2.95	$1.85
37	$1.41	$1.90	$6.04	$2.10	$3.10	$1.93
38	$1.55	$1.84	$6.04	$2.25	$3.29	$2.04
39	$1.72	$1.75	$6.04	$2.42	$3.52	$2.16
40	$1.91	$2.89	$6.04	$2.62	$3.78	$2.22
41	$2.13	$2.77	$6.04	$2.83	$4.10	$2.33
42	$2.36	$2.70	$6.04	$3.08	$4.44	$2.47
43	$2.62	$2.71	$6.04	$3.37	$4.80	$2.60
44	$2.89	$2.72	$6.04	$3.67	$5.20	$2.78
45	$3.19	$4.02	$6.04	$4.00	$5.65	$2.96
46	$3.50	$4.01	$6.04	$4.29	$6.16	$3.17
47	$3.84	$4.01	$6.04	$4.62	$6.73	$3.41
48	$4.19	$4.01	$6.04	$4.91	$7.37	$3.78
49	$4.58	$4.02	$6.04	$5.41	$8.12	$4.19
50	$5.01	$7.07		$5.87	$8.89	$4.63
51	$5.51	$6.82		$6.42	$9.79	$5.13
52	$6.08	$6.62		$7.00	$10.80	$5.75
53	$6.74	$6.43		$7.84	$11.95	$6.45
54	$7.48	$6.17		$8.79	$13.23	$7.32
55	$8.28	$12.38		$9.88	$14.68	$8.46
56	$9.15	$12.13		$11.31	$16.38	$9.94
57	$10.06	$11.96		$12.78	$18.18	$11.51
58	$11.02	$11.65		$14.39	$20.19	$13.34
59	$12.05	$11.26		$16.20	$22.45	$12.72
60	$13.20	$16.26		$12.79	$22.08	$13.04
65	$21.52	$24.22		$21.96	$29.80	$21.69

Rates shown include waiver-of-premium through age 59.

*Includes any applicable policy fees, and dividends, which are not guaranteed. *Policyholders signing up after age 30 will pay higher rates than shown here,* because they will not have accumulated the same dividends. Fidelity Union rates apply to entry at any age.

[1]From preceding table, see text. Does not include waiver-of-premium.

[5]Five-year renewable (to 70) term; minimum $10,000, maximum $53,000.

[3]Twenty-year renewable (to 65) term; maximum $20,000. Per-$1,000 rates for $10,000 coverage somewhat higher. Renewal beyond age 50 *very* expensive.

much credit for dividends.) Why pay the New England Life $10,182 for $200,000 of coverage between the ages of 30 and 44, say, when the Prudential will provide it for $3,850 less? And for $8,380 less in the following 10 years? Is their advertising *that* good?

NEW YORK'S INSURANCE DEPARTMENT TO THE RESCUE!

With Saviors Like This . . .

When the Gerber Life story appeared in somewhat different form as a magazine article, it prompted a larger than usual number of letters. One, from an agent of the Equitable, is worth quoting because it typifies the kind of well-intentioned but emotional, illogical and ill-conceived arguments that life insurance sales people spend millions of hours making every year. It read:

> There are wide variations in the prices of equal amounts of insurance in each company. So what! Each policy is structured differently to accomplish different financial goals; our products are as varied as a sweater manufacturer's—we have cashmere, wool and cotton. [The policies compared were all essentially of one type—cotton. The point was, is, to avoid paying cashmere prices for them.] The author says that people are not likely to die in their 20's and 30's. True. But how about those that do? My 22 year old sister-in-law did, following childbirth. Does your author suggest that the family didn't need insurance protection?
>
> Don't ask a wife if her husband's insurance was too expensive—ask a widow.

Far from advising people in their twenties and thirties not to buy insurance, the story suggested that those with a need for insurance should stretch the amount they can afford by shopping for the least expensive policies. For $200 a year a young man or woman can obtain $100,000 of term insurance protection—or less than $20,000 of whole life. It pays to understand the difference. Term insurance may not be the answer for every young couple (more on that later), but why not "ask a widow" how it feels to have received one-fifth what she might have if only her husband had taken the trouble to

---

[4]Annual renewable (to 70) term. Minimum, $50,000. Rates for females set back three years.

[5]Yearly renewable (to 70) term. Rates based on $100,000 coverage of a standard male life. Rates for females set back three years.

[6]Annual renewable (to 70) term; minimum $100,000. Rates for females set back about four years.

shop for the best buy and to buy term insurance instead of the much more heavily touted whole life?

Another agent sent a carefully written, closely typed two-page attack on stories like mine, to which I replied with an equally painstaking rebuttal. That elicited an even longer letter. Where does this agent find the time to write these things? I wondered. I later discovered that for his first letter the agent had simple instructed his secretary to type half of an article from an industry handout. Between the salutation and the sincerely, there it was, word for word. It had taken him all of thirty seconds— and his secretary perhaps half the morning. His second letter merely repeated the procedure with the second half of the article.

It was a recipe for persuasion not uncommon in the selling of life insurance: a dollop of dogma mixed with a dash of deception and delivered at higher cost than necessary. (Why not just send a photocopy of the article?)

It is precisely this failure to think independently that makes the army of 250,000 life insurance agents such a powerful force. Like crusaders set on an enthusiastic, unquestioning course, they knock down anything in their paths. No wonder the F.T.C. got its knuckles rapped for looking into the life insurance business.*

Most of the letters to the editor were only what you would expect. Insurers and agents were highly critical; the Savings Bank Life Insurance people loved it. Perhaps most interesting, therefore, because it was not so predictable, was the response of New York's Insurance Department—the people's watchdog, funded with the people's tax dollars, established in 1859 and long considered one of the very best of the state insurance departments. The department found the story . . . naively irresponsible.

Down to the New York State Insurance Department trotted the errant reporter. For two hours he met with the chief of the department's life insurance division, a dignified, fastidious, unexcitable man who had been toiling in the insurance field since before the reporter was born. With the patience of a forgiving grandparent, the chief of the New York State Insurance Department life insurance

---

*"For it is the absence of . . . knowledge on the part of the salesman that allows him to abound with zest and fervent sales enthusiasm. He sallies forth under the false, but honest, belief that he is engaged in the most humanitarian, benevolent . . . mutual non-profit business on earth . . ."—James B. Epperson, *Like a Thief in the Night*, 1939.

division explained that, actually, far from being cheaper than Gerber's, Beneficial National Life's rates were among the highest in the state. Yes, he said; it was right there in the *Consumers Shopping Guide for Life Insurance* that his department published.

(In an effort to help New Yorkers make intelligent comparisons among competing policies, no fewer than 50,000 of these booklets had been mailed out over the prior three years. Unfortunately, quite a few of those 50,000 had gone not to insurance buyers but to agents in search of helpful statistics, which left several million New York insurance buyers untouched by the *Shopping Guide*. But the department seemed pleased with its effort, nonetheless.)

The chief had checked Beneficial's cost index, he said, comparing it with Gerber's, and had found that Beneficial's renewable term insurance was actually more expensive.

This produced considerable consternation on the part of the errant reporter.

Far from feeling that Gerber was in any way taking advantage of consumers, or bemoaning his inability to make it stop, New York's chief of life insurance regulation (second only to the state insurance superintendent himself) began thumbing through his *Shopping Guide* for the page that showed how Beneficial's policy was more expensive than Gerber's. Meanwhile, the reporter was pointing to the actual offers described in his magazine story and asking how $66.48 could possibly be considered less than $23.04.

On went the thumbing—leading one to wonder how, if it was difficult for the chief of the life insurance division of the New York State Insurance Department to use the guide, the consumers for whom it was intended were likely to fare—until at length: "There," he said, pointing to one cost index. "There," he said, pointing to another. "Beneficial's renewable term policy cost index is much higher than Gerber's." In fact, he said, having had a few days to research all this prior to the reporter's visit, *Beneficial's term insurance was about the highest-priced of any in the state.*

The errant reporter, pointing again to the columns of numbers in *his* table, began to grow a bit bug-eyed. They were comparing, in effect, two numbers. To the untrained eye, $23.04 would have appeared to be a smaller number than $66.48. But to the chief of the New York State Insurance Department life insurance division, backed by the computer-generated cost indices this department had developed to make life insurance shopping easy and intelligible, it was not. It was as though an apprentice meteorologist were sitting opposite the chairman of Yale's meteorology department, watching rain fall out the window behind the professor while the professor, peering at his instruments, insisted otherwise.

Minutes ticked by. Master and apprentice began repeating themselves. Finally, reason dawned. The Beneficial National number in the *Shopping Guide* had nothing whatever to do with the policy in question. It referred *not* to the inexpensive "group" plan described in the article and offered to millions of credit-card holders, but to a high-priced policy Beneficial offered individuals. Their rates for *this* policy, which they did not advertise or offer widely, were very poor. The chief was comparing the *wrong policies*. He had had time to study the article; he had had time to prepare for his meeting with the reporter—and yet at the meeting he was maintaining that the Beneficial National deal was actually more expensive for the consumer than Gerber's.

When finally it came clear that the cost index he was using to compare Beneficial with Gerber was for a policy other than the one Beneficial had been urging on New Yorkers—*other* than the one detailed in the magazine article that the department had taken such exception to—he said, simply, Well, you can't compare *those* two policies, they are apples and oranges.

No. McIntosh apples and Delicious apples, perhaps, but not apples and oranges.

I run through all this, I repeat, not to recommend Beneficial National, by any means, nor further to berate Gerber. It was merely an accident in my mailbox that led me to pick these two offers to make my point. Yet this meeting with the people's life insurance regulator was remarkable. In the isolated, arcane world of insurance, this man was tops. When it came to analyzing an insurer's reserves or to assuring that no life insurance policies were offered in New York that could not sustain themselves, thereby protecting the public from insurance company failures, he was, surely, a regular James Bond. Forget forests and trees—*this* dedicated public servant, I have no doubt, knew even the leaves. But when it came to looking at two policies being pitched aggressively to the people of his state, on TV and through the mails, his considered opinion was that $66 was less than $23 and that *New York* magazine and the Federal Trade Commission, among others, were way off base in their calls for reform. After all, an enterprising consumer need only write to the Insurance Department for a free copy of the *Shopping Guide*, wait three weeks, and then, with a bit of tenacity, locate the very same figures the chief had found, whereupon he would have known that Beneficial's policy was expensive, not cheap.

And the New York Insurance Department is among the best in the country!

(When you read that an insurer is "licensed to do business in 49 states and the Commonwealth of Puerto Rico," or some such, it is not Alaska or North Dakota the insurer has overlooked—it's New York. To escape New York's tough regulations, to which they must conform *nationwide* if they are to do business in the state, many companies stay out. They set up subsidiaries to do business in New York, instead.)

The best criticism of the Gerber story came from a sophisticated chartered life underwriter (an agent with an insurance degree) who wrote:

> Unquestionably, the industry deserves all that it is getting [by way of criticism]. As a matter of fact, it has been long overdue. However, there are some excellent companies that offer superior products. There are some (not many, unfortunately) excellent practitioners that put together people's needs with product; they design essential estate plans, viable business buy-out agreements and a myriad of highly sophisticated programs life insurance based. Many widows, orphans and businesses are around today because some good planning was done in the past.

Quite right. When it comes to life insurance, there are at least two very different markets. There is the rarefied world of insurance for those with complex estate problems; for them, like it or not, the convolutions of the U.S. tax code require the counsel of talented specialists—tax attorneys, tax accountants and, despite their obvious conflict of interest (being biased toward the product they sell), life insurance salesmen.

There are, however, another 30 or 50 million people who have dependents, most of whom should thus carry life insurance, but whose insurance requirements are *not* complex. (Even though their incomes may be high.) It is they for whom saving $50 or $250 a year—or stretching their insurance dollars to buy an extra $25,000 or $50,000 of coverage—is important. And it is they, largely, whom America's army of a quarter-million life insurance salesmen serves.

14

TOO MANY SALESMEN
The Slow Death of Whole Life

*Such is life insurance at a glance,—a thing which has
grown upon the country like a prodigious dream, having
palaces, powers, and potentates of its own, with incomes that
little kings might envy.*
—Elizur Wright, 1877

Life insurance, it is frequently said, is not bought—it's sold. An eminently postponable purchase, it covers a contingency most people would just as soon not contemplate. It was not a product that Americans immediately clamored to have.

The first life insurance societies were formed in England in the years between 1692 and 1720. In America, life insurance became available to the clergy through the Presbyterian Ministers Fund, founded in 1759 (still in existence), and the Episcopal Corporation, founded ten years later (subsequently merged). But it would be another eighty years before the product attained even limited acceptance among America's general public. Ironically, public resistance to life insurance was in part religious: it seemed to some to thwart God's will. As late as 1832, William Bard, president of the New York Life Insurance and Trust Company, would have to struggle to convince countrymen of the soundness of his undertaking. Life insurance was not "an impious attempt to prevent the will of Providence," he argued, "but a wise and prudent endeavour." At the time, the New York Life had just 150 policies in force.

250

"Life insurance was new to the public of that day," writes historian J. Owen Stalson; "its inquiries into family and personal health, its concern with death, its numerous 'declarations' and associated papers, its investigations of risks—all these matters suggested to a diffident and suspicious public that it was a difficult, involved, overly intimate business, not one to be approached lightly."*

Even by 1841, the Pennsylvania Company, capitalized 29 years earlier at a munificent $100,000, had only 210 lives under contract. Nor would it grow, for the company rigidly eschewed the notion of personalized selling.

And then came the mutual insurers. Wrote Stalson: "Life insurance as protection is one thing—it has its attractions; but life insurance as profitable investment, in addition to protection, is something much better. So thought the public which greeted the 'pioneer' companies in the middle 1840's; those companies were all mutuals, and, in the hearty welcome which the public accorded them, all their predecessors were quickly forgotten."

One advantage of mutuality, besides the obvious attraction to policyholders of "insurance at cost," was the ease of entry it allowed entrepreneurs. Establishing a stockholder-owned life insurer required substantial capital. Not so a mutual. A patent admirer of the life insurance industry, but a realist as well, Stalson held that "Mere mutuality, no matter how perfectly achieved, could never have won for life insurance the following which aggressive marketing programs have indisputably won for it. . . . Something else focused the attention of the new organizers upon the marketing function in life insurance. What was that something? Plainly, the need for an income from which they could pay themselves . . . salaries." And so it began. Without sales there would be no salaries for the insurance executives; without growth in sales, no growth in salaries. Profits were secondary. Altruism ran a distant third.

"Although they probably did not relish pure mutuality," writes Stalson of the entrepreneurs who, had they had the capital, would have preferred to own their creations outright, "they rightly foresaw in the prospective success of a mutual of their own founding a personal gain in position, security, and income which was not lightly to be set aside."

Marketing Life Insurance, the definitive history. Copyright © 1969, The McCahan Foundation, Bryn Mawr, Pa. All rights reserved. Reprinted by permission.

Growth was rapid. New companies were formed year after year, then month by month. New England Life was founded in 1835 (but did not truly begin to function until the mid 1840s). The Mutual Life of New York was founded in 1842, the New York Life in 1843, the State Mutual of Massachusetts in 1844, the Mutual Benefit of New Jersey in 1845, the Connecticut Mutual in 1846. Agents were recruited, newspaper advertising blossomed. Commissions on the sale of whole life insurance were sweetened, doubling from 5 to 10 percent of the first year's premium (and 5 percent thereafter). Within a decade, commissions would double again, to 20 percent of the first year's premium, and then triple, to today's 55 or 60 percent. (Sales overrides to supervisors and general agents typically boost commissions to 90 percent or more of the first year's premium, followed by 7½ percent of each of the following nine years' premiums.)

The beauty of whole life was, in part at least, that no one outside the actuarial department had any notion what it should cost. What did it matter, anyway, customers of mutual companies were lulled into thinking, since any overcharges would be returned to them as dividends? And so there was cash by the barrelful with which the industry could expand. Companies competed not to provide the best values but to attract the best salesmen, enroll the most policyholders, build the tallest headquarters.

Term policies were available, but the emphasis, as today, was on whole life. Because whole life commissions are figured not just on the "protection" element of the premium but on the savings element as well, a salesman can easily earn five times as much selling whole life as selling a like amount of term. (In contrast to the 55 or 60 percent of first-year premium an agent typically earns on a whole life policy, the commission on term policies averages under 40 percent of the—much lower—first-year premium.)

The need for some sort of "Truth in Life Insurance," along the lines of Truth in Lending, was as apparent a hundred years ago as it is today. The Federal Trade Commission staff report of 1979 had little more to say on the subject than had been said by Massachusetts reformer Elizur Wright a century before. That the life insurance industry has managed so long to keep its product from becoming a readily intelligible "commodity," subject to the same sorts of competition as, say, a savings account or mortgage, is no mean tribute to its power, inertia, arrogance and intransigence. Wrote Wright of whole life in 1877: "As things are mixed in the policy which ought to be kept separate (the protection element and the savings element), and as the knowledge of what is going on under it from year to year is necessarily almost wholly on one side, if anywhere, the facility for swindling in life-insurance is so great, that the wonder is that it should ever be conducted with any degree of honesty." And yet Wright never doubted the value of life insurance. "Provided the game is fairly understood on both sides, fairly played, and no risk run, except what is necessary to secure the desired indemnity, human science has never devised a more admirable plan for securing at the same time the benefit of association and the independence of the individual."*

What's more, as a by-product of providing financial security, the whole life industry served a second great function. Like the banking industry, it served to funnel dimes and dollars from millions of individual savers into great chunks of capital to be invested in building the nation. The insurers actually *sold* thrift and saving, door to door, sucking capital out of people's pockets like a giant financial vacuum cleaner poised just above tree level and run from town to town.

With time, the early whole life policies were refined. Policy loans were introduced; policies were made "incontestable" after a period of years; life insurance for substandard risks became available at increased rates; 30-day grace periods were introduced to keep policies from lapsing if premium payments were made late. The most important reform was the provision for cash values. Until Elizur Wright waged his successful campaign for reform, non-payment of a whole life premium meant not just that the protection element of the policy would lapse but that the savings element to which one had contributed by his early-year overpayments would be lost as well.

Wright's zeal had been kindled on a visit to London's Royal Exchange in 1844, where he saw life insurance policies on very old men being sold to speculators "apparently of Hebrew persuasion," who would profit by taking over the premium payments the old men could no longer afford to keep up, waiting for the day of decease to collect the face value of the policy. This was done, Wright was told,

---

Traps Baited with Orphan; or, What Is the Matter with Life Insurance.

"because the companies made it a rule *'never to buy their own policies.'* " Never, that is, to pay out any cash upon surrender or lapse of a whole life policy, no matter how long it had been kept in force. "A poor rule it seemed to me! I had seen slave auctions at home. I could hardly see more justice in this British practice. . . . I resolved, if I ever returned to America, it should be otherwise here, if my voice could avail."

Avail it did. It became a requirement that cash values, payable upon surrender of a policy, be written into whole life contracts. That way, if an old man could no longer keep up his premiums, he could in effect sell back his policy to the company for a partial refund— its surrender value.

The extent to which a group of policyholders manages to keep its policies in force, a crucial element in the life insurance equation, is called its "persistency." A company whose policyholders tend to lapse their policies at an above average rate is said to experience poor persistency. It is an expensive problem, because it amounts to a huge waste of selling effort and expense. Imagine paying out 90 percent of a policyholder's first-year premium payments in commissions to agents and supervisors, only to have the policy canceled the next year. When this happens, there is little left over to contribute to the costs of running the enterprise. Neither does it work out well for the policyholder. A 30-year-old male who buys a $100,000 whole life contract from the Prudential at an annual premium rate of $1,420 (compared with about $200 for a term policy of equal size) receives no payment whatever if he surrenders his policy after the first year, and only $462 if he drops it after two years.

And people do drop their policies. The table to the right shows just how bad the problem had become by 1980 (with 1981 proving even worse).

After the Civil War, poor persistency plagued the fledgling life insurance industry. In the grand American tradition of "turning a lemon into lemonade," someone hit on the notion of "tontine insurance policies"—and here a little background is in order.

One of the more intriguing financial schemes tied to life expectancy is the tontine. Where life insurance provides for one's heirs in the event of premature demise, tontines provide for *oneself* in the event of exceptionally long life. The prize comes from living rather than dying (and so holds special appeal for the purchaser). Provi-

HE WHO LAPSE LAST

Voluntary Termination Rate
Ordinary Policies in Force in the United States

Year	Policies In Force Less Than 2 Years	Policies In Force 2 Years or More	All Policies In Force
1951	9.4%	2.2%	3.2%
1955	11.4	2.5	3.8
1960	14.5	3.7	5.2
1965	15.4	3.5	5.1
1970	19.3	3.9	5.9
1975	20.9	4.5	6.7
1980	22.4	5.8	8.1
1981 (est.)			9.0

sions vary, but in the typical tontine each participant will make one lump sum contribution at the outset. As years pass and participants die off, the shares of those who remain grow correspondingly larger, all the while accumulating interest. The pie grows bigger and there are fewer people left to eat it. When only one participant remains, the entire fortune is his.

The very first tontine was organized (perpetrated?) in 1689 by the French government. A total of 1.4 million livres was collected and "loaned" to the treasury. Interest on the loan was paid to the tontine's subscribers. As their number shrank, there was that much more interest for those who remained. The sole survivor 37 years later was a merry widow indeed at 96. According to Richard Shulman, her interest payments, on an investment of 300 livres, came to some 73,500 livres a year. But France was none the worse for the scheme, either. When the widow died later that year, the government's obligations ceased. The 1.4 million livres paid into the tontine was forever the property of France.

It was nearly two hundred years later, in 1867, that tontine and semitontine life insurance policies began to sweep America. Pioneered by Henry Hyde's Equitable Life Assurance Society, then only eight years old, these policies pledged to *accumulate* their dividends rather than disburse them. Then, after ten, fifteen or twenty years (depending on the policy chosen), a policyholder would receive his accumulated dividends—*plus his share of the dividends forfeited by others who had died or allowed their policies to lapse.* Poor persistency was turned into a selling point. Not only could you earn dividends on your own policy, but on those of other policyholders as well. The Equitable's sales grew explosively, with the New York Life quick to follow.* The Mutual Life of New York reluctantly joined the fray in 1879. Between them, these three mutuals were writing more than half the life insurance in the United States. (Sixty years later they would still account for 42 percent of the life insurance in force.) The Connecticut Mutual, meanwhile, one of the very few insurers that refused to write such policies, languished.

The Connecticut Mutual's Jacob L. Greene, appalled by the sweeping tontine movement, assessed the life insurance industry in 1876:

> . . . from 1860 to 1872 about two hundred and fifty life insurance companies were chartered in the different States. . . . New plans of insurance, new ways of paying premiums, new methods of applying a surplus as yet unearned, were devised with wonderful fertility of invention, and urged with great plausibility to people who could really fathom none of them. The point of every new plan seemed to be that by it alone could more than a dollar's worth of insurance be got from a dollar; or rather, that a dollar's worth could be got from less than a dollar—appealing to the desire of many to get something for nothing. . . . But above all, the new companies began raising the rates of commissions to agents enormously, paying large salaries in addition to commissions often times . . . all with the effect of permanently and greatly increasing the cost of insurance. . . . No scheme was too worthless to find promoters and believers; premises in the baldest contradiction of facts were assumed for fair mathematical results; . . . people were made to believe that a simple insurance transaction was somehow going to be the most profitable investment for themselves individually; companies whose premiums were

---

*James Garfield, America's first lefthanded president and its second to be assassinated, left his widow $50,000 under Tontine Investment Policy #149056 issued by the New York Life. (There is no record of Abraham Lincoln's ever having been insured.) William McKinley, assassinated in 1901, also had $50,000 of insurance with the New York Life, but it was not of the tontine variety. Meanwhile, a check in the amount of $4,750 was delivered by an agent of that same company to Elizabeth B. Custer on November 16, 1876. It is not clear what it was about their leader that persuaded Custer's subordinates to seek insurance, but heavily insured they were. The New York Life paid out more in connection with Custer's massacre—$40,000— than it had paid as the result of any single battle of the Civil War.

eaten up by extravagance, held out the prospect of unexampled
returns of surplus; . . . In short, in the management of a multi-
tude of companies, not only was there wanting intelligence, skill,
prudence, moral courage, and common fairness; but the very
opposite of these qualities were pre-eminent.

From the seed of the wind came the harvest of the whirlwind.
. . . Small dividends, and oftener none at all, where the greatest
hopes had been excited, destroyed the motive upon which too
many had been induced to take policies. One and another, in
rapid succession, disappointed, disgusted, chagrined, and feeling themselves cheated, dropped their policies; and one by one
the companies began to disappear; the managers of some, for a
profit, selling the wreck of their trusts to others, to be again
manipulated for personal profit and at further loss to the policy
holders; others have died of pure inanition; others have gone
under the ban of the law; and yet others remain, moribund, and
a disgrace to the business.

Excess and irresponsibility characterized the management of mutual insurers throughout the remainder of the century, climaxed, as
the nineteenth gave way to the twentieth, in the much celebrated
extravagances of James Hazen Hyde. The son of the Equitable's
charismatic founder, Hyde was off at Harvard when he was first
appointed to the Equitable's board of directors. (Imagine—a college student on the board of an august financial institution! But
Hyde senior controlled the board and its appointments.) His passion
was for all things French, not for insurance, but the younger Hyde
nevertheless assumed the vice presidency of the Equitable at 23. At
27, he became chairman of the finance and executive committees.
He drew a salary of $100,000 plus expenses, courtesy of the poli-
cyholders he supposedly served; he pocketed fees from his service
as a director of no fewer than forty-five companies in which the
Equitable had invested policyholder funds; and he manipulated investment of the Equitable's $400 million in assets to his personal
advantage. To indulge his passion for horses he employed eighty
stablemen, whom he took, with his horses, annually to France. In
1905, he invited 600 guests to a Louis XVI–style costume ball that
was estimated to have cost $200,000.

The following year there was held the most exacting investigation
of the life insurance industry to that time—or since. (It was also
around this time that New York's insurance superintendent, Louis
F. Payn, was not reappointed. "Being a frugal man," it was noted,

"out of his seven thousand dollars a year salary he has saved enough to borrow nearly half a million dollars from a trust company, the directors of which are also the directors of an insurance company.")

Obviously, the excesses and outrages of the life insurance industry today incline more toward subtlety than in the days before New York State's Armstrong investigation. But this is the heritage of the industry. Much less of it would have been possible—and would be possible today—if customers were better able to assess the value, and compare the prices, of what they were buying. A truly competitive marketplace imposes a discipline no team of regulators can provide.

But to have a competitive marketplace, buyers must be able to compare prices. Most elements of the industry, while paying lip service to this notion, oppose it on fundamental grounds. Unless they happen to be the low-cost producers, they know that adequate cost disclosure would cause drastic cutbacks in their comfortable businesses. Look what disclosure would do to flight insurance sales. Or look what it would have done to the incredible growth of the Prudential Insurance Company of America.

The Prudential got a relatively late start among today's giants, having been founded in 1878; but it caught up fast. In its early years, the Prudential prospered by imitating its British namesake in the sale of so-called industrial or debit insurance. These are the tiny face-amount policies, still sold in some of America's poverty pockets, that promise $500 or $1,000 at death (or today a bit more) to assure a decent burial. Under the terms of these whole life policies, the insurance agent comes by in person, weekly, to collect the 50 cents or dollar that is due, checking off payments in his debit book. For the poor who could save in no other way, it was argued, this was worthwhile insurance. Yet these policies were, and are, grotesquely inefficient. Of each dime "saved," perhaps a penny went to pay the actual cost of insurance, and a penny or two more built up "cash value"—but most of the dime went to expenses, overhead and profit. Horror stories abound of families being sold five and ten such penny-ante policies—on the lives of their children, no less, instead of their breadwinner—when the coverage was not needed, or when the same dollars, combined to purchase a single term policy, could have purchased five or ten or twenty times more coverage. (Today, even more horror stories filter up from the fringes of the life and health insurance industry with regard to the sale of worthless and near worthless health policies to confused and helpless old people.) There were still 98 million home-service life insurance policies in force in 1980 (62 million industrial policies and 36 million of the more modern monthly debit plans), with an average face value of less than $1,600 each.

LIFE INSURANCE IS SOLD IN INEFFICIENT LITTLE CHUNKS
Average Size Life Insurance Policy
In Force in the United States

Year	Ordinary*	Group	Industrial
1920	$ 1,990	$ 960	$150
1930	2,460	1,700	210
1940	2,130	1,700	240
1950	2,320	2,480	310
1960	3,600	4,030	390
1970	8,110	6,910	500
1980	11,920	13,410	620

*Includes both whole life and term.
Sources: Spectator Year Book and American Council of Life Insurance.

Consider the cost of macaroni and cheese. How much are you paying for the macaroni, how much for the cheese? The two together may go for $1.39, but what you're paying for the cheese depends on what you choose to think you're paying for the macaroni—and vice versa.

Whole life is the same way. It is made up of two ingredients, life insurance and a savings plan, but you are charged only one price. The bill is not itemized. If you knew what you were being charged for insurance, you would know how much of your premium is really a savings deposit—and could then determine what sort of a return your savings were earning.

The sensible way to compare whole life policies is to assume that the insurance portion of the contract is being provided at the lowest term insurance rates readily available. What's left is savings.

But because the price of insurance rises each year as you grow older, the savings portion of your premium falls. This alone puts the calculations required to analyze the rate of return on a whole life policy out of range of the average consumer. But to provide such valuable information would not be at all difficult for an insurer.

The problem is that for comparisons to be meaningful, insurers must all use the same assumption about the cost of macaroni. Instead, of course, an insurer's inclination is to assume you are buying *expensive* macaroni. That makes the cheese look cheap.

In its 1979 report on life insurance—the one that caused such commotion—the staff of the Federal Trade Commission analyzed rates of return on the savings portion of whole life policies available to a 35-year-old male in 1977. It used as its assumption for macaroni term insurance rates that were low-priced but readily available. Here were the rates of return it found would be earned, on average, from the policies it examined, depending on the length of time they were held. After five years: *minus* 8.36 percent. After ten: 1.43 percent. After twenty: 4.12 percent. And after 30 years: 4.45 percent. These were the returns for participating policies. The rates on non-participating policies were worse.

Consumers Union surveyed 110 of the leading life insurers to analyze the rates of return of their whole life policies. It, too, used a low (but not lowest) price of macaroni—a table of term insurance rates developed by the Society of Actuaries. The table at right, drawn from the excellent *Consumers Union Report on Life Insurance* (Fourth Edition), which I highly recommend, shows a small sampling of the many policies CU's actuaries analyzed, and the returns you would have earned on each had you kept them in force for 9 years, for 19 years or for 29 years. (CU chose these odd time spans to foil companies that might have designed their policies to look good at the traditional 10-, 20- and 30-year comparison points.) Those marked with an asterisk were among the highest-yielding in their respective categories when CU did its survey, but the sampling that follows is by no means an endorsement of any policies. Rather, it is offered as an illustration of how mediocre whole life is as a savings vehicle. Financially speaking, anyway. (Psychologically, whole life has advantages: forced savings, a specific plan to follow in an otherwise complicated world, pride in sticking to that plan—perhaps even a feeling of affinity with the insurance company.)

Much is made of the fact that the interest earned on whole life cash values is sheltered from taxes. You pay no tax until the policy is surrendered, and even then are taxed only on the amount by which what you get back exceeds what you paid in (less dividends). Generally, little or no tax is due. Neither is tax due if you die. The insurer keeps your savings and pays out the face value of the policy to your beneficiary.

For someone in the 50 percent tax bracket, earning 4 percent tax free is as good as earning 8 percent after tax.

But while this definitely makes the low returns from whole life

SAMPLE WHOLE LIFE YIELDS

Company/Policy	Yield on Savings Element if Held for:			Annual Premium
	9 Years	19 Years	29 Years	
$25,000 Non-participating Policies:				
Allstate Life Exec. Plan, age 25				
non-smoker	0.03%	3.99%	3.98%	$ 249
smoker	−0.63%	3.69%	3.78%	$ 254
Travelers Ordinary Life, age 25	0.93%	3.61%	3.14%	$ 293
Conn. General Ord. Life, age 25	−6.04%	1.75%	2.28%	$ 309
Aetna Whole Life, age 35	−1.27%	2.86%	3.19%	$ 392
J.C. Penney Value Select, age 45	−0.50%	2.91%	3.33%	$ 575
Hartford Life Whole Life, age 45	−1.89%	2.13%	2.79%	$ 613
$25,000 Participating Policies:				
*Mass. SBLI, age 25	8.54%	7.97%	7.85%	$ 236
*New England Mutual, age 25	3.64%	6.26%	6.45%	$ 296
*Mass. Mutual Convertible Life, age 25	3.40%	5.98%	6.08%	$ 302
Prudential, Modified Life 3, age 25	1.20%	4.91%	5.40%	$ 400
New York Life, age 25	2.23%	5.10%	5.54%	$ 374
John Hancock Paid Up at 85, age 25	−1.75%	3.74%	4.68%	$ 394
Equitable, Adjustable Whole Life, age 35	1.66%	4.85%	5.27%	$ 526
$100,000 Participating Policies:				
*Northwestern Mutual, age 25	2.58%	5.36%	5.98%	$1411
Equitable, Adjustable Whole Life, age 25	1.98%	5.15%	5.55%	$1445
Metropolitan Life, Whole Life, age 25	−2.60%	4.03%	5.06%	$1272
*Phoenix Mutual, non-smokers, age 35	3.26%	5.78%	5.94%	$2062
Franklin Life Exec. Select II, age 35	−1.70%	3.44%	4.22%	$2272
Manhattan Life Challenger, age 35	−1.02%	3.58%	4.16%	$2316
Prudential Estate 20, Whole Life, age 35	0.24%	3.99%	4.79%	$2043
State Farm "Est. Protector" (L95), age 45	0.31%	4.29%	4.56%	$2542
State Farm Whole Life, age 45	−1.56%	3.59%	4.40%	$3048

*Based on a sampling of evaluations by Consumers Union of several hundred life insurance policies: see *The Consumers Union Report on Life Insurance* (Fourth Edition).

policies more attractive than they look, they still don't look all that attractive. (Had the F.T.C. and CU assumed even lower term insurance rates in their calculations, the savings yields would have looked still less attractive.) The industry boasts of this tax advantage as though it should somehow be given credit for the tax laws. It's wonderful (I think) that cash value life insurance gets favorable tax treatment—thank you, Congress—but why should it not provide good yields as well?

THE SLOW DEATH OF WHOLE LIFE

There have been books before. *Like a Thief in the Night, The Billion Dollar Bookies, The Mortality Merchants, Pay Now Die Later, The Great American Insurance Hoax, The Life Insurance Conspiracy, What's Wrong with Your Life Insurance, How Your Life Insurance Policies Rob You*—they have struck the industry like BBs against a battleship. The same year Elizur Wright's *Traps Baited with Orphan* was published in Massachusetts—1877—New York's state legislature held hearings and compiled a record fairly bulging with industry misconduct. Rather than clean up their act, the companies chose to clean up the record. They had it edited. When a troublemaker named Manning somehow secured and published the authentic stenographic transcript, the industry bought up the whole printing, then tranquilized Manning with an annual retainer. (Whence the expression, "Every Manning has his price.")

A century later, in 1981, the life insurance industry faced problems not so easily brushed aside.

(A contrarian could have seen it coming. There had been in 1979 and 1980 a rash of insurance company takeovers at record prices. Everyone had to own a life insurance company, even if it meant paying twice book value to buy it. It was a classic market top: a good time to sell, not buy.)

The worst sustained inflation in the nation's history had pushed interest rates to unthinkable levels. The whole life policyholder who had slaved to pay the premiums on a $25,000 policy now found, twenty or thirty years later, that his slaving had been largely in vain. The $25,000 would still be paid if he died—but what was $25,000 in 1981? The great middle class, long content with whole life's taxfree 2 or 3 percent yield even if 5 percent was available down the street (few knew of the disparity, and what difference did it really make?), suddenly couldn't pass a bank window without seeing promises of 15 percent and 18 percent interest on sums as small as $1,000. The yields on good whole life policies had climbed to a tax-sheltered 6 or 7 percent, if held for ten or twenty years, but how attractive was that? And who could afford whole life premiums, anyway, now that a pound of hamburger cost $2.39? (And who could tell a good whole life policy from a bad one?)

Suddenly—after a century—the whinings of the whole life critics had begun to fall on responsive ears. Attention once focused on other things had come to be focused on the unsoundness of paper money and on ways to beat inflation. Whole life was not one of them. With alarming speed, insurance buyers were shifting from whole life to term. Bad enough that selling term insurance instead of whole life was like selling a motorbike instead of a Buick. What really hurt was that term insurance, being simple and comprehensible, lent itself to price comparisons. To competition! People began shopping for the best buys, squeezing profit margins even further.

Policyholders already stuck with whole life policies—in the same boat as investors holding pre-inflation bonds—had their own ways of squeezing the industry. Some were simply dropping their policies. Others began borrowing against them. Prudent souls who in the past had borrowed against their insurance only as a last resort were now, with equal prudence, exploiting the disparity between the rate at which they could borrow from the Prudential (5 or 6 or 8 percent) and the rate at which they could lend to Uncle Sam (15 or 16 percent). On $30,000 cash value, it came to $2,100 to $3,300 a year, completely risk free.*

To combat the avalanche of policy loans, most of which, experience showed, would never be repaid, the industry began lobbying state capitols for laws allowing them to charge the going rate of interest on newly issued policies. But even where successful, that was no help in staunching the outflow of funds to existing policyholders.

---

*To gamble the proceeds of a policy loan on anything riskier than Treasuries would be to jeopardize the security the whole life contract was purchased to provide. Note, too, that this scheme is *decidedly less attractive* for taxpayers who don't itemize their deductions. They are taxed on interest earned, but receive no deduction for interest paid.

The problem was not that insurers were losing money lending policyholders their own savings at 8 percent. They were not. The problem was liquidity. Like everyone else in 1981, life insurance companies were very rich—they just didn't have any money. Some had to borrow cash in the open market at 17-plus percent to lend to policyholders at 6 or 8 percent. (When they did *that*, they lost money.) The last time the industry found itself so strapped was the depression.

Roosevelt's famous "bank holiday" the day after his inauguration in 1933 is well remembered. Less well remembered is the response of the life insurance industry. Policy loans and lapses had already climbed to record levels, as desperate families looked to the cash value in their policies as the ultimate safety net. Now, with the banks closed, the rush to tap life insurance cash values threatened to become a stampede. Within two days of Roosevelt's order, New York State legislators passed a law prohibiting life insurers from paying cash to their policyholders. Only death benefits would still be paid and, "in cases of dire need," up to $100. Otherwise, cash values, like bank deposits, were frozen solid. Other states quickly followed. It was a national insurance holiday. But where the banks were truly closed to withdrawals and deposits, life insurers had shut off only withdrawals. Premiums were still payable when due. And where 92 percent of the nation's bank deposits were back on stream within days of Roosevelt's order, the life insurance freeze remained in effect for months. (During this time, an officer of the Chase National Bank called the president of the Equitable Life Assurance Society—himself a Chase director—to ask that an exception be made for the Secretary of the Treasury. The Secretary of the Treasury, William H. Woodin, had accumulated $68,000 in cash values with the Equitable—and he *wanted* it. Tough luck for the Secretary of the Treasury.)

Well protected by its regulators, the life insurance industry sailed through the depression. The 1980s may actually prove to be more difficult. More stormclouds:

By raising the level beneath which estates escaped tax—and eliminating entirely tax on estates passing from one spouse to another—Ronald Reagan's 1981 tax bill eliminated, too, one of the

major appeals of life insurance (lucrative big-ticket whole life policies in particular): namely, its usefulness in paying estate taxes. By
one estimate, the number of taxable estates was due to fall from
56,000 a year in 1981 to just 6,000 a year by 1986. Suddenly, there
was far less reason for rich people to buy life insurance.

Even more threatening was the blossoming in 1981 of a life
insurance product, "universal life," that for the first time actually
separated *savings* from *protection,* so you could see which was
which, and that paid attractive rates of interest to boot. There were
some drawbacks to universal life (interest rates could fall; some
plans were more straightforward than others; it provided less discipline than whole life; there was still a "load" levied on each dollar
deposited as savings); but it threatened to cut deeply into traditional
whole life sales—and profits. It was, quite simply, a better deal.

Given various brand names by the companies that began offering
it, universal life was (naturally) the innovation of an industry out-
sider, the life insurance arm of E.F. Hutton. It hung in large measure
on a letter ruling from the I.R.S. that accepted the plan as one of
insurance, rather than investment, and so allowed the savings element of the plan to mount tax free. "Most insurance policies are
backed by low yield pre-inflation investments," Hutton advertised.
"Ours are current, allowing a higher return. [And] we simply keep
a smaller percentage for our services, leaving more for you."

Hutton's plan guaranteed only a 4 percent rate of interest, but
promised to pay more on all but the first $1,000 of cash value when
investment performance allowed. In 1981, it was paying about 11
percent. There was a one-time sign-up charge of $252 plus $1.08
for each $1,000 of coverage purchased; and a 7½ percent sales
charge on every premium, like the load of a mutual fund. But this
was peanuts in comparison to the commission on a whole life plan.
The Hartford, meanwhile, was charging $200 more up front, but
just 5 percent of each premium. On October 1, 1981, it raised its
declared interest rate to 12 percent. Life of Virginia was charging
more, but stressed that its yield was indexed to prevailing interest
rates, not left to management discretion. *(Note that all these yields
are in fact lower, when the sales charges are taken into account.)*

Already there are dozens of universal life plans on the market; by
the time you read this, there will be many more. Most of the large
traditional insurers, at the same time as they were lobbying to scuttle

universal life by having its favorable tax status rescinded, were rushing to launch competitive plans of their own. (The same contrarian encountered a few pages back would say this means we are about to enter a period of deflation, when interest rates will drop precipitously; universal plans will be paying no more than traditional whole life; and the real question will concern the financial strength of the institution behind the plan. But even so, the sales and expense charges of universal life would likely remain lower than those of whole life.)

As usual, it will pay to shop around. Administration and insurance fees vary significantly on universal life plans as do interest rates. And there are other important differences as well. But if it's hard to compare the relative merits of universal life policies, it's easy to compare them, as a class, with traditional whole life plans. By and large, with universal life you lose less of the first year's premium to sales commissions; your cash value earns a higher rate of return. You can pay premiums in any amount and at any time you like, after the first one, just as you would make voluntary deposits to a savings plan, provided only that you keep enough cash value in the plan to cover the cost of your term insurance protection. Not only may you borrow against your cash value, you can also *withdraw* a portion of it permanently. You can choose an option that will pay your beneficiary both the death benefit *and* your cash value if you die. You can increase your coverage, upon passing a physical, without paying new first-year charges. You will receive an intelligible annual statement showing exactly what you've paid in, what your cash value has earned (and how that was calculated), what was deducted for insurance and what was deducted for expenses.

And so here was perhaps the largest storm cloud of all: aggressive price competition from nontraditional sources.

The financial landscape was in the midst of a dramatic rationalization, in 1981, with the lines between banks, insurers and brokers growing increasingly fuzzy. Stockbrokers were selling life insurance (and why not?); the Prudential, through Bache, was selling stocks. American Express, parent of Fireman's Fund Insurance, had bought stockbroker Shearson Loeb Rhoades, which itself was looking to acquire a life insurer and had, in any event, through its credit card/ money market fund hook-up, become something of a national bank. As had Merrill Lynch. Sears, the huge credit card company, was selling life insurance through Allstate and gearing up to offer a money market fund of its own. It, too, planned to become an enormous financial services conglomerate. Meanwhile, the banks themselves—about the only ones on this list restricted in how they could attract depositors or where they could do business—were sending group insurance offers to their credit cardholders and lobbying like mad to be allowed into the fray.

Not all the life insurers had begun gearing up to offer universal life. But even those that would wait and see had begun trying, as term insurance began handily to outsell whole life, to make their whole life plans more attractive. Premium rates were lowered; dividend scales were increased; and some companies, like Northwestern Mutual, were voluntarily adding to the face amount of policies already in force at no increase in premium.

The life insurers would boast that in a decade when everyone else was raising prices, they had managed to lower theirs. The implication was that belt tightening and skillful management were responsible. Instead, of course, people were simply living longer (which reduces the cost of providing life insurance) and, even more important, interest rates were soaring (which reduces it still further). It was as if Merrill Lynch were taking credit for lowering the price at which it sold long-term bonds.

But if the life insurers deserved little credit for our increased longevity or for record interest rates, neither, in truth, could they be blamed for our inflation. They had accepted as a basic assumption the long-term financial stability of the nation; had depended on the notion that in America you could plan decades ahead—and had helped the country to do so. Were the insurers fools throughout the forties, fifties and sixties for lending money to home buyers at rates that now seem cheap? Or for buying the bonds that enabled corporations and municipalities to build for the future?

Clearly not.

And yet it took this external shock, a prolonged inflation that was never supposed to happen in America, to force to the surface and to public attention problems for which the industry *could* be blamed.

In 1981, there were more than 250,000 life insurance agents in America working, primarily, to sell whole life insurance. By 1990, if reason prevails, there may be fewer than 50,000, catering mostly to well-heeled prospects with complicated tax and estate problems.

The traditional whole life policy may be largely a thing of the past. This is not to say that the rest of us will go uninsured—any more than the absence of elevator operators in most buildings forces us to walk up the stairs. We will have insurance, just as we have elevator service. But it will be provided more efficiently.

15

HOW GOD WOULD RESTRUCTURE THE INSURANCE INDUSTRY

A Few Modest Proposals

[Ours is] an industry that's spent the last hundred years mostly listening to itself.
—**Aetna Life & Casualty advertisement, 1980**

If the insurance industry has nearly a million redundant employees; if it provides barely half the bang we should get for our auto insurance buck; if life insurance purchasers cannot understand what they're buying and if credit life insurance buyers are provided a product that in some states pays as little as 28 cents on the dollar—what should we do? On whom can we rely to set things straight?

State regulation—a $150 million annual enterprise—leaves much to be desired. After a 1980 hearing on auto insurance in New Mexico, throughout which a consumer advocate kept arguing that insurers' *investment income* should be taken into account in the setting of rates, New Mexico's insurance commissioner pulled the consumer advocate aside.

"You keep talking about investment income," he said, slightly

269

embarrassed. "What's investment income?"

In North Carolina, in 1981, three of the eleven members of the Senate Insurance Committee owned and operated insurance agencies. A fourth was a director of Columbus Standard Life. In the House, four of seventeen committee members owned and operated insurance agencies; two more were lawyers representing insurance companies.

A 275-page report issued by the General Accounting Office in October 1979, found "serious shortcomings" in the way states were regulating insurance. "Insurance regulation," it said, "is not characterized by an arms-length relationship between the regulators and the regulated."

Arms length? Here is a photo that appeared in the *National Underwriter*. It shows two executives celebrating the attainment by National Home Life of $5 billion life insurance in force. A proud achievement. A milestone. They are cutting a big cake, each with a hand on the knife. Are they the president and sales director of National Home? No, they are the president of National Home and Missouri's chief insurance regulator. (That was in 1980. A new chief regulator has since been recruited from Alexander & Alexander, one of the giant national insurance brokerage firms. The old commissioner returned to the private practice of law, representing insurance companies.) The party, incidentally, was held at the office of the state insurance department.

GAO found that about half the state commissioners had been previously employed by the industry and that roughly the same proportion joined it after leaving office.

The semiannual meetings of the National Association of Insurance Commissioners—held, like any other industry bash, in places like Mexico City and at the Waldorf Astoria Hotel, and announced by brochures an airline could be proud of—draw as many as 1,500 industry representatives and their spouses. Also 200 to 300 state regulators. The industry spends $2 or $3 million to attend each meeting. Hospitality suites abound. According to the GAO, the NAIC's model laws and regulations, which many states adopt in full, are drafted "with advisory committees composed entirely of insurance company representatives."

The problem is not one of malicious disregard of the public good but of common assumptions and comfortable relationships. It is a club. (Prominent *non*members: Pennsylvania's former commissioner, Herb Denenberg, Massachusetts' brilliant ex-commissioner, James Stone, New Jersey's politically ambitious James Sheeran.) Most of its members are nice guys. Robert J. Bertrand was a nice guy in 1966, when he was employed by the Wisconsin legislature to help revise that state's insurance laws; he was a nice guy in 1967, when he went to work for State Farm; he was a nice guy in 1969, when he left State Farm to become deputy New York insurance commissioner; and he was a nice guy in 1973, when, still in New York, he switched from regulating to lobbying. (Among his clients: State Farm.)

Thomas A. Harnett, meanwhile—also a very nice guy—quit as New York's chief regulator in 1977 because the pay was too low ($47,800). He went to work for the Travelers Insurance Companies ($100,000). In truth, he had taken the regulatory post in the first place only after a lot of urging. It wasn't his fault the governor had decided an attorney who represented insurance company interests, and who would likely represent them again after his stint as a regulator, was the best man for the job.

The "revolving door" is by no means unique to the insurance industry, but nowhere more pervasive. In four out of five states, the insurance commissioner is a political appointee. Politically powerful, the industry can often, in effect, appoint its own regulators. Joseph M. Belth, professor of insurance at Indiana University and a modern-day Elizur Wright, has probably done more to reform deceptive life insurance sales practices than any other living American. Meticulous in his research and assertions almost to the point of obsession, he has never been asked to serve as a state regulator nor even to participate as a member of an NAIC advisory committee. The industry doesn't like him.

Insurance companies and state regulators both oppose federal regulation. Insurers would rather risk the occasional maverick state regulator, and incur the cost of conforming to fifty different sets of regulations, than chance regulation by a federal agency they could not dominate.

And dominate they do. "I once asked a friend in the game how come the Connecticut Insurance Department only had twenty-nine examiners," says a former state regulator, "and he said, 'Because the Travelers doesn't want them to have thirty.'"

It's hard to believe that the nation's insurance buyers would not benefit from a measure of federal oversight. Indeed, one has the feeling that it is this threat, more than anything else, that has gotten state regulators to go as far as they have in standing up to the industry.

In the meantime, there are two things you can do. First is to buy your insurance judiciously and to advise friends to do likewise. The industry cannot long offer unneeded or overpriced insurance if people will not buy it. Second is to support the National Insurance Consumer Organization (344 Commerce Street, Alexandria, VA 22314). It's tax-deductible.

"Look," says former Federal Insurance Administrator* J. Robert Hunter, NICO's full-time president. "As things stand now, a fellow gets appointed commissioner of some state and he wants to do a good job. He wants to hear both sides of each issue and then make a fair decision. He feels judicial. So he holds hearings, and first one side comes in to tell its story (the industry)—*and that's all that comes in.*" No one, typically, comes in with an opposing point of view. NICO has begun to fill the void. In addition to Hunter, NICO's two principals are James Hunt, former Vermont commissioner, and Howard Clark, former South Carolina commissioner. These are capable, knowledgeable people who, if their first year's efforts are indicative, can actually make a difference. Nor am I troubled by the likelihood that NICO's consumer advocacy will from time to time prove excessive. The industry, I feel sure, will be able to stand up for its legitimate interests against the onslaught of two full-time and two part-time professionals.

CALLING IN THE BIG GUNS

If instead of our having to rely for leadership on the National Association of Insurance Commissioners the Lord Himself could be persuaded to spend a few minutes on the case, there are a few things He would do. They would ruffle a few feathers, but when has that ever stopped Him? Rather than get mired in years of committee meetings, He'd size up the situation, entrust as much of the job as possible to the free market, and *leave*. ("Further conversation will accomplish nothing," advises the claims manual.)

The next morning:

---

*The Federal Insurance Administration oversees federal insurance programs, like flood insurance, but has no authority, or budget, to deal with the insurance industry at large.

I. Savings banks, commercial banks, *and anyone else* who could satisfy regulators as to the financial soundness and safeguards of their undertaking, would be allowed to sell life insurance. Savings Bank Life Insurance, for one, would not be limited to New York, Massachusetts and Connecticut, nor to $30,000, $53,000 and $10,000 of coverage. The state legislators who retain these limits are simply bowing to the pressure of an industry that, naturally enough, fears low-priced competition.

II. For competition to work, life insurers would be required to disclose, in a simple, prominent, standardized format, what they were charging each year for the macaroni (insurance protection) and, on policies that include a savings component, the rate of interest they were crediting each year to the cheese. So long as the industry insists this can't be done, consumers should buy inexpensive term insurance and do their saving elsewhere.

III. To protect low-income consumers, easy prey for high-powered salesmen, minimum coverages would be established. It's not enough to print on an insurance policy that only 20 cents of each premium dollar will be paid in claims if the prospect can barely read. Why not ban sales of whole life policies under $10,000 and term insurance under $25,000? Policies smaller than that are ordinarily *so* uneconomical as to represent, ipso facto, a terrible buy. Exceptions would be made where it could be demonstrated that at least 60 cents of each protection premium dollar would be paid in claims and that, with respect to savings, interest would be at least 3 percent for policies kept in force five years or more. If stockbrokers can be required to "know their customers" and not to sell them securities inappropriate to their financial situations, why should not life insurers be prevented from selling to the poor policies that pay out 30 cents on the dollar or earn a negative rate of interest for the first ten years?

IV. Similarly, credit life policies would be subject to a minimum pay-out requirement on the order of 75 or 80 cents. If it is not inappropriate for states to impose price ceilings on credit life insurance—*as most already do*—why would it be inappropriate to *lower* those ceilings to provide the public decent value?

American's life insurance industry, a giant sales machine, is all but unchanged over the last century. But when the machine took shape, the world was different. Television had not been invented (television is a powerful sales tool); there were no credit cards (in 1981, four out of five adult Americans carried at least one); there was no such thing as computer-driven direct-mail marketing. Nor were there Social Security or company life insurance and pension plans (which reduce a family's dependence on life insurance), nor any appreciable income tax. For all its evils, one advantage of the income tax is that it can itself be a most persuasive sales tool. Tens of millions of people can be induced to save for their future security simply by giving them a tax break for doing so. (To wit: IRA and Keogh plans.)

The industry maintains that insurance must be sold—and sold the same way it's been sold for a century. But inflation and increased customer sophistication have pushed more and more buyers toward low-priced term coverage. Where getting a young father to part with $1,500 a year may require several visits to his home and a certain amount of throttling, selling a like amount of term insurance for $300 may not. Whatever ill this may bode for such fathers later in life, when term premiums climb drastically (but when the need for insurance may be much less), or for the nation's formulation of large stable pools of inexpensive capital (read on), it does suggest that insurance may not be as tough a sale as once it was considered. Even a whole life product may not be so tough to sell if it is intelligible, low-cost and high-yielding, on the order of universal life. "For the first time in my memory," said a senior vice president of the Hartford in September 1981, "potential buyers are contacting *us* to purchase life insurance."

Finally, almost every family now has a bank account. Certainly anyone who can afford life insurance does. It's hard to walk two blocks anywhere in America without stumbling over a bank branch. At no significant incremental cost, the banks could reach virtually every family in the country *monthly,* via the bank statement, to sell the very real virtues of life insurance. Bank branch displays could extol the product and direct those with inadequate coverage to a bank officer trained in life insurance counseling. (Very little training would be required to address the needs of 99 percent of American families competently.)

We no longer live in the 1890s, or even the 1940s. Why are we still selling life insurance as if we did?

Allowing the banks, and others, to compete in the sale of life insurance (in Japan, the post office sells it) would destroy the cherished American agency system. Why? Simply because the banks could deliver the product with an efficiency the traditional life insurer cannot. Sophisticated agents would still be required to arrange group sales and to service the complicated, big-dollar cases. And a certain number of insurance agents would doubtless be recruited by the banks to serve as experts at their branches. The difference would be that where many such agents had spent countless hours addressing envelopes (yes, those handwritten envelopes with their offers of a free road atlas in exchange for your birthdate are, as often as not, addressed by the life insurance specialist himself), making cold phone calls and driving from appointment to appointment all week just to make one sale—now they might spend several hours a day actually helping people to buy life insurance.

People today buy savings certificates without a salesman having driven out to their homes; so might they buy life insurance.

Life insurance is an industry entirely dominated by salesmen. Terrific salesmen, inspired salesmen, salesmen trained to believe (with some reason) that whole life is second only to religion as a man's anchor in life, second only to the Constitution as an anchor for our society. Listen to Coy Eklund, once a lieutenant colonel on General Patton's staff and now chairman of the Equitable, in a speech to senior agents in July 1978: "I promise you a trip to glory," he said, "a place high on the mountainside, where, like an eagle perched at the peak, you can one day look back on your accomplishments with a deserved sense of personal pride." He planned to build "an enterprise so good, so wholesome, so galactic in its value to the people of this nation that our efforts will be heralded by our successors for a hundred years to come."

It would be too easy to scoff at such rhetoric. The people at the Equitable, and at the Metropolitan, and at the Prudential, are to be admired for their salesmanship and dedication. They are to be admired, too, for their contributions to community projects. It is the insurance men and women, not the journalists or even the consumer advocates, by and large, who toil for the United Fund and head up Boy Scout troops.

Even so, the only legitimate argument *against* adequate life insurance cost disclosure and wide open competition from the banks, et al, is this: *Less might be sold.* With life insurance recognized for what it is, a financial commodity, its price would be lower. Many would thus find their insurance dollars stretching to buy greater coverage. But others, without a skilled salesman to grab them by the lapel and thrust a pen into their hands, would never get around to buying coverage at all. To the extent people were thus less well insured, their heirs would suffer. And to the extent less money were saved nationwide (with the money that would have gone into insurance premiums going, instead, into consumption), the country as a whole would suffer. The life insurance sales army has functioned for a century as a seller of saving.*

And so the one—and only—legitimate argument against life insurance reform is that it would damage the nation's enormous and costly life insurance sales force and ultimately impair the nation's ability to generate capital through the sale of whole life insurance. If people saw what a bad deal they were getting, goes the argument, in essence, they would buy less life insurance. (Or if sales costs *were* cut back sharply, so better deals *could* be offered, there would not be the marketing muscle to *sell* those better deals. So still we would generate less capital.)

But great as is our need for a higher rate of saving in this country, it hardly seems reasonable that in order to encourage it we should purposely keep consumers in ignorance, knowing that if they knew the truth they would not stand for it. And keep qualified entrants out of the competition, knowing that if they entered it, they might win.

Later that same day:

V. A letter like the one on page 202 would go out over His signature, *in stone,* to every licensed driver, introducing the new nationwide no-fault pay-as-you-drive auto insurance system. The response would be overwhelming. (Forget Mailgrams; I'm talking *tablets.*)

And why not? There are only two things auto insurers do. They sell and process policies; and they settle claims. The first function

---

*But assume that by allowing the life insurance sales force to shrink by 200,000, leaving 50,000 highly trained salesmen to sell group plans and to counsel the "carriage trade," you actually did lower the nation's already disastrously low savings rate, from around 5 percent in mid 1981 to, say, 4.5 percent. There would be two ways you could then get the savings rate back up. Which one makes more sense? You could *rehire* those 200,000 sales reps, and have them sweat blood trying to sell whole life policies, as they do now, committing about 400 million man-hours annually to the task. Or you could simply change a few words in the tax code—and *save* the 400 million man-hours. For example, you could raise the ceiling on contributions to tax-deferred retirement plans (IRAs) from the current $2,000 to, say, $3,000. Such a simple change would boost saving dramatically. And efficiently.

is totally unnecessary. Because we want everyone to carry auto insurance, we needn't sell it to them one at a time. The second function, settling claims, *is* important. But a true no-fault system would cut claims settlement costs dramatically. Result: for the same dollars we pay now, we would get nearly double the benefits. (And they would be more equitably distributed.) Just by reorganizing the system. Praise the Lord.

One hesitates to suggest "socialist" grand plans like this one. But insurance is itself a cooperative enterprise, socialist in nature; a sharing of risk. We may not be eager to share our kitchens, *a la* the Soviet design, but we are more than willing to share our risks. Here—have some of mine.

Much of our insurance is *already* provided in group, state-wide or even national plans. Beyond that, a huge chunk is provided by mutuals. Mutual insurers, while stanchions of capitalism, are nonetheless at root socialist institutions. So it would be a little silly to deny ourselves an efficient, equitable auto insurance system on the grounds that it were somehow unAmerican.

VI. Companies and individuals would begin self-insuring more of the risks they could bear themselves, taking a page from the Equitable Life Assurance Society itself. The Equitable's headquarters at 120 Broadway in New York burned to the ground on January 9, 1912. It was not insured. "Henry B. Hyde had decided that the Society was capable of carrying its own risk on its building," explains the company historian, "and it was estimated that over a period of a quarter of a century he had saved about $3 million by so doing; and the old building was valued at considerably less than $3 million."

VII. Banks would begin offering Self-Insurance Accounts (page 156)—a good way for them to draw deposits and a good way for us to "buy" insurance (for the small risks) that returned more than a dollar for every dollar in "premiums" deposited.

VIII. The I.R.S. would call a press conference to announce a dramatic reversal. Companies would henceforth be permitted to deduct as business expenses reasonable reserves for self-insurance. They would still insure against risks they could not afford to bear, but no longer have a tax incentive for insuring against those they could afford. The proper amount for any given company to deduct as a self-insurance premium would be open to debate—but so are many items in a corporate tax return.

IX. Homeowners and fire policies would be rewritten to take the profit motive out of arson. Where insurance proceeds were not to be used to rebuild a property, only legitimate market value (up to the limits of the policy) would be paid. A property owner could get no more by torching his building than by putting it up for sale.

X. A simple, standardized, prominently displayed disclosure statement would suddenly appear on the sales literature of every insurance plan offered to the public, like the one on page 293. Insurance regulators could request documentation behind the estimates shown, just as TV advertisers must be able to back up *their* claims.

Oh, yes. The federal government would be allowed to look in on the insurance industry from time to time, and everyone on Earth would get a free one-year subscription to *Consumer Reports*. In the meantime. . . .

16

HOW TO BUY INSURANCE

A Brief Consumer's Guide

AUTO INSURANCE

1. Shop around. Don't forget to call such direct writers as State Farm, Nationwide Mutual, Wausau Insurance and GEICO. If you live in California, be sure to call 20th Century Insurance. If you qualify to be a 20th Century policyholder—only preferred risks are accepted—you could cut your current insurance premiums in half.

2. Choose the highest deductibles you can afford, particularly if you itemize your tax deductions. Unreimbursed casualty losses above $100 are tax-deductible; Uncle Sam and your local income tax man become your coinsurers at no charge. Because filing claims can boost your insurance rates substantially, it's generally best to absorb small losses yourself, holding insurance in reserve for the really big loss that, with luck, will never occur.

3. The highest deductible of all, of course, is not to buy collision or comprehensive coverage at all. This makes sense for owners of older cars with low resale values. Also for owners of expensive new cars—if they're very wealthy.

279

4. Many auto insurers offer discounts—if you ask. These include discounts for non-smokers, non-drinkers and graduates of driver-education programs; discounts for teen-age drivers with good grades, for families whose youthful drivers go away to school (leaving the insured vehicle behind) and for families in which the only driver is a woman aged 30 to 64; discounts for vehicles driven less than 7,500 miles a year and for vehicles equipped with air bags, automatic seatbelts or anti-theft devices; discounts if you car-pool; discounts if you insure two or more vehicles with the same company (you'll typically save about 15 percent by doing this); and discounts for drivers who haven't caused an accident in the past few years.

At State Farm, in many states, drivers earn a 5-percent discount after three years' unblemished record, 10 percent after six years. Drivers who have had, within the past three years, an accident for which the company paid out $200 or more and in which no third-party was at fault are charged 10 percent extra. Two such accidents, 30 percent extra. Three or more, 80 percent. (These discounts and surcharges apply to liability, medical payments and collision coverages only.) An adult suburban Chicago resident who drove a 1981 Oldsmobile Cutlass sedan for pleasure only, and who carried a typical package of coverages, paid a basic premium of $464.64 a year. But it could run from as low as $432.08 (had he been accident-free for six years) to as high as $726.88 (if he had had three or more accidents). *If* State Farm chose to renew the policy at all.

In buying automobile insurance under the current system, you are buying six separate coverages:

Most important by far is *bodily injury* (BI) liability coverage. It protects you if you—or anyone else driving your car with your permission—injure pedestrians, people in other cars, or guests in your own car. It also covers you, and family members living with you, if you or they have an accident while driving someone else's car. Bodily injury coverage provides for your legal defense in the event of a lawsuit, and for payment of whatever settlement is made—up to the limits of the policy.

Property damage (PD) liability insurance works just the same way, only it covers damage to other people's *property*.

Liability coverages are typically expressed in a string of three numbers. If you select "10/20/5" coverage, then you are covered up to $10,000 for any person you damage, up to $20,000 for the whole lot of them (even if you've injured eleven); and up to $5,000 for damage to their property. You are underinsured. Even "100/ 300" bodily injury coverage may not be enough to shield you from liability in a serious accident.

Collision coverage pays you, regardless of fault, for damage to your car if it should hit something (other than a bird or an animal) or turn over. It is limited to the value of your car at the time of the accident. In filing accident reports, you may wish to draw inspiration from these: "The guy was all over the road. I had to swerve a number of times before I hit him." "I pulled away from the side of the road, glanced at my mother-in-law and headed over the embankment." "The indirect cause of the accident was a little guy in a small car with a big mouth."

If you suffer property damage in a collision that was not your fault, you have a choice. (Say you have $500-deductible collision coverage.) You may collect from your own insurance company (which may then go after the other driver's insurance company for the full value of your loss and, if successful, return the $500 it deducted from your loss). Or you may file a claim for the full loss directly with the other driver's insurance company, which, if it agreed its policyholder was at fault, would pay your loss out of the policyholder's property-damage coverage. Naturally, your insurer would prefer you did the latter.

Comprehensive coverage reimburses you in the event of fire or theft, "glass breakage, falling objects, missiles, explosion, earthquake, windstorm, hail, water, flood, vandalism or malicious mischief, riot or civil commotion, or collision with a bird or animal." You may also be entitled to payment for personal belongings that were in the car, and for reimbursement for a rental car for a limited period of time.

Medical payments coverage pays medical expenses that you, and all members of your family living with you, may incur, whether riding in your own car or in someone else's, or if hit by a car. It also covers guests riding in your car or in some other car you are driving with the owner's permission. Typical limits are $1,000 or $5,000 per person. If your family already has good medical insurance, you can save money by skipping this coverage.

Uninsured motorist coverage protects you and family members living with you (and guests riding in your car) if injured through the fault of an uninsured or hit-and-run driver, or one whose insurance company goes broke before settling your claim. If it wasn't the other party's fault, you don't collect.

Personal injury protection (PIP) is offered or required in no-fault states. Depending on the state, it may provide just a few thousand dollars of coverage up to (in Michigan, New Jersey and Pennsylvania) unlimited medical expenses and certain other benefits. But because you can still be sued under these so-called no-fault laws for injury you do others, you will still need liability coverage.

HOMEOWNERS INSURANCE

1. Shop around. It's easy to get price quotations over the phone; and you should feel free to request a copy of the policy—and to read it—before committing yourself.

2. Choose the highest deductibles you can afford.

3. Do not allow the limits of your policy to fall behind the actual cost of rebuilding your home. (This excludes the cost of the land and foundation.) In the event of a fire or tornado, you would want to be able to rebuild. *And in the event of a partial loss, your insurer will not cover you fully unless you've insured your home for at least 80 percent of its replacement cost.* Needless to say, this is very important. If the replacement cost of your house has climbed to $100,000 but you still carry only $60,000 of coverage, most companies will pay only three-quarters of your partial loss. (Because $60,000 is only three-quarters of 80 percent of the home's replacement cost.) Or even less. An Aetna Life & Casualty spokesperson gives this example: "Let's say your 15-year-old house is insured for 80 percent of its current replacement cost when the roof blows off. We estimate the normal life of a roof at 20 years. But we'll pay you on a replacement cost basis, so you get a brand-new roof. But suppose you were not insured for a full 80 percent. In that case, we'd likely pay you the price of a new roof minus 15 years' depreciation." Quite a difference.

Claims-payment policies vary from insurer to insurer and from state to state. For structural damage, most do pay replacement cost, which is just what it sounds like. "Actual cash value," on the other hand, which sounds good, isn't. Under this formula, depreciation is subtracted from the estimated replacement cost. Market value,

PERILS AGAINST WHICH PROPERTIES ARE INSURED UNDER THE VARIOUS HOMEOWNERS POLICIES

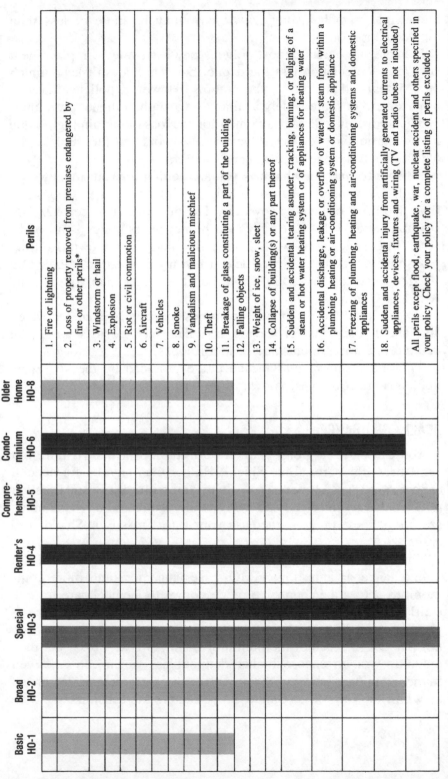

Perils	Basic HO-1	Broad HO-2	Special HO-3	Renter's HO-4	Comprehensive HO-5	Condominium HO-6	Older Home HO-8
1. Fire or lightning							
2. Loss of property removed from premises endangered by fire or other perils*							
3. Windstorm or hail							
4. Explosion							
5. Riot or civil commotion							
6. Aircraft							
7. Vehicles							
8. Smoke							
9. Vandalism and malicious mischief							
10. Theft							
11. Breakage of glass constituting a part of the building							
12. Falling objects							
13. Weight of ice, snow, sleet							
14. Collapse of building(s) or any part thereof							
15. Sudden and accidental tearing asunder, cracking, burning, or bulging of a steam or hot water heating system or of appliances for heating water							
16. Accidental discharge, leakage or overflow of water or steam from within a plumbing, heating or air-conditioning system or domestic appliance							
17. Freezing of plumbing, heating and air-conditioning systems and domestic appliances							
18. Sudden and accidental injury from artificially generated currents to electrical appliances, devices, fixtures and wiring (TV and radio tubes not included)							
All perils except flood, earthquake, war, nuclear accident and others specified in your policy. Check your policy for a complete listing of perils excluded.							

Dwelling and Personal Property

Dwelling only

Personal Property only

*Includes as a peril in traditional forms of the homeowners policy; as an additional coverage in the simplified (HO-76) policies.

Courtesy of the Insurance Information Institute.

meanwhile, which insurers *don't* pay, may be more or less than replacement cost.

For loss of contents, most policies pay cash value—replacement cost less depreciation less the deductible. That doesn't leave much on a 5-year-old stereo. Maybe nothing. However, policies that pay replacement cost are widely available at a slightly higher premium.

Most policies will not pay much for the loss of certain high-value items, particularly jewelry, silverware, artwork and furs, unless you have purchased special coverage ("floaters").

Be sure to find out what it is you are getting for your money.

4. Homeowners policies include liability coverage. Choose at least $100,000 of liability coverage. The difference between $25,000 coverage and $100,000 on my own homeowners policy is all of $4 a year. I consider it $4 well spent, particularly as my own dwelling sits above another. One good leak from my Jacuzzi onto their Old Masters, and the $100,000 would be gone faster than you can say Albrecht Dürer.

5. Inquire about discounts for homes recently built or renovated and about discounts for having installed such devices as smoke detectors, alarm systems and deadbolt locks.

The chart summarizes the coverage provided by the six basic homeowners coverages, known as HO-1 through HO-6.

HEALTH INSURANCE

You can't beat a group plan, if you qualify for one. If not, you can't beat Blue Cross/Blue Shield. Rather than sign up for special cancer coverages, "medigap" plans or mail-order hospitalization policies that promise you $50 a day while you're laid up—the mails are full of these things—increase your Blue Cross/Blue Shield coverage.

Those not covered at work should also consider joining a health maintenance organization. HMO's, serving more and more communities across the country, provide complete medical care for one (fairly large, but fixed) annual fee.

"Major medical" policies, sold by life insurance companies, do not pay out as much of the premium dollar as Blue Cross, but they do allow you to choose higher deductibles, which can save you money; and their rates may be attractive for young people, inasmuch as with Blue Cross/Blue Shield the young tend to subsidize the old.

It's important that you check—now, while you are healthy—just how much of a major illness or operation your present insurance would cover. (Don't forget that your spouse's coverage may cover you, and the children, as well.) If your coverage is limited to $25,000, say, you are underinsured.

The problem in buying supplementary coverage is that it is difficult to avoid at least some duplication. Duplicate coverage is a complete waste, because most policies will not pay a claim already covered by another. The aggressively advertised policies that *will* pay an extra $50 or $100 for each day you're hospitalized, regardless of other coverage, only return about 50 cents on the premium dollar, if that. For advice on supplementary health insurance, consult your employer's personnel department or an experienced insurance agent.

If you have to leave a group plan, because you've quit your job or been laid off, you will generally have thirty to ninety days to convert your coverage to an individual policy with the same carrier. This is a valuable option, because whatever conditions or illnesses you might have contracted would still be covered. With a new plan—if you could qualify for one at all—"pre-existing conditions" might not be covered for a year or more.

Finally, in buying individual policies, try to find one that is "guaranteed renewable," regardless of the number or severity of claims you file.

DISABILITY INSURANCE

This is a tough one. Companies are growing increasingly leery of writing it, because the claims are so hard to verify and can be so expensive to fight even if denied. And people who do buy the coverage find themselves paying not only for legitimate disabilities, the insurer's expenses and profit, but also for the claims of those who are not truly disabled. The veteran claims adjuster referred to in Chapter 8 once had to investigate the disability claim of a Southern Alabama hog trader with a bad back. He got numerous affidavits attesting to the fact that the claimant was still actively buying and selling hogs; he filmed the man loading and unloading hogs from a truck; he was very nearly murdered when the fellow found out what was going on. And *still* the adjuster had to pay the man $3,000 to obtain a final settlement of the claim. It was cheaper than going to court.

That was many years ago, but in principle, if not degree, the same sort of thing happens all the time.

Yet this is one area in which millions of people are underinsured. They're covered if their pipes freeze and burst, but not if they become permanently disabled. Financially speaking, permanent disability is truly a fate worse than death. Most disabled workers will receive workers' compensation insurance if their injury was work related and Social Security benefits even if it wasn't. But that still may leave a lot to be desired. One widely accepted way to increase your chance of obtaining disability insurance at reasonable rates is to choose a six-month or full year waiting period, like a deductible, only after which would benefits start.

CREDIT INSURANCE

Unless you are elderly or in poor health, don't buy it. The same money will stretch a lot farther simply purchasing a regular term insurance policy.

AUTO RENTAL INSURANCE

A good buy when the roads are icy, or if, even in good weather, you average about three accidents a year. Otherwise, forget it. You are automatically covered against major loss when you rent a car or truck; it is the small loss they are trying to get you to insure against.

LIFE INSURANCE

Anyone whose dependents would suffer financially if he or she died has a compelling reason to buy life insurance.

But how much? What kind? For many people, these questions are not so thorny as insurance counselors might have them think. Simply put, many people who need life insurance—young families in particular—need more than they can afford. Therefore, they have not the luxury of choosing between whole life and term—they should simply buy as much inexpensive renewable term insurance as they can.

Fortunately, comparing term insurance policies is relatively easy. You simply call half a dozen life insurers and ask what they charge someone your age and sex for renewable term insurance in the

amount you want. Then choose one. You may not be able to pin-
point the absolute best buy. There may not even *be* one clear-cut
best buy. (How can you tell whether a dividend-paying term policy
will pay more or less in dividends than illustrated? You can't. How
can you value the advantage of a policy guaranteed renewable
through age 70 versus one renewable through age 65? You can't.)
But at least you can avoid paying 20 percent or 50 percent or 200
percent more than you need to for the protection you want. Use the
rates on page 244 as a benchmark.

For most people, it's about as simple as that: Buy renewable term
insurance as inexpensively as possible to tide you over the years
when your children are young and your earnings and assets relatively
low. Shop around, and do your level best not to buy your coverage
piecemeal. As with toothpaste, four 2-ounce tubes cost a great deal
more than one 8-ounce tube.

It may make sense to sign up for the waiver-of-premium rider, at
modest additional cost. It relieves you of the obligation to pay premiums while disabled, and, like a car radio, is an option not everyone needs but most people buy. The accidental-death-and-dismemberment rider may appeal to you, also, but it is rarely geared to pay
out a good return. One "benefit" offered free in most term policies
is the guaranteed right to convert the term policy to whole life. This
is like guaranteeing you the right when you buy a GE hot plate to
come back at any time and buy, at full price, the six-burner range
they were dying to sell you in the first place.

You may also wish to inquire as to each insurer's "Best's" rating
to gauge its financial strength. A.M. Best & Co. rates 250 of the
1365 life insurers in its 1980 edition A +; 279 of them A; 167 B +;
111 B; and 84 C + or C. The remainder have either not been in
business for the requisite five years or are otherwise ineligible for a
Best's rating. With so many top-rated insurers to choose from, there
is no need to deal with other than those rated A +. This is of
particular importance with regard to whole life, universal life and,
to a lesser extent, dividend-paying term policies.

What term insurance *doesn't* do is help you to save money—
neither for retirement nor for the years when life insurance becomes
crushingly expensive.

One solution to this problem is whole life insurance. It has provided millions of people with a steady, disciplined means of saving.
The cash values it accumulates and against which policyholders may

borrow have been, for many, an invaluable last resort in times of financial difficulty—a reserve tank to draw on with one engine out in a blinding rain fifty miles from land. Today, of course, inflation has played a cruel joke on the millions who accepted returns of 2 percent and 4 percent and 6 percent on their insurance dollars—the purchasing power of which, over the last dozen years, has badly eroded. (With any sort of reasonable luck, we will avoid the sort of hyperinflationary experience that has appeared from time to time throughout history—indeed, it may be a deflationary spiral we have next to avoid—but the German experience is always worth remembering. Oil economist Walter Levy tells of a life insurance policy his father had taken out in Germany in 1903. He cashed it in after twenty years of faithful payments and bought a single loaf of bread.)

An alternative to buying whole life insurance is to "buy term and invest the difference"—taking what you save over the cost of whole life and investing it yourself. If you are careful, you are likely to build up at least as much "cash value" as you would have with a whole life policy, possibly a great deal more.

A second alternative is to choose as your savings vehicle one of the new universal life plans described in Chapter 14. They provide much less discipline to save but, currently, much higher interest (and, hence, incentive).

Insurers assume that, *sans* their discipline, you will *not* buy term and invest the difference, as so frequently recommended; you will buy term and *spend* the difference. Often they are right. They further assume that, having spent the difference—whether on a home or home improvements, clothing, vacations, an automobile or tuition—you will have nothing worthwhile to show for it.

There is much to be said for denying oneself pleasures early in life so as to be able enjoy them later. How much more satisfying gradually to see one's level of physical comforts and security rise than to suffer humiliation and deprivation in later years! But it is also true that we are only young once; that even luxuries like beach houses and tennis courts may appreciate in value as fast as a whole life policy; that despite the iron discipline of the whole life contract a significant portion of whole life buyers—unable or unwilling to keep up with the high premiums—drop their policies after just a few years, thereby losing not only their insurance but also much of the cash invested in the policies; and that the threat of inflation, now or in the distant future, is such that even a man or woman who does contribute faithfully to the whole life plan can never be certain that a lifetime of denial will not amount to naught or next to it.

The least expensive way, by far, to meet immediate insurance needs is obviously term insurance. If you can afford, as well, to set money aside for the future, one way of doing it is with whole life. Another (better) is universal life. But before you do anything else you should determine just how much insurance coverage it is you want to carry.

How Much Life Insurance Do You Need?

• If you are single with no dependents, you need little or none. The great push to sell college students life insurance is not entirely unlike the selling of ice to Eskimos, except that a lot more insurance is sold that way than ice.

• If you are married, with a hopelessly incompetent spouse, a family history of heart disease, and a host of little children, you should carry a great deal of insurance. Less if your spouse has a reliable income. Less still if you have fewer children or if those children have wealthy and benevolent grandparents. And still less once those children have grown up.

• If you are very rich, you need no insurance at all, except as it is helpful in paying off estate taxes. If you *live* richly off a high income but own outright little more than a deck of credit cards and some cardigan sweaters, it will take a lot of insurance to keep from exposing your dependents to an altogether seamier side of life when you are gone.

What you want, ideally, is enough insurance, when combined with whatever other assets you may have, to pay for what are euphemistically called "final expenses" (deathbed medical expenses not covered by other insurance, funeral expenses, and possible post-mortem emergencies like an illness of the surviving spouse, payment of bills you didn't know had been incurred, auto repair, and so on), and then enough in addition to replace the income you had been kicking into the family till. So that, financially, anyway, you will not be missed.

For final expenses and a cushion for emergencies, experts advise allowing an amount equal to roughly half one year's gross salary, or, to be on the safe side—particularly if your income is under

$15,000—a full year's income. Obviously, someone anticipating a $350 cremation need allow less for final expenses than someone who would prefer a more elaborate undertaking. (In parts of California, to the horror of funeral directors nationwide, the proportion of cremations to traditional burials has risen to nearly 50 percent.)

But whatever you allow for "final expenses" is nothing compared to what will be needed to replace your income. True, you won't have to replace all of it—just the after-tax portion you were actually taking home. And not even that much, because, with you gone, there will be one less mouth to feed, one less theater ticket to buy. (Not to mention the savings on commuting expenses, cigarettes, medical and dental expenses, gambling losses, the subscription to *Business Week,* insurance premiums, gifts, charitable contributions, clothing, laundry, golf balls, toiletries and cosmetics.) Your surviving dependents will need anywhere from 60 to 75 percent of your current take-home pay in order to live as well, or nearly as well, as they were living before. So if you were earning $30,000 a year and taking home $23,000, your family might maintain roughly the same living standard on $14,000 to $17,000 a year.

A portion of this replacement income will be provided tax-free by Social Security benefits. The typical $5,000-10,000 annual benefit a widow with one or more dependent children receives will go a long way toward replacing 60 percent of the deceased's after-tax income. Thus, low-income families need not rely nearly as much on insurance as higher-income families, so long as they are covered by Social Security.

How much of an "endowment" will it take to make up the gap between Social Security payments and what you actually need? Let's say your take-home pay is $23,000, of which you would like to replace $16,000; and that Social Security would in your case amount to $9,000 (until the children are grown). The gap is $7,000 a year.

To provide your surviving spouse $7,000 a year for 20 years would require a lump sum of $80,000—*if he or she could invest that money to return, after taxes, 6 percent.* To provide a $7,000 annuity that would last *40* years under the same assumptions would require $105,000.

But what about inflation? What if $7,000 in 1996 buys only a so-so steak dinner for two at The Palm? What you really want is to provide $7,000 a year of purchasing power.

It's relatively easy to earn 6 percent after taxes when inflation is running at 12 percent. The only hitch is that in real terms you lose money every year. The best "true return" most people can hope for, after taxes and *after* inflation, is in the neighborhood of a mere 3 percent a year. And even that's no cinch.

With that in mind, the table below shows the lump sums required to provide various levels of after-tax annual income for varying lengths of time. It assumes these lump sums will be invested to return 3 percent after taxes—the true return, after inflation, your heirs might hope to earn. Naturally, if they could earn a higher return, less insurance would be required. To illustrate this, I have included in parentheses figures that assume an 8 percent after-tax return. But, as I say, unless your heirs are extraordinarily clever in investing these proceeds (or reckless but lucky), they will only be able to earn such a high rate if inflation, too, is running at a high rate—in which case the real value of each year's income will shrink and shrink and shrink.

HOW MUCH INSURANCE YOU MUST CARRY TO PROVIDE

This Much Annual Income	For This Many Years			
	10 years	20 years	30 years	40 years
$2,500	$21,000 ($17,000)	$37,500 ($25,000)	$50,000 ($27,500)	$57,500 ($30,000)
$5,000	$42,500 ($33,500)	$75,000 ($50,000)	$100,000 ($55,000)	$115,000 ($60,000)
$7,500	$64,000 ($50,000)	$112,500 ($75,000)	$150,000 ($85,000)	$172,000 ($90,000)
$10,000	$85,000 ($67,000)	$150,000 ($100,000)	$200,000 ($112,500)	$230,000 ($120,000)
$15,000	$128,000 ($100,000)	$225,000 ($150,000)	$300,000 ($170,000)	$345,000 ($180,000)

Note: Main entries assume proceeds will be invested to earn 3 percent after inflation and taxes; parenthetical entries—8 percent.

If these figures look overwhelming (and they do), remember that they may be reduced by the value of assets you already own, and that the income they will provide sits on top of Social Security benefits. Also, your spouse could remarry; your spouse could go to work; once the children are grown, they could provide support as well. Furthermore, it is not inconceivable that your family could be happy with a more modest life-style than they now enjoy.

Nine Simple Steps to Your Answer

1. Determine the 60–75 percent portion of your current annual take-home pay your family would need to live nicely without you.   (Annual Replacement Needs) _____

2. Subtract from this the approximate annual Social Security benefit your family would receive if you died today.   (Annual Social Security) –_____

3. The difference is the annual gap you will want your life insurance to make up.   (Annual Gap) ========

4. Consult the table on page 291 to find the approximate "endowment" you would need to close this gap for the desired number of years.   (Endowment Required) _____

5. Add to this a provision for "final expenses" equal to 50 or even 100 percent of a full year's gross salary.   (Final Expenses) +_____

6. The total of steps 4 and 5 is the maximum amount of insurance coverage you would need.   (Gross Insurance Needed) _____

7. From this you should subtract the value of other assets you may own, such as savings accounts, stocks and bonds, a pension or profit-sharing plan at work, a group life insurance policy at work (do not include equity in your home, as you will not want your heirs to have to sell it or to increase the mortgage).   (Other Assets) –_____

8. Finally. adjust downward for such intangibles as wealthy grandparents, or a spouse who is resourceful, employable, or likely to remarry. Adjust downward, also, to the extent—if any—you feel your family would be happy with even less than the 60–75 percent of your current take-home pay you figured on above. If, for example, they could manage in a less expensive home, subtract the difference between what they could get for your present one and what the new one would cost.   (Intangible Adjustments) –_____

9. This is roughly the amount of life insurance you   (Net Life
    should, if at all possible, be carrying. Review these   Insurance
    calculations as your circumstances change.   ======   Needed)

How Much Life Insurance Do Your Children Need?

In 1980, Nationwide Life Insurance Company of Columbus, Ohio, ran ads in *Newsweek* and *Money* showing a young girl learning to boogie. The headline: FOR $46.50, YOU COULD GIVE HER 4 DISCO LESSONS FROM MR. RUDOLPH. OR A $10,000 ESTATE OF HER OWN. "Right now," Nationwide confided, "she might very well prefer the disco lessons. But you know there are things in life more permanent than the Latin Hustle." Nationwide offered $10,000 of term insurance for young women aged 15 to 22, for $46.50 a year. But very few 15-year-old girls (or children of any sort) have the financial responsibilities to require their carrying *any* life insurance—so the product being sold so persuasively was, for most buyers, of very dubious value. Additionally (and to me this is rather a telling point), *of your $46.50, only $4.50 or so was likely to be paid out in benefits*—while more than $40 would go to expenses and profit.

There were no disclosure statements in the ads, but if there had been, they might have looked like this:

It Is Expected That
APPROXIMATELY 8 CENTS
Of Your Premium Dollar Will Be Paid Out In Benefits
The Rest Goes to Cover Our Expenses, Overhead and Profit

If a child dies—God forbid—a family's finances *improve*. Once funeral expenses are paid, there will be a very substantial *decrease* in family expenses. Not that there will be any comfort in this, but it does make one question the need to insure children. It is *breadwinners* who need insurance.

Furthermore, a very large proportion of the teenage deaths that occur are the result of auto accidents. So it is not unlikely that the child would already be covered for medical and funeral expenses by existing automobile insurance.

Finally, it is *not* true that "it pays to start an insurance plan early," even before you have any dependents—except in two limited respects:

• By signing up early you protect against the possibility of not being able to qualify for it at some later date. However, *very* few people in their twenties and thirties—and for that matter forties and fifties—are in such poor health that they cannot get insurance.

• With whole life, you do begin building a nest egg earlier; the excess cash you pay the insurance company has more time to grow. (For it is only when you reach later life that, actuarially speaking, you are in any serious danger of dying.) Also, you may be spreading your payments out over a greater number of years, depending on the nature of the policy. Thus, each year's payment is smaller. Similarly, the payments on a 30-year home mortgage are smaller than those on a 20-year mortgage. But that certainly doesn't make the home any cheaper! In fact, the bank hits you pretty hard for the extra ten years' interest.

That people actually sign up for such plans—in significant numbers—is evidenced by the sales pitch of the Globe Life and Accident Insurance Company of Oklahoma City. Chairman and chief executive officer R.K. Richey writes in his personalized form letter (to a San Diego couple, in this instance): "Already some 600,000 parents across the country . . . have shown a preference for our particular plans which are for young people under 26 years old." Globe offered a plan that allowed you to buy $5,000 of term coverage for your daughter for $22 the first year, and $40 each year thereafter up to age 26, at which time the plan was convertible to a whole life policy. Of the $40 annual premium, just $5 or so, as with Nationwide, pays for protection.

"Renting Vs. Owning"

Buying term insurance is like renting a house, buying whole life like owning one. It is a persuasive analogy. But when homes are overpriced and good rental units are available at cheap rates (with guaranteed renewable leases), it makes sense to rent.

Net Cost

Insurance agents like to compare whole life with term insurance to show how, over the long run, whole life is cheaper. Here is a flier written by a highly successful general agent to inspire junior colleagues. It compares a 35-year-old buying $100,000 yearly renewable term (first year premium: $229) with another buying a non-participating whole life policy (level premium: $1,325). After thirty-six years, at age 71, the sum of term premiums paid ($51,441) would have surpassed the total of whole life premiums ($49,025). By age 98, assuming the term insurance had been faithfully renewed, total premiums would have been $825,714, versus just $83,475 for whole life. "Sure term is an easy sale," summarizes the general agent. "So are counterfeit thousand dollar bills when offered to trusting, unsuspecting prospects. Worthwhile living does not come easy."

But neither does $10,227—the extra cost of whole life in the first ten years of this example. Compounded at 7 percent after taxes to age 71, that difference would become an $89,212 fund, versus cash value in the whole life policy less than one-third as great.

A whole life plan that actually paid a good rate of interest *could* be a good investment. But "net cost" comparisons like the one above that fail to take into account the time value of money, that fail to disclose the rate of interest at which one's early-year overpayments are compounded, are worth exactly nothing.

Replacing Old Policies

If you have a life insurance policy purchased in the 1950s or 1960s, when interest rates were low and mortality relatively high—particularly if it is a non-participating policy—it will often make sense to drop it (having first secured the coverage you need somewhere else).

If yours is a term insurance policy, the comparison is simple. Replace it if you can find a comparable policy at a significantly lower rate. If it is a whole life policy, write the company to ascertain its surrender value, the premiums that will be due in each of the next twenty years and the projected year-by-year growth in cash value. Compare that, year by year, with current alternatives. An experienced life insurance agent may help you with this comparison; but shop around before accepting his assessment at face value.

Deposit Term, Variable Life

All kinds of life insurance policies are devised in hope of luring your dollars. Deposit term was one such, great for the agent but not the buyer. Variable life offers a fixed death benefit, but cash values that depend on the insurer's stock market savvy.

Rule of thumb: The more trimmings an insurance plan has and the harder someone is pitching it, the faster you should run. You may (conceivably) be passing up a good product; but there are other good products available that *are* comprehensible. Stick with simple value.

appendixes

A. THREE HORRIBLY UNFAIR JOKES YOU CAN TELL ABOUT LAWYERS
(With Space to Append Three More of Your Own)

Most attorneys are exemplary citizens. Had we but a few of them, everything might be fine. It is as a *group* that their swollen ranks are gumming everything up.Thus, whenever one has a chance to disparage attorneys—not *specific* attorneys, but attorneys in general—one owes it to the graduate students of tomorrow to do so. *Engineering* school is where we need to have them apply, or perhaps biotechnology school or culinary school or even business school—but not law school. With that thought in mind:

St. Peter is at his post, greeting heaven's new arrivals and assigning them living quarters. First in line is the Pope. St. Peter directs him to heaven's equivalent of one of those $6-a-night roadside motel rooms. No phone, no TV—nothing. Next in line is a lawyer. St. Peter assigns him to a two-bedroom suite. Sauna—the works. The third man can't restrain his curiosity. "St. Peter, forgive me . . . I mean, the *Pope,* for God's sake! And some lawyer?" He gestures weakly at their respective accommodations.

"My son," St. Peter replies calmly, "we have seventy-five popes up here. We've never had a lawyer."

A doctor, an architect and a lawyer—classmates from college—were relaxing at their club. Talk turned to their respective dogs, each of which, apparently, was most remarkable. Boast followed boast, tempers flared, and finally it was decided to see just what was what.

The doctor called to his beagle. "Hippocrates," he said, "do your stuff." Whereupon Hippocrates ran to the back door of the club, rooted around the garbage, and in several quick trips returned with a pile of bones. *Which he assembled in the form of a human skeleton.* Beaming, the doctor waited for congratulations. But the architect said, "Hey, that's nothing. Sliderule, get over here." Sliderule, an English sheepdog much in need of shearing, came loping over. "Do your stuff, Sliderule." Whereupon Sliderule *tore* into the bones, added a few more from around back of the club, and in less than a minute had assembled a near-perfect model of the Taj Mahal. The architect grinned uncontrollably. Both he and the doctor turned to look at the lawyer.

"Bullshit," called the lawyer to his Doberman. "Do your stuff." Whereupon Bullshit ate all the bones, the beagle and the sheepdog.

(You:) Do you know how to save five drowning lawyers?
(They:) No.
(You:) Good!

B. HOW TO FIGURE YOUR SOCIAL SECURITY BENEFITS

Social Security is the largest insurance plan of all. Where the life insurance industry paid out $40 billion in life, health and retirement benefits in 1981, the Social Security Administration paid out more like $150 billion.

There is no way to know exactly what your Social Security benefits will be when you (or yours) begin to collect them. However, you can probably get a pretty good idea by looking to see what they would be *now*, were you to retire, die or become disabled today.

Social Security benefits are likely to rise with the cost of living. But in *real dollars, real buying power*, it's reasonable to assume that the payments will neither increase (how could we afford it?) nor decrease sharply (how could Congress allow it?). The operative word here would seem to be "sharply," because clearly the squeeze is on. As national demographics tilt ever more heavily toward older Americans, there will be ever fewer workers to support ever greater numbers of retirees. Thus, it is likely the retirement age will gradually be pushed back, and that benefits, expressed as a measure of buying power, have peaked.

Social Security benefits are tied to how much you have paid in to the system. What's more, in the case of death benefits, the payout to your surviving spouse will depend in part on your age at death and on the composition of your family. Therefore, the examples below are to be taken as *only the roughest guideline* of what you might expect.

The figures assume, at the low end, that the worker has averaged about $4,000 in Social Security-taxed earnings a year since 1950; and, at the high end, that the worker has in all years earned at least as much as the top income level on which Social Security tax was levied. (As recently as 1965, only the first $4,800 of earnings was subject to Social Security tax. By 1981, that figure had climbed to $29,700.)

EXAMPLES OF ANNUAL *TAX-FREE* INCOME FROM SOCIAL SECURITY

Recipient	Amount
Worker retiring at 65, with no dependents	$4,466–8,124
Worker retiring at 65, with dependents	$7,636–14,216
Disabled worker, no dependents	$2,760–7,728
Disabled worker with dependents	$3,276–11,592
Widow or widower at 65	$4,466–8,124
Widow or widower caring for one child	$4,140–11,592
Widow or widower caring for more than one child	$4,140–13,531

To qualify for benefits, no one needs credit for more than ten years of work covered by social security. The length of credit required ranges down to as little as 1½ years for people who become disabled or die in their early twenties.

If you are within several years of retirement, don't rely on the rough guidelines above. Write or call any of the 1,300 Social Security offices around the country and ask for the booklet and forms that will help you make a closer estimate.

C. ACCIDENTS AND DISASTERS FOR A RAINY AFTERNOON

PESTILENCE.

More than half a million Americans died of Spanish influenza in 1918—nearly ten times the number who died fighting World War I. The flu, which was actually Chinese in origin, killed an estimated 21.6 million people worldwide.

VOLCANIC ERUPTION.

The eruption of Krakatoa in Indonesia in 1883, the largest in recorded history, killed 36,000 people (mostly as a result of waves up to 120 feet high) and was heard 3,000 miles away. Fire alarms were pulled in Connecticut, so intense were the sunsets that ensued.

VEHICULAR CONCUSSION.

In 1896, when there were four automobiles in the United States, two were in St. Louis. They collided. Both drivers were hurt, one seriously.

DROWNING.

A 90-foot storage tank in Boston's North End burst on January 15, 1919, releasing 2 million gallons of molasses in a 20-foot tidal wave. Buildings were knocked from their foundations; twenty-one people drowned. Horses, mired in molasses, had to be shot.

ROOF COLLAPSE.

With the American Institute of Architects 1979 convention going great guns just a few blocks away, the roof of Kansas City's award-winning Kemper Arena collapsed in a heavy rainstorm. News reached Helmut Jahn, the arena's designer, in town to receive another AIA citation, in the midst of a banquet. "It's just terrible," he said.

MALPRACTICE.

A West German surgeon removed the only kidney of a 16-year-old boy, mistaking it for a tumor.

WILDLIFE.

A large sturgeon jumped out of the water, smashing through the windshield of an onrushing speedboat and knocking the driver unconscious. The boat, reports Aetna, ran into a tree.

Also: A policyholder tormented by mosquitoes finally "leaped out of bed and sprayed the little winged devils into oblivion." In the morning he realized he had grabbed a cannister filled with red enamel paint.

In Illinois, meanwhile (October 2, 1979), the State Supreme Court upheld a workers' compensation award for injuries to a metalworker who, in attempting to step up on a bench to swat a cockroach, slipped and hurt his toe. The Supreme Court held that his action, while not directly related to his employment duties, was nonetheless reasonable and compensable.

SEX.

A 37-year-old employee of an American autoparts manufacturer, on assignment in Birmingham, England, collapsed and died in March 1979 after having sex with a female co-worker. It was determined that vapors from a space heater in her flat had been the cause. A Michigan administrative law judge ruled that although their meeting had been held after normal working hours, and off company premises, the man's family was eligible for workers' compensation benefits. "The deceased's work assignment in England exposed him to situations and hazards that were different in nature and degree from those found in Michigan," wrote the judge.

TRAIN WRECKS.

True disaster buffs will have on their shelves the profusely illustrated *Train Wrecks,* by Robert C. Reed (Bonanza Books/Crown Publishing, New York). Did you know that there were 138 train wrecks in 1853 alone? Or that Isaac Dripps invented the cow-catcher in 1833? Chapters include: "The Horrors of Travel," "Derailments," "Head On Collisions," "Rear End Collisions," "Bridge Disasters," "Runaways" and "Boiler Explosions."

The very first railroad death occurrred on June 17, 1831, on the South Carolina Road—at 135 miles, the world's longest—"when the fireman, annoyed by the loud hissing noise of steam escaping from the safety valve, simply held the valve down."

A generation later, Dr. John T. Hannigan, stone deaf and a resident of Columbus, New Jersey, would be out in his surrey and fail to heed the insistent whistle of an oncoming train. The train struck one of Hannigan's horses and derailed, killing twenty-three. Dr. Hannigan was unhurt.

The very best train wreck, however, you may actually have witnessed. It occurred in *The Wrong Box,* a British comedy, in which the engineers of two old-fashioned trains find themselves locomotive to locomotive, head to head, suspended some feet off the ground after a terrible crash. The camera pans slowly over the wreckage sprawled out behind each of them, then comes in tight on the two men, unhurt but dazed. Says one of them: "We 'aven't 'eard the last of *this,* I'll wager."

SHIPWRECK.

When the *Andrea Doria* was rammed broadside by the steel-reinforced bow of the *Stockholm* in June 1956, in thick fog off Nantucket, Linda Morgan, 14, woke to find herself unharmed on the bow of the *Stockholm.* Her sister, asleep a few feet below, on the lower bunk, was killed.

FURTHER READING.

Indispensable and in paperback is *The Great International Disaster Book,* by James Cornell (Pocket Books, 1979), the teaser for which alone is worth the price of admission:

> Our Worst Fears Come True. Our Bravest Moments Captured. The Great Fire of London in 1666. The two-pound hailstones that killed 23 people in Russia. The bizarre plane collision that dumped 120,000 pieces of mail and an apparently unhurt 11-year-old passenger on the streets of Brooklyn. [Apparently unhurt, he died the next day.] This encyclopedia contains not only a complete record of the world's great disasters, but also the causes [TWA and United collided in a snowstorm], the consequences [most of the mail was never delivered], and how to survive them [if a tornado is coming and no underground shelter is available, get into the bathtub].

Largest U.S. Disasters

	Type and Location	No. of Deaths	Date of Disaster
Floods:	Galveston tidal wave	6,000	Sept. 8, 1900
	Johnstown, Pa.	2,209	May 31, 1889
	Ohio and Indiana	732	Mar. 28, 1913
	St. Francis, Calif. dam burst	450	Mar. 13, 1928
	Ohio and Mississippi River valleys . .	380	Jan. 22, 1937
Hurricanes:	Florida	1,833	Sept. 16–17, 1928
	New England	657	Sept. 21, 1938
	Louisiana	500	Sept. 29, 1915
	Florida	409	Sept. 1–2, 1935
	Louisiana and Texas	395	June 27–28, 1957
Tornadoes:	Illinois	606	Mar. 18, 1925
	Mississippi, Alabama, Georgia	402	Apr. 2–7, 1936
	Southern and Midwestern states . . .	307	Apr. 3, 1947
	Ind., Ohio, Mich., Ill. and Wis. . . .	272	Apr. 11, 1965
	Ark., Tenn., Mo., Miss. and Ala. . .	229	Mar. 21–22, 1952
Earthquakes:	San Francisco, earthquake and fire . .	452	Apr. 18, 1906
	Alaskan earthquakes-tsunami hit Hawaii, Calif.	173	Apr. 1, 1946
	Long Beach, Calif. earthquake	120	Mar. 10, 1933
	Alaskan earthquake and tsunami . . .	117	Mar. 27, 1964
	San Fernando-Los Angeles, Calif. earthquake	64	Feb. 9, 1971
Marine:	*Sultana* exploded, Mississippi River . .	1,547	Apr. 27, 1865
	Empress of Ireland ship collision, St. Lawrence River	1,024	May 29, 1914
	General Slocum burned, East River . .	1,021	June 15, 1904
	Eastland capsized, Chicago River . . .	812	July 24, 1915
	Morro-Castle burned, off New Jersey coast	134	Sept. 8, 1934
Aircraft:	Crash of scheduled plane near O'Hare Airport, Chicago	273	May 25, 1979
	Two-plane collision over San Diego, Calif.	144	Sept. 25, 1978
	Two-plane collision over New York City	134	Dec. 16, 1960
	Two-plane collision over Grand Canyon, Ariz.	128	June 30, 1956
	Crash of scheduled plane in New York City	113	June 24, 1975

Sources: *National Almanac, World Almanac, Official Associated Press Almanac,* National Fire Protection Association, Chicago Historical Society, Texas Inspection Bureau, American Red Cross, U.S. Bureau of Mines, National Oceanic and Atmospheric Administration, city and state boards of health, and the Metropolitan Life Insurance Company.

Courtesy, National Safety Council, *Accident Facts.*

	Type and Location	No. of Deaths	Date of Disaster
Railroad:	Two-train collision near Nashville, Tenn.	101	July 9, 1918
	Two-train collision, Eden, Colo. . . .	96	Aug. 7, 1904
	Avalanche hit two trains near Wellington, Wash.	96	Mar. 1, 1910
	Bridge collapse under train, Ashtabula, Ohio	92	Dec. 29, 1876
	Rapid transit train derailment, Brooklyn, N.Y.	92	Nov. 1, 1918
Fires:	Peshtigo, Wis., and surrounding area forest fire	1,152	Oct. 9, 1871
	Iroquois Theatre, Chicago	575	Dec. 30, 1903
	Cocoanut Grove Nightclub, Boston . .	492	Nov. 28, 1942
	North German Lloyd Steamships, Hoboken, N.J.	326	June 30, 1900
	Ohio Penitentiary, Columbus	320	Apr. 21, 1930
Explosions:	Texas City, Texas, ship explosion . . .	561	Apr. 16, 1947
	Port Chicago, Calif., ship explosion . .	322	July 18, 1944
	New London, Texas, school explosion .	294	Mar. 18, 1937
	Eddystone, Pa., munitions plant explosion	133	Apr. 10, 1917
	Cleveland, Ohio, gas tank explosion . .	130	Oct. 20, 1944
Mines:	Monongha, West Va., coal mine explosion	361	Dec. 6, 1907
	Dawson, New Mexico, coal mine fire .	263	Oct. 22, 1913
	Cherry, Ill., coal mine fire	259	Nov. 13, 1909
	Jacobs Creek, Pa., coal mine explosion	239	Dec. 19, 1907
	Scofield, Utah, coal mine explosion . .	200	May 1, 1900

D. INSURANCE YOU MAY NOT HAVE KNOWN YOU HAD

Most American families are covered by Social Security in the event of death or disability. Examples of benefits will be found on page 302.

In addition, 88 percent of all salaried and wage-earning Americans in 1981 were covered by workers' compensation for job-related injuries and illnesses.* Each state has its own rules, but in most, disabled workers received two-thirds of their pre-disability wage, up to certain limits—tax-free. The table at right shows the ceilings on weekly benefits payable to permanently disabled workers. In all but a few states, the same weekly benefits were paid during periods of *temporary* total disability, as well as to the spouse and children of workers killed on the job. If a plant foreman in Pittsburgh falls into a blast furnace, or a Philadelphia bank executive is murdered by an irate loan applicant, his spouse will collect (on top of Social Security, life insurance and the rest) $13,624 a year in workers' compensation benefits, tax-free, for life or until she remarries.

There are also lump sum benefits paid for certain injuries. To see how much more valuable a thumb is if it is attached to a federal employee, rather than some other worker, see the table on the two pages that follow.

---

*The definition of "job-related" grows ever broader. A secretary unhinged by the discovery of her boss's dead body was awarded benefits, as was the widow of a judge whose death was held to be related to the enormity of his case backlog. Coverage was even awarded to the widow of a Michigan man who died after making love to a co-worker, after hours, at her flat. (See page 304.)

STATE	PERMANENT TOTAL DISABILITY (Maximum Weekly Benefits)			STATE	PERMANENT TOTAL DISABILITY (Maximum Weekly Benefits)		
	1970	1981	Increase		1970	1981	Increase
Alabama	$ 50	$148	196%	Nebraska	55	180	227%
Alaska	83	859	935%	Nevada	66	245	269%
Arizona	154	204	32%	New Hampshire	67	213	218%
Arkansas	49	126	157%	New Jersey	91	199	119%
California	52	175	237%	New Mexico	48	222	363%
Colorado	60	245	308%	New York	80	215	169%
Connecticut	84	285	239%	North Carolina	50	210	320%
Delaware	75	175	133%	North Dakota	59	213	261%
D.C.	70	456	551%	Ohio	56	275	391%
Florida	56	228	307%	Oklahoma	43	155	260%
Georgia	50	110	120%	Oregon	63	261	314%
Hawaii	113	235	109%	Pennsylvania	60	262	337%
Idaho	43	198	360%	Rhode Island	70	217	210%
Illinois	71	376	430%	South Carolina	50	216	332%
Indiana	57	140	146%	South Dakota	50	191	282%
Iowa	56	384	586%	Tennessee	47	119	153%
Kansas	56	170	204%	Texas	49	133	171%
Kentucky	56	233	316%	Utah	47	230	389%
Louisiana	49	163	233%	Vermont	61	208	241%
Maine	73	322	341%	Virginia	62	213	244%
Maryland	85	248	192%	Washington	81	205	152%
Massachusetts	70	245	250%	West Virginia	66	262	300%
Michigan	104	181	74%	Wisconsin	79	249	215%
Minnesota	70	244	249%	Wyoming	35	362	934%
Mississippi	40	98	145%	**Fed'l Employees**	**405**	**723**	**103%**
Missouri	58	150	159%	**Cost of Living**			**135%**
Montana	60	219	265%				

For additional lump-sum payments, see "An Eye for an Ear," pages 310-11.

AN EYE FOR AN EAR

1981 LUMP SUM WORKERS' COMPENSATION BENEFITS

IN THIS GROUP OF STATES, COMPENSATION FOR TEMPORARY
DISABILITY IS ALLOWED IN ADDITION TO ALLOWANCE FOR SCHEDULED INJURY

Jurisdiction	Arm At Shoulder	Hand	Thumb	First Finger	Second Finger	Third Finger	Fourth Finger	Leg At Hip	Foot	Great Toe	Other Toes	One Eye	Hearing One Ear	Hearing Both Ears
Alabama	$32,856	$25,160	$9,176	$6,364	$4,588	$3,256	$2,368	$29,600	$20,572	$4,736	$1,628	$18,352	$7,844	$24,124
Alaska	43,680	33,600	10,400	6,440	4,200	3,500	2,100	40,320	28,700	5,320	2,240	22,400	7,280	28,000
Arizona	43,725	36,437	10,931	6,559	5,101	3,644	2,915	36,437	29,150	5,101	1,822	21,862	14,575	43,725
Arkansas	25,200	18,900	7,560	4,410	3,780	2,520	1,890	22,050	15,750	3,780	1,260	12,600	5,040	18,900
California	29,488*	21,770	3,797	1,680	1,680	1,260	1,260	32,288*	16,870	2,117	420	10,553**	3,157	21,770
Colorado	17,472	8,736	4,200	2,184	1,512	924	1,092	17,472	8,736	2,184	924	11,676	2,940	11,676
Connecticut	88,920	71,820	27,075	15,390	12,540	8,835	7,410	67,830	56,430	11,970	3,705	66,975	14,820	44,460
Delaware	43,800	38,544	13,140	8,760	7,008	5,256	3,504	43,800	28,032	7,008	2,628	35,040	13,140	30,660
D.C.	142,347	111,323	34,218	20,987	13,687	11,406	6,844	131,397	95,529	13,687	7,300	72,998	93,724	91,248
Florida	No schedule. Benefits paid according to degree of impairment and loss of earnings.													
Georgia	24,750	17,600	6,600	4,400	3,850	3,300	2,750	24,750	14,850	3,300	2,200	13,750	6,600	16,500
Hawaii	73,320	57,340	17,625	10,810	7,050	5,875	3,525	67,680	48,175	8,930	3,760	37,600	12,220	47,000
Idaho	36,300	32,670	13,310	8,470	6,655	3,025	1,815	24,200	16,940	5,082	847	21,175	—	21,175
Illinois	88,438	71,503	26,343	15,053	13,172	9,408	7,527	75,266	58,331	13,172	4,516	60,213	14,113	56,450
Iowa	88,250	67,070	21,180	12,355	10,590	8,825	7,060	77,660	52,950	14,120	5,295	49,420	17,650	61,775
Maine	66,434	54,808	16,608	10,629	9,301	6,643	5,647	66,434	54,808	8,304	3,322	33,217	16,608	66,434
Maryland	74,400	62,000	24,800	9,920	8,680	7,440	6,200	74,400	62,000	9,920	2,480	62,000	31,000	62,000
Massachusetts*	6,750	5,250	—	—	—	—	—	6,000	4,500	—	—	6,000	4,500	12,000
Michigan	56,490	45,150	13,650	7,980	6,930	4,620	3,360	45,150	34,020	6,930	2,310	34,020	2,310	34,020
Minnesota	65,880	53,680	15,860	9,760	8,540	6,100	4,880	53,680	40,260	8,540	3,660	39,040	20,740	41,480
Mississippi	19,600	14,700	5,880	3,430	5,940	1,960	2,970	17,150	12,250	5,940	980	9,800	3,920	14,700
Montana	30,660	21,900	8,212	4,380	4,052	2,738	1,642	32,850	19,710	4,052	1,752	18,068	4,380	21,900
Nebraska	40,500	31,500	10,800	6,300	5,400	3,600	2,700	39,700	27,000	5,400	1,800	22,500	9,000	(*)
Nevada	No schedule. Degree of disability determined in relation to whole man.*													
New Hampshire	45,582	37,275	10,650	6,603	5,538	4,047	2,769	45,582	32,163	5,538	2,130	26,838	11,076	45,582
New Jersey	48,161	29,255	4,583	3,055	2,444	1,833	1,222	45,972	24,412	2,444	917	23,882	2,820	18,574
New Mexico	44,300	26,688	12,182	6,202	4,873	3,766	3,101	44,300	25,472	7,752	3,101	28,795	8,860	33,225
North Carolina	50,400	42,000	15,750	9,450	8,400	5,250	4,200	42,000	30,240	7,350	2,100	25,200	14,700	31,500
North Dakota	10,000	10,000	3,250	2,000	1,500	1,000	800	9,360	6,000	1,200	480	6,000	2,000	8,000
Ohio	30,938	24,062	8,250	4,812	4,125	2,750	2,062	27,500	20,625	4,125	1,375	17,188	3,438	17,188

State	19,200	15,000	4,800	2,400	2,200	1,000	600	15,000	13,500	1,800	400	10,000	6,000	19,200
Oregon	67,704	52,948	16,275	9,982	6,510	5,425	4,340	67,704	44,485	8,246	2,170	34,720	13,020	43,400
Rhode Island	47,520	42,120	14,040	8,640	7,560	5,400	4,320	42,120	30,240	7,560	2,160	21,600	17,280	35,640
South Carolina	38,200	30,560	9,550	6,685	5,730	3,820	2,865	30,560	23,875	5,730	1,910	28,650	9,550	28,650
South Dakota	23,800	23,800	7,140	4,165	3,570	2,380	1,785	23,800	14,875	3,570	1,190	28,650	8,925	17,850
Tennessee	28,611	19,125	10,251	6,426	5,202	2,601	1,224	19,125	13,464	3,978	612	18,360	7,650	15,300
Utah	44,720	44,720	10,400	6,656	5,200	4,160	2,496	44,720	36,400	5,200	2,080	26,000	10,816	44,720
Vermont	42,600	37,275	12,780	7,455	6,390	4,260	3,195	37,275	26,625	6,390	2,130	21,300	10,650	21,300
Virginia	36,000	36,000	12,960	8,100	6,480	3,240	1,620	36,000	25,200	7,560	2,760	14,400	10,650	28,800
Washington	41,933	41,933	13,978	6,989	4,892	3,494	3,494	41,933	24,461	6,989	2,796	23,063	17,472	45,427
West Virginia	35,000	28,000	11,200	4,200	4,150	1,820	1,960	35,000	17,500	5,833	1,750	19,250	3,850	23,100
Wisconsin	34,944	29,470	10,629	7,005	3,623	3,623	1,960	32,611	24,156	4,831	1,691	22,707	9,662	—
Wyoming	36,234	32,611	10,629	7,005	3,623	3,623	1,960	32,611	24,156	4,831	1,691	22,707	9,662	—
Federal Employees	**225,507**	**176,358**	**54,209**	**33,248**	**21,683**	**18,070**	**10,842**	**208,161**	**148,170**	**27,466**	**11,564**	**115,645**	**37,585**	**144,556**
Longshoremen	142,347	111,323	34,218	20,987	13,687	11,406	6,844	131,397	95,529	13,687	7,300	72,998	23,724	91,248

IN THIS GROUP OF STATES, COMPENSATION FOR TEMPORARY DISABILITY IS ALLOWED IN ADDITION TO SCHEDULED INJURY WITH CERTAIN LIMITATIONS AS TO PERIOD

State														
Indiana	18,750	15,000	4,500	3,000	2,625	2,250	1,500	16,875	13,125	4,500	2,250*	13,125	5,625	15,000
Kansas	35,700	25,500	15,750	5,400	5,100	3,400	2,550	34,000	21,250	5,100	1,700	20,400	5,100	18,700
Missouri	20,880	15,750	5,400	4,050	3,150	3,150	1,980	18,630	13,500	3,600	1,260	12,600	3,960	15,120
New York	32,760	25,620	7,875	4,830	2,625	2,625	1,575	30,240	21,525	3,990	1,680	16,800	6,300	15,750
Pennsylvania	107,420	87,770	26,200	13,100	10,480	7,860	7,336	107,420	65,500	10,480	4,192	72,050	15,720	68,120

IN THIS GROUP OF STATES, COMPENSATION FOR TEMPORARY DISABILITY IS DEDUCTED FROM THE ALLOWANCE FOR SCHEDULED INJURY

No schedule. Permanent partial disability benefits paid at 66-2/3% of wages up to 425 weeks according to degree of disability.

State														
Kentucky	32,600	24,450	8,150	4,890	3,260	3,260	1,630	28,525	20,375	3,260	1,630	16,300	—	—
Louisiana	22,500	18,000	5,400	3,150	2,700	1,800	1,350	22,500	18,000	2,700	900	18,000	9,000	27,000
Oklahoma	18,000	18,000	5,400	3,150	2,700	1,800	1,350	18,000	18,000	2,700	900	18,000	9,000	27,000
Texas	26,600	19,950	7,890	5,985	3,990	2,793	1,995	16,625	13,300	3,990	1,330	13,300	—	19,950

Calif. *Plus life pension up to $64.21 weekly.
**If unable to wear artificial eye.

Ind. *Second toe—$2,250, third toe—$1,500, fourth toe—$1,125, fifth toe—$750.

Mass. *Benefits fixed at amount reflected in chart. Proportional benefits for functional loss of use of arm, hand, leg, or foot.

Nebr. *Permanent total loss of hearing is compensated as permanent total disability.

Nev. *Each 1% of impairment is compensated by 1/2% of worker's monthly wage up to maximum (= $1,061.24 as of 7/1/80), payable for 5 years or until age 65, whichever is later.

Source: U.S. Chamber of Commerce
In addition to these lump sum benefits, workers' compensation laws also provide extensive medical and rehability benefits, weekly or monthly benefits for temporary or total disability, and benefits to spouse and children in the event of fatal accidents. For an excellent summary of the laws and benefits, write for the Analysis of Workers' Compensation Laws, U.S. Chamber of Commerce, Washington, D.C. 20062. Updated annually in March.

E. MORBID STATISTICS

**EXPECTATION OF LIFE
AT BIRTH IN THE UNITED STATES (YEARS)**

Year	White			All Other			Total		
	Male	Female	Total	Male	Female	Total	Male	Female	Total
1900 . .	46.6	48.7	47.6	32.5	33.5	33.0	46.3	48.3	47.3
1910 . .	48.6	52.0	50.3	33.8	37.5	35.6	48.4	51.8	50.0
1920 . .	54.4	55.6	54.9	45.5	45.2	45.3	53.6	54.6	54.1
1930 . .	59.7	63.5	61.4	47.3	49.2	48.1	58.1	61.6	59.7
1940 . .	62.1	66.6	64.2	51.5	54.9	53.1	60.8	65.2	62.9
1950 . .	66.5	72.2	69.1	59.1	62.9	60.8	65.6	71.1	68.2
1960 . .	67.4	74.1	70.6	61.1	66.3	63.6	66.6	73.1	69.7
1961 . .	67.8	74.5	71.0	61.9	67.0	64.4	67.0	73.6	70.2
1962 . .	67.6	74.4	70.9	61.5	66.8	64.1	66.8	73.4	70.0
1963 . .	67.5	74.4	70.8	60.9	66.5	63.6	66.6	73.4	69.9
1964 . .	67.7	74.6	71.0	61.1	67.2	64.1	66.9	73.7	70.2
1965 . .	67.6	74.7	71.0	61.1	67.4	64.1	66.8	73.7	70.2
1966 . .	67.6	74.7	71.0	60.7	67.4	64.0	66.7	73.8	70.1
1967 . .	67.8	75.1	71.3	61.1	68.2	64.6	67.0	74.2	70.5
1968 . .	67.5	74.9	71.1	60.1	67.5	63.7	66.6	74.0	70.2
1969 . .	67.8	75.1	71.3	60.5	68.4	64.3	66.8	74.3	70.4
1970 . .	68.0	75.6	71.7	61.3	69.4	65.3	67.1	74.8	70.9
1971 . .	68.3	75.8	72.0	61.6	69.7	65.6	67.4	75.0	71.1
1972 . .	68.3	75.9	72.0	61.5	69.9	65.6	67.4	75.1	71.1
1973 . .	68.4	76.1	72.2	61.9	70.1	65.9	67.6	75.3	71.3
1974 . .	68.9	76.6	72.7	62.9	71.2	67.0	68.2	75.9	71.9
1975 . .	69.4	77.2	73.2	63.6	72.3	67.9	68.7	76.5	72.5
1976 . .	69.7	77.3	73.5	64.1	72.6	68.3	69.0	76.7	72.8
1977 . .	70.0	77.7	73.8	64.6	73.1	68.8	69.3	77.1	73.2
1978* . .	70.2	77.8	74.0	65.0	73.6	69.2	69.5	77.2	73.3
1979* . .	70.6	78.3	74.4	65.5	74.5	69.9	69.9	77.8	73.8

Source: National Center for Health Statistics, U.S. Department of Health and Human Services.
*Provisional Data
Courtesy, American Council of Life Insurance.

WHO DIES, WHO COLLECTS

Analysis of Payments to Beneficiaries Under
Ordinary Life Insurance in the United States

	Percent of Policies			Percent of Amount		
	May 1969	May 1973	April 1977	May 1969	May 1973	April 1977
SEX OF INSURED						
Male	78.8	77.0	75.4	91.1	89.2	88.6
Female	21.2	23.0	24.6	8.9	10.8	11.4
Total	100.0	100.0	100.0	100.0	100.0	100.0
AGE OF INSURED AT DEATH						
Under 25	4.0	3.4	3.0	4.1	3.4	3.2
25–34	2.0	2.5	2.5	4.2	5.5	6.0
35–44	4.7	4.3	3.7	8.4	9.2	8.7
45–54	12.2	11.8	10.5	18.7	18.2	17.5
55–64	24.4	23.3	21.7	25.5	24.5	25.1
65–74	26.9	27.2	28.0	19.8	21.7	21.4
75 or Older	25.8	27.5	30.6	19.3	17.5	18.1
Total	100.0	100.0	100.0	100.0	100.0	100.0
RELATIONSHIP OF BENEFICIARY TO INSURED						
Husband	8.2	8.6	9.1	3.2	3.9	4.4
Wife	54.1	51.5	52.0	57.9	54.1	58.2
Child or Children	16.1	17.7	18.0	9.5	11.0	10.6
Other Relatives	12.0	11.6	10.9	9.4	7.8	8.3
Estate or Trust	5.9	6.9	6.3	9.7	9.7	9.0
Institution	.6	.6	.6	1.4	1.7	1.4
All Other	3.1	3.1	3.1	8.9	11.8	8.1
Total	100.0	100.0	100.0	100.0	100.0	100.0
DURATION OF POLICY WHEN IT BECAME A CLAIM						
Less Than 1 Year	1.8	1.9	1.5	3.4	4.2	3.8
1 to 5 Years	7.4	7.0	6.2	13.6	14.2	15.2
5 to 10 Years	9.7	9.0	8.5	14.7	15.2	16.2
10 to 20 Years	18.2	20.1	21.1	22.4	23.2	24.1
20 to 30 Years	20.3	17.0	16.6	16.6	15.3	15.5
30 Years or More	42.6	45.0	46.1	29.3	27.9	25.2
Total	100.0	100.0	100.0	100.0	100.0	100.0

Source: American Council of Life Insurance. Update available January 1982.

TAKE TWO ASPIRIN AND CALL ME IN THE MORNING

Leading Causes of Death
Total U.S., by Age

	No. of Deaths	Death Rate*		No. of Deaths	Death Rate
All Ages	1,899,597	878	Firearms	344	1
Heart disease	718,850	332	Other	1,159	3
Cancer	386,686	179	Cancer	1,733	5
Stroke**	181,934	84	Congenital anomalies .	676	2
Accidents	103,202	48			
Motor-vehicle . .	49,510	23			
Falls	13,773	6	**15 to 24 Years** . . .	47,986	117
Drowning	7,126	3	Accidents	25,619	63
Fires, burns . .	6,357	3	Motor-vehicle . . .	18,092	44
Other	26,436	13	Drowning . . .	2,150†	5
			Poison (solid, liquid)	709	2
Under 1 Year	46,975	1,485	Firearms . . .	665	2
Anoxia	10,604	335	Other	4,003	10
Congenital anomalies .	8,420	266	Suicide	5,565	14
Complications of preg-			Homicide	5,196	13
nancy and childbirth .	5,786	183			
Immaturity	3,714	117			
Pneumonia	1,665	53	**25 to 44 Years** . . .	103,042	182
Accidents	1,173	37	Accidents	23,460	41
Choking	275	9	Motor-vehicle . . .	13,031	23
Motor-vehicle . .	253	8	Drowning	1,690†	3
Mech. suffocation .	206	6	Poison (solid, liquid)	1,349	2
Fires, burns . .	159	5	Fires, burns . . .	1,081	2
Other	280	9	Falls	956	2
			Other	5,353	10
1 to 4 Years	8,307	69	Cancer	16,753	30
Accidents	3,297	27	Heart disease	14,392	25
Motor-vehicle . . .	1,219	10			
Drowning	650†	5			
Fires, burns . .	608	5	**45 to 64 Years** . . .	437,795	1,000
Choking	168	1	Heart disease	153,652	351
Falls	121	1	Cancer	132,514	303
Other	531	5	Stroke**	22,926	52
Congenital anomalies .	1,066	9	Accidents	19,167	44
Cancer	631	5	Motor-vehicle . .	8,000	18
			Falls	2,245	5
			Fires, burns . .	1,481	4
5 to 14 Years	12,579	35	Drowning	940†	2
Accidents	6,305	17	Surg. complications	865	2
Motor-vehicle . .	3,142	9	Other	5,636	13
Drowning . . .	1,110†	3	Cirrhosis of liver . .	17,166	39
Fires, burns . .	550	1	Suicide	8,368	19

	No. of Deaths	Death Rate*		No. of Deaths	Death Rate
65 to 74 Years . . .	445,595	3,054	**75 Years and Over** . .	797,318	8,941
Heart disease	182,354	1,250	Heart disease	366,141	4,106
Cancer	115,587	792	Stroke**	116,753	1,309
Stroke**	37,896	260	Cancer	116,675	1,308
Diabetes mellitus . .	9,611	66	Pneumonia	30,487	342
Accidents	9,006	62	Arteriosclerosis . . .	23,683	266
Motor-vehicle . . .	3,060	21	Accidents	15,175	170
Falls	1,995	14	Falls	7,762	87
Fires, burns . . .	843	6	Motor-vehicle . . .	2,713	30
Surg. complications .	767	3	Surg. complications .	1,030	12
Choking	447	3	Fires, burns . . .	1,023	11
Other	1,894	13	Choking	723	8
Pneumonia	8,335	57	Other	1,924	22
Cirrhosis of liver . .	6,208	43	Diabetes mellitus . .	13,993	157
			Emphysema	6,190	69

Source: Deaths are for 1977, latest official figures from National Center for Health Statistics, Public Health Service, U.S. Department of Health, Education and Welfare.

*Deaths per 100,000 population in each age group. Rates are averages for age groups, not individual ages.

**Cerebrovascular disease.

†Partly estimated.

Courtesy of *Accident Facts,* published by the National Safety Council.

Deaths Among Holders of Individual Life Insurance Policies
By Cause, 1945–1980

Cause of Death	1945	1955	1965	1970	1975	1980
Cardiovascular-renal Disease .	49.3%	57.2%	53.9%	52.1%	49.8%	47.9%
Cancer	14.8	18.6	19.2	20.1	21.4	23.2
Pneumonia and Influenza . .	3.1	2.0	3.1	3.3	2.8	2.6
Tuberculosis (all forms) . . .	2.8	.5	.2	.1	—	—
Diabetes	1.5	.9	1.1		1.0	.9
Other Diseases*	18.2	12.3	13.6	14.5	16.2	17.0
Total Natural Causes . .	89.7	91.5	91.1	91.1	91.2	91.6
Motor Vehicle Accidents . .	2.3	3.1	3.6	3.5	3.0	3.3
Other Accidents	5.9	3.2	3.2	3.1	3.1	2.6
Suicide	1.9	2.0	1.8	1.7	1.8	1.6
Homicide	.2	.2	.3	.6	.9	.9
Total External Causes . .	10.3	8.5	8.9	8.9	8.8	8.4
Total All Causes	100.0%	100.0%	100.0%	100.0%	100.0%	100.0%

Note: A small number classified as "War Deaths" is included in "Other Diseases" in the data for 1965; in other years the category is excluded. *Source: American Council of Life Insurance.*

*Includes those causes not specified.

SLIPPERY WHEN WET

	Deaths	Deaths per 100 Million Vehicle Miles
TOTAL U.S.	**51,083**	**3.4**
Total Rural Roads		**4.8**
Total Interstates		**1.6**
Selected States		
California	5,542	3.5
Nevada	354	6.0
North Dakota	128	2.5
Texas	4,168	3.8
Louisiana	1,196	5.3
Virginia	1,016	2.6
Michigan	1,822	2.7
Illinois	2,017	3.2
Pennsylvania	2,150	3.0
Selected Turnpikes		
Florida Toll Roads	12	1.1
Florida Turnpikes	25	1.8
Illinois Tollway	20	0.6
Indiana East–West Turnpike	12	1.7
Kansas Turnpike	12	2.2
Kentucky Parkways	14	1.7
Maine Turnpike	9	2.0
Kennedy Memorial Hwy. (Md.)	6	1.2
Massachusetts Turnpike	15	1.1
New Hampshire Turnpike	2	0.4
Atlantic City Expy. (N.J.)	4	1.4
Garden State Pkwy. (N.J.)	28	1.0
New Jersey Turnpike	37	1.3
New York State Thwy.	40	0.9
Hutchinson River Pkwy. (N.Y.)	0	0.0
Saw Mill River Pkwy. (N.Y.)	4	1.6
Ohio Turnpike	38	2.4
Oklahoma Turnpikes	17	1.7
Pennsylvania Turnpike	29	1.0
Dallas North Tollway (Tx.)	0	0.0
Richmond Expy. Sys. (Va.)	1	1.4
Richmond–Petersburg (Va.)	2	0.3
Va. Beach–Norfolk Expy. (Va.)	2	0.6
West Virginia Turnpike	28	11.8

Source: Turnpike traffic authorities; International Bridge, Tunnel and Turnpike Association, Federal Highway Administration. Data are for 1979.

Motor Vehicle Deaths

Year	Deaths	Year	Deaths
1915*	6,800	1972	56,278
1925*	21,800	1973	55,511
1935	36,369	1974	46,402
1945	28,076	1975	45,853
1955	38,426	1976	47,038
1960	38,137	1977	49,510
1965	49,163	1978	51,083
1970	54,633	1979*	52,300
1971	54,381	1980*	53,300

*Estimated.   Source: National Safety Council.

Auto Claim Payments*

Year	Bodily Injury	Property Damage
1970	$1,676	$320
1971	1,852	346
1972	1,926	355
1973	2,125	375
1974	2,472	397
1975	2,646	445
1976	2,583	490
1977	2,890	544
1978	3,123	622
1979	3,559	715

*Including all loss adjustment expenses. Data exclude most states which have no-fault automobile insurance laws and are for private passenger car liability claims only.
Source: Insurance Services Office. Courtesy of Insurance Information Institute

1975 Chevrolet Impala 4-door Sedan damaged in:

| | April, 1975 | | February, 1981 | |
	Parts	Labor*	Parts	Labor**
Front Bumper	$196.68	$ 34.27	$ 446.91	55.78
Radiator Grill	81.35	20.35	181.10	33.12
Hood Panel	159.10	14.99	343.69	24.40
Front Fender (one side)	147.66	39.63	294.40	64.49
Total	$584.79	$109.24	$1,266.10	$ 177.79

*$10.71 an hour.   **$17.43 an hour.

Sources: Parts costs, Motor Crash Estimating Guides, April, 1975 and February, 1981; labor costs, Allstate Insurance Company.
Courtesy of Insurance Information Institute.

KEY HEALTH INSURANCE STATISTICS

(year-end 1979)

Americans covered by private health insurance:

for hospital expense	183 million
for surgical expense	174 million
for physician's expense	164 million
for major medical expense	148 million
for dental expense	70 million
for disability (lost wages)	66 million
for long-term disability (lost wages)	20 million
by insurance company group policies	94.3 million
by insurance company individual policies	34.4 million
by Blue Cross/Blue Shield	86.1 million
by other plans	19.1 million

Premiums paid to:

Blue Cross/Blue Shield & related plans	$30.3 billion
Insurance companies	$35.8 billion

Benefits paid by:

Blue Cross/Blue Shield & related plans	$27.7 billion
Insurance companies	$29.6 billion
Medicare	$29.3 billion
Medicaid	$20.0 billion

Government share of national health costs: 43.1%.
Average hospital stay: 7.6 days.

Source: Source Book of Health Insurance Data, 1980–1981.

LIFT WITH YOUR LEGS, NOT YOUR BACK

WORK INJURIES BY BODY PART

Disabling work injuries in the entire nation totaled approximately 2,300,000 in 1979. Of these, about 13,200 were fatal and 80,000 resulted in some permanent impairment.

Injuries to the trunk occurred most frequently, with thumb and finger injuries next, according to State Labor Department reports.

Eyes	110,000
Head (except eyes)	140,000
Arms	210,000
Trunk (includes back)	670,000
Hands	160,000
Fingers	340,000
Legs	300,000
Feet	110,000
Toes	50,000
General	210,000

Source: National Safety Council.

U.S. FIRE LOSSES,*

Year	Property	Loss Per Capita
1950	$ 649,000,000	$ 4.29
1960	1,108,000,000	6.19
1970	2,328,000,000	11.41
1978	4,008,000,000	18.34
1979	4,851,000,000	22.04
1980	6,400,000,000†	27.82

*Including allowances for uninsured and unreported fires.
†National Safety Council estimate.
Source: Insurance Services Office.

CRIMES AGAINST PROPERTY, 1980

Crime	No. of Offenses	Property Loss
Robbery	548,809	$ 333,127,000
Burglary	3,759,193	3,315,608,000
Larceny/Theft	7,112,657	2,183,586,000
Vehicle Theft	1,114,651	3,209,080,000

Source: Federal Bureau of Investigation

WHERE THE PROPERTY/CASUALTY PREMIUM DOLLAR GOES

Year	Losses +	Loss Adj. Expense =	Loss Ratio +	Sales Costs +	Other Expense =	Combined Ratio
1974	66.2%	9.3%	75.5%	14.2%	14.0%	103.7%
1976	66.0	9.4	75.4	13.2	12.7	101.3
1978	61.1	9.0	70.1	13.1	12.7	95.9
1980	65.3	9.5	74.9	12.7	13.7	101.4
1974–1980	64.4	9.3	73.7	13.1	13.1	99.9

How to read this table. Losses are what you and your lawyer get to split. Eventually. The losses shown here (about 65 cents of each premium dollar) are paper losses, some of which may not be paid out for years. In the meantime, the insurer earns interest. The combined ratio represents, in effect, the total cost to the insurer of getting your money to invest. In some lines, only a few months pass before claims are paid. In others, years may pass.

Savings banks from 1974 through 1980 were paying $1.06 or more to borrow $1 for a year. They had to earn enough on that borrowed $1 to pay back $1.06 at the end of the year, pay all their salaries and overhead and advertising and insurance premiums and then make a profit. Property/casualty insurers, during the same period, were paying 99.9 cents, on average, to borrow that same $1. (See boldface, above.) And that was after making you pay all salaries, rent, sales commissions, and so forth. The interest earned on your $1 was all gravy. In 1980, it came to $11.7 billion.

Source: Derived from A.M. Best Company data, Aggregates & Averages.

F. STATE INSURANCE COMMISSIONERS

National Association of Insurance Commissioners, 350 Bishops Way,
Brookfield, Wisconsin 53005, 414-784-9540

Alabama	Tharpe Forrester, Montgomery 36130	205-832-6140
Alaska	Kenneth C. Moore, Juneau 99811	907-465-2515
American Samoa	Patricia G. Trammel, Pago Pago 16797	
Arizona	J. Michael Low, Phoenix 85007	602-255-4862
Arkansas	William H. L. Woodyard III, Little Rock 72204	501-371-1325
California	Robert Quinn, Los Angeles 90005	213-736-2551
Colorado	J. Richard Barnes, Denver 80203	303-866-3201
Connecticut	Joseph C. Mike, Hartford 06115	203-566-5275
Delaware	David Elliott, Dover 19901	302-736-4251
D.C.	James R. Montgomery III, Washington 20001	202-727-1273
Florida	Bill Gunter, Tallahassee 32301	904-488-3440
Georgia	Johnnie L. Caldwell, Atlanta 30334	404-656-2056
Guam	Jose R. Rivera, Agana 96910	
Hawaii	Dr. Mary Bitterman, Honolulu 96811	808-548-7505
Idaho	Trent M. Woods, Boise 83720	208-334-2250
Illinois	Philip R. O'Connor, Springfield 62767	217-782-4515
Indiana	Donald H. Miller, Indianapolis 46204	317-232-2386
Iowa	Bruce W. Foudree, Des Moines 50319	515-281-5705
Kansas	Fletcher Bell, Topeka 66612	913-296-3071
Kentucky	Daniel B. Briscoe, Frankfort 40601	502-564-3630
Louisiana	Sherman A. Bernard, Baton Rouge 70804	504-342-5328
Maine	Theodore T. Briggs, Augusta 04333	207-289-3101
Maryland	Edward J. Birrane, Jr., Baltimore 21202	301-659-4027
Massachusetts	Michael Sabbagh, Boston 02202	617-727-3333
Michigan	Nancy A. Baerwaldt, Lansing 48909	517-374-9724
Minnesota	Michael D. Markman, St. Paul 55101	612-296-6907
Mississippi	George Dale, Jackson 39205	601-354-7711
Missouri	C. Donald Ainsworth, Jefferson City 65102	314-751-2451
Montana	Elmer V. Omholt, Helena 59601	406-449-2996
Nebraska	Walter D. Weaver, Lindoln 68509	402-471-2201
Nevada	Patsy Redmond, Carson City 89710	702-885-4270
New Hampshire	Frank Whaland, Concord 03301	603-271-2261
New Jersey	James J. Sheeran, Trenton 08625	609-292-5363
New Mexico	Vincente B. Jasso, Santa Fe 85701	505-827-2451
New York	Albert B. Lewis, New York 10047	212-488-4124
North Carolina	John R. Ingram, Raleigh 27611	919-733-7343
North Dakota	J.O. Wigen, Bismarck 58505	701-224-2444
Ohio	Robin L. Ratchford, Columbus 43215	614-466-2691

Oklahoma	Gerald Grimes, Oklahoma City 73105	405-521-2828
Oregon	Josephine M. Driscoll, Salem 97310	503-378-4271
Pennsylvania	Michael L. Browne, Harrisburg 17120	717-787-5173
Puerto Rico	Rolando Cruz, San Juan 00904	809-724-6565
Rhode Island	Thomas J. Caldarone, Jr., Providence 02903	401-277-2223
South Carolina	Robert T. Smith, Columbia 29204	803-758-3266
South Dakota	Henry J. Lussem, Jr., Pierre 57501	605-773-3563
Tennessee	John C. Neff, Nashville 37219	615-741-2241
Texas	E. J. Voorhis, Austin 78786	512-475-2273
Utah	Roger C. Day, Salt Lake City 84102	801-533-5611
Vermont	George A. Chaffee, Montpelier 05602	802-828-3301
Virginia	James W. Newman, Jr. Richmond 23209	804-786-6077
Virgin Islands	Henry A. Millin, St. Thomas 00801	809-774-2991
Washington	Dick Marquardt, Olympia 98504	206-753-7301
West Virginia	Richard G. Shaw, Charleston 25305	304-348-3354
Wisconsin	Susan Mitchell, Madison 53702	608-266-3585
Wyoming	John T. Langdon, Cheyenne 82002	307-777-7401

BIBLIOGRAPHY

BASIC REFERENCES (ANNUALS)

Accident Facts. Chicago: National Safety Council.
Analysis of Workers' Compensation Laws. Washington: U.S. Chamber of Commerce.
Argus F.C.&S. Chart. Cincinnati: National Underwriter Company.
Best's Aggregates & Averages. Oldwick, New Jersey: A.M. Best & Company.
Information Please Almanac. New York: Simon & Schuster.
Insurance Facts. New York: Insurance Information Institute.
Life Insurance Fact Book. Washington: American Council of Life Insurance.

PERIODICALS

I am greatly indebted to the reporting and analysis of countless journalists on whose work I have based much of my own. Among the periodicals which proved most helpful: *Business Insurance, The National Underwriter,* Professor Joseph Belth's excellent *Insurance Forum* (a monthly life insurance newsletter; Box 1333, Bloomington, IN 47402), *ICPI Reports* (tales of scuttled scams; house organ of the Insurance Crime Prevention Institute, Westport, Connecticut), *The American Lawyer* (special thanks to Jane Berentson), *Institutional Investor* (especially Neil Osborn and Lynn Brenner), *Forbes, Business Week, Fortune, Money, Time* and *U.S. News & World Report*. Also, of course, *The Wall Street Journal* and the New York *Times*. Special thanks, also, to Robert D. Shaw, Jr., Patrick Riordan and William R. Amlong for their fine series in the Miami *Herald*. And to the editors of *Consumer Reports,* whose work on insurance has been uniformly outstanding.

BOOKS AND REPORTS

All-Industry Research Advisory Committee. *Automobile Injuries and Their Compensation in the United States*. Two Volumes. March 1979.

322

Allstate Insurance Company. *Insurance Handbook for Reporters*. Northbrook, Illinois: Allstate, 1979.

Bach, Karl. *Selling Is Simple*. San Francisco: Advance Books, 1979.

Belth, Joseph M. *Life Insurance: A Consumer's Handbook*. Bloomington: Indiana University Press, 1973.

Bishop, George A. *Capital Formation through Life Insurance*. Homewood, Illinois: Richard D. Irwin, 1976.

Bladen, Ashby. *How to Cope with the Developing Financial Crisis*. New York: McGraw-Hill, 1980.

Brackenridge, R.D.C. *Medical Selection of Life Risks*. London: Undershaft Press, 1977.

Brown, Antony. *Lloyd's of London*. New York: Stein and Day, 1974. Originally published as *Hazards Unlimited*. London: Peter Davies, Ltd.

Buley, R. Carlyle. *The Equitable Life Assurance Society of the United States, 1859–1964*. Two Volumes. New York: Appleton-Century-Crofts, 1967.

Consumers Union Report on Life Insurance. Fourth Edition. New York: Holt, Rinehart and Winston, 1980.

Cornell, James C., Jr. *The Great International Disaster Book*. New York: Pocket Books, 1979.

Dacey, Norman F. *What's Wrong with Your Life Insurance*. New York: Crowell-Collier, 1963.

Davidson, James D. *The Squeeze*. New York: Summit Books, 1980.

Defoe, Daniel. *Essay on Projects*. London: 1697.

Epperson, James B. *Like a Thief in the Night*. Los Angeles: James B. Epperson, 1939.

Fisher, George R. *The Hospital That Ate Chicago*. Philadelphia: The Saunders Press, 1980.

Florida Association of Insurance Agents. *The Florida Agents' Manifesto; Object: Survival*. Tallahassee: 1973.

Gollin, James. *Pay Now, Die Later*. New York: Random House, 1966.

Goulden, Joseph C. *The Million Dollar Lawyers*. New York: G.P. Putnam's, 1978.

Healy, John J. *A Game of Wits*. New York: David McKay, 1975.

Hoffman, William. *The Stockholder*. New York: Lyle Stuart, 1969.

Holtom, Robert B. *Restraints on Underwriting: Risk Selection, Discrimination and the Law*. Cincinnati: The National Underwriter Co., 1979.

Huebner, S.S., and Black, Kenneth, Jr. *Life Insurance*. Ninth Edition. Englewood Cliffs, New Jersey: Prentice-Hall, 1976.

Hunt, James H. *Taking the Bite out of Insurance: How to Save Money on Life Insurance*. Washington, D.C.: National Insurance Consumer Organization, 1981.

Hunter, Robert. *Taking the Bite out of Insurance: Investment Income in*

Ratemaking. Washington, D.C.: National Insurance Consumer Organization, 1981.

Insurance Information Institute. *Sharing the Risk: How the Nation's Businesses, Homes and Autos Are Insured*. New York: 1981.

James, Marquis. *Biography of a Business, 1792–1942: Insurance Company of North America*. Indianapolis: Bobbs-Merrill, 1942.

Kaye, Barry. *How to Save a Fortune on Your Life Insurance*. Los Angeles: Carol Press, 1981.

Lee, J. Finley, et al. *Entering the Twenty-First Century: An Insurance Forecast*. Tallahassee: Florida Association of Insurance Agents, 1979.

Mackay, Charles. *Extraordinary Popular Delusions and the Madness of Crowds*. London: 1841 (New York: Harmony Books, 1980).

Massachusetts Division of Insurance. *Automobile Insurance Risk Classification: Equity and Accuracy*. Boston: 1978.

Miller, Nicholas F., Jr., et al. *Private Passenger Automobile Insurance Risk Classification*. A Report of the Advisory Committee to the National Association of Insurance Commissioners, May 1979.

New York Insurance Department. *Automobile Insurance . . . For Whose Benefit?* A Report to Governor Nelson A. Rockefeller, 1970.

North American Reassurance Company. *Life Underwriting*. New York: North American Reassurance.

O'Brien, Francis J. *The Fabulous Franklin Story*. Springfield, Illinois: The Franklin Life Insurance Company, 1972.

O'Connell, Jeffrey. *The Lawsuit Lottery*. New York: The Free Press (Macmillan), 1979.

————. *The Injury Industry and the Remedy of No-Fault Insurance*. Urbana: University of Illinois Press, 1971.

Orren, Karen. *Corporate Power and Social Change: The Politics of the Life Insurance Industry*. Baltimore: Johns Hopkins University Press, 1974.

Payne, Gaylord L. *Life and Health Insurance Handbook*. Homewood, Illinois: Richard D. Irwin, 1973.

Pileggi, Nicholas. *Blye, Private Eye*. Chicago: Playboy Press, 1976.

Reliance Insurance Companies. *Judicial and Miscellaneous Bond Underwriting and Production Guide*. Philadelphia.

Reynolds, G. Scott. *The Mortality Merchants*. New York: David McKay, 1968.

Riegel, Robert; Miller, Jerome S.; and Williams, C. Arthur, Jr. *Insurance Principles and Practices: Property and Liability*. Sixth Edition. Englewood Cliffs, New Jersey: Prentice-Hall, 1976.

Shulman, Richard. *The Billion Dollar Bookies*. New York: Harper's Magazine Press, 1976.

Spielmann, Peter, and Zelman, Aaron. *The Life Insurance Conspiracy,*

Made Elementary by Sherlock Holmes. New York: Simon and Schuster, 1979.

Stalson, J. Owen. *Marketing Life Insurance: Its History in America.* Cambridge: Harvard University Press, 1942 (Homewood, Illinois: Richard D. Irwin, 1969).

Stewart, Richard E. *Insurance and Insurance Regulation.* Collected Speeches, 1968–1980.

Stryker, Perrin. *The Incomparable Salesmen.* New York: McGraw–Hill, 1967.

Wandell, William H. *The Control of Competition in Fire Insurance.* New York: Columbia University doctoral dissertation, 1935.

Wright, Elizur. *Traps Baited with Orphan; or, What Is the Matter with Life Insurance?* Boston: James R. Osgood and Company, 1877.

GOVERNMENT PUBLICATIONS

Abuses in the Sale of Health Insurance to the Elderly. Hearings and Staff Study by the House Select Committee on Aging, November 1978.

Cancer Insurance: Exploiting Fear for Profit (An Examination of Dread Disease Insurance). Report (Together With Additional Views) by the Select Committee on Aging, March 1980.

Life Insurance Cost Disclosure. Staff Report to the Federal Trade Commission, July 1979.

Life Insurance Marketing and Cost Disclosure. Hearings before the Subcommittee an Oversight and Investigations of the House Interstate Commerce Committee, August 1978. Report (Together With Dissenting Views), December 1978.

State No-Fault Automobile Insurance Experience, 1971–1977. U.S. Department of Transportation, June 1977.

INDEX